THE

# CONRAN BEGINNER'S GUIDE TO DECORATING

# THE CONRAN BEGINNER'S GUIDE TO DECORATING

JOCASTA INNES
& JILL BLAKE

Stoddart

Brackets indicate North American terminology.
Always follow either all metric or all imperial measurements.



First published in 1988 by
Stoddart Publishing Co. Limited
34 Lesmill Road
Toronto, Canada
M3B 2T6

Published in the U.K. by
Conran Octopus Limited
37 Shelton Street
Covent Garden
London WC2H 9HN

**Canadian Cataloguing in Publication Data**
Innes, Jocasta.
The Conran beginner's guide to decorating
ISBN 0-7737-2165-7
1. Interior decoration. I. Blake, Jill. II. Title.
III. Title: Beginner's guide to decorating.
NK2115.I66 1987 747 C87-094197-6

Printed and bound in Hong Kong

# Contents

Part I

# THE KEY

One of life's great satisfactions is the moment when you first turn your own key in your own lock and step inside your own home, your mind full of plans and ideas – plus the inevitable reservations about how and when you are going to carry them out. The key to decorating success is confidence: both in your ideas and practical ability.

This book will be an indispensable guide. The second section, 'The Inspiration', helps you focus on what style you're aiming for, while the following chapters take you step by step through the stages of planning out the changes you've decided on, preparing the ground and finally tackling the projects themselves.

Meanwhile, you have moved in and are impatient to make your mark on the place. So this opening chapter does something different. It shows you the short-cuts which enable you to *avoid* the dreaded square one where so many well-intentioned beginners come unstuck. It details a wealth of decorating solutions that are especially relevant to people in rented locations where it's not possible to make drastic changes, but useful too to new home-owners working on a first staging-post rather than the home of a lifetime. They are also good emergency tactics for people planning to renovate, but who meanwhile need some habitable space fast.

And if, as often happens, some of these short-term expedients are still in use ten years later, perhaps that just goes to show how valuable they are.

*A jumble of second-hand furniture can be transformed with a few coats of paint to create an effect that is fresh and homogeneous. This might be a good way of giving furniture you are stuck with a new lease of life, while it gets away from the functional look of some bathrooms.*

Taking over a small rented flat or apartment can arouse exactly the same feelings as moving in to your very own first home. The nesting instinct makes you want the place to feel personal and yours, but the look of the place in the cold light of day, with all its cracks and chips, its wildly patterned wallpaper and lack of sunshine, is a shock. Of course you want to make your mark and put it all to rights, but where does an absolute beginner start, and what with, let alone when?

Or maybe you're a home-owner intending eventually to strip everything back to basics and do it all properly, but in the meantime you need a base – quickly. It's psychologically important to feel at home, and the sooner you can establish one room as a retreat from the clutter and turmoil of work in progress the better. It may be jumping the gun in terms of the strict schedule of operations, but since jobs invariably take longer then you expect them to, it's a wise investment of time. If your base camp is 'done properly' and acts as visible proof of what you're aiming for, so much the better; otherwise, go for the quick cover-up approach, and tell yourself that at least you will be really getting to know the place before undertaking any major changes.

You may not have two sticks of furniture to rub together or you may be lumbered with clumsy great pieces already there; you may be free to make radical changes or (with someone else as landlord) have to tread carefully and compromise. The most obvious make-yourself-at-home tactics are to spread some of your own possessions around you, but unsympathetic surroundings can make them look forlorn and out of place. Get to work on the background so that your favourite things stand out. Block out ugly patterns or depressing colour schemes with one of the cover-up strategies outlined below – or just with paint.

Whether a room is sparsely furnished or cluttered, some kind of 'unification' principle helps bring it all together – disparate elements work if they have something in common, such as a positive colour scheme or a theme based on neutral colours and natural materials. They can be pulled together visually by

taking a good idea and repeating it, like using the same fabric and cushions on different-shaped chairs, or the same plants or flowers in different places. One way of glamorizing a makeshift interior, for a special occasion perhaps, is to go overboard with fairly low-cost props – a hideous sofa or chair can be hidden under a colourful quilt or rug. Heap lots of coloured cushions together, light a whole row of candles, or splash out on a profusion of plants or (better still) cut flowers.

Using 'props' in this way is taking a leaf out of the photographic stylists' notebook. Their expertise is about making instant transformations in room sets, and they have a wealth of useful tips. They go for cosmetic changes rather than serious facelifts. As in make-up jargon, this means camouflage and disguise for the elements you don't like or can't change, and highlights or some flattering emphasis to the good points.

The strategy for improving a temporary place – a rented flat or apartment – is of course ultimately different from the way to go about improving the place that belongs to you. It is quixotic or extravagant to put substantial amounts of money or time into setting temporary accommodation to rights, sanding floors and building in cupboards. The canny approach is to invest any spare cash in portable removable items. A good rug, some well-designed lamps, a few prints, a nest of stacking chairs are things that will upgrade a dismal room, and you will be grateful for

*Opposite left: An unused window could be the place for a treatment such as this. Translucent fabric is hung over a pole, then loosely knotted and hooked onto the handle of the window.*

*Opposite right: If yours is not yet a permanent house, use movable things for your decoration. A jumble of toning fabrics will remind you of home almost anywhere.*

*Below left: Candlelight reflected in a mirror is one of the oldest tricks in the book – and still one of the best and most successful ones.*

*Below right: Awkward corners and battered fixtures can be brightened up with houseplants.*

them when you move on, perhaps into your own first real home.

For short-term storage, find adjustable shelving on track systems which need the minimum number of holes drilled in walls. Second-hand kitchen wall cabinets are often cheap and roomy and look reasonable when cleaned up and given a lick of paint. Hammer finish paint, which dries with a ripply metallic finish, is the beginner's friend, because you can get away with one coat and the effect is cool and smart. A metal trunk or chest flat enough to double as a coffee table will swallow bulky things, and car spray-paints make a quick colour transformation.

An architect's solution for storage in fitted kitchens offers a longer-term idea. Plan a run of deep, wall-mounted shelving all around the walls, using sturdy chipboard (particle board) or blockboard (lumbercore board) edged with timber. Make the countertop wider and tile the top, or cover it with sheets of steel, zinc or laminate. The shelves can eventually be closed off with tongue-and-groove or alternatively louvred doors, but in the short term fabric curtains will conceal their contents prettily and cheaply.

Fabric cover-ups are another favourite with the stylists. Fabric wraps are the best disguise for lumpy furniture in any case, but the idea can be extended to walls. It will hide the scars where you have removed some ugly shelving or wall cupboards, and generally give a room a softer, warmer feel. Use a heavy-duty staple gun to secure lengths of plain canvas, ticking, printed bedspreads or old textiles, over as much of the walls as you can reach. A smaller panel of colourful fabric or a dhurry stapled to the wall behind a bed will 'zone' the area as a place for relaxing. Wrap more fabric round chairs and tables, and a room immediately looks

*Above: An unusual lighting system provides the unifying theme for this rather unsophisticated kitchen. Lightbulb sockets are mounted onto wooden strips (hollowed out at the back to carry the cables), then nailed to the wall under the windows for night-time lighting.*

*Left: A single, expensive, perfect item will raise the standard of a decorative scheme, and be a sensible way of using a tight budget. Here the lamp compensates for a folding chair and cheap cover.*

brighter. Any fabric will do, but things complete in themselves – bedspreads, old kelims, chenille table covers, even sheets – are a portable investment as well as doing away with the need to neaten raw edges. If you fancy a Bedouin tent effect, suspending more fabric over part of the ceiling (again with staples, or by hooking sewn-on loops over hooks in the ceiling) will change a room's look dramatically.

Fabric is the traditional and time-honoured cover-up for windows. But lined curtains and valances, even blinds and shades, are expensive to buy and slow to make. A simple length of fabric, sari, bedspread or a striped sheet, draped and pinned over poles, feels fresh and casual. Try to repeat the fabric somewhere in the room. Drops of fine cotton diffuse light pleasantly, a disarming alternative to sheer curtains if you need some kind of screen. Knotting and looping back simple fabric treatments at windows keeps the casual look going but gives a slightly more 'finished' effect. These *ad hoc* and inexpensive expedients can be retained in a gradually civilized environment until you are ready to set about making your 'real' curtains in your chosen fabric.

Two of the stylists' most cherished props are plants and lighting. Have you noticed how the room sets in glossy magazines are always bushy and burgeoning with plants? That is one key: plants import variety, colour and the indefinable charm of living green, especially helpful to morale in a confined urban space. Big, bushy ones look most handsome but are expensive; at the other end of the scale come seasonal flowering plants like geraniums that can be used in greater profusion. Massing smaller plants makes them look more than the sum of their parts. You can also try mixing flowering with foliage plants for a dramatic effect. Plants with variegated leaves can also add texture to a display. Watertight containers make life easier: use an old zinc bath with a layer of peat or gravel inside to hold a collection of pots. Use large Chinese ceramic containers with saucers for larger plants. Either way, plants seem to exert a screening and beautifying effect quite disproportionate to their actual size, and as long as they have the light and water they need, they will thrive quite happily in temporary quarters.

Like plants, good lighting seems to add new dimensions to a room. Even without sophisticated built-in schemes designed by experts, a variety of light sources will enable you to warm up a cold-looking interior, suggest intimacy, expand a confined space, designate different areas for different uses, and much more besides. The first step is to remove or adapt the classic dangling central ceiling light which shows up every blemish and bleaches the colour and cosiness out of a room. If you need light over a table or desk an *ad hoc* solution is to fit a longer cord to the existing ceiling fixture and carry this across to a ceiling hook above the place you need lit. Use a spot, paper lantern or metal shade according to the type of light required; it's relatively easy to install a dimmer to the light switch for the option of a different sort of mood lighting.

Make as much use as possible of small free-standing lamps. The cords can be a nuisance, but they do come in bright colours that make them look less depressing and sufficiently conspicuous to be safe. Uplighters wash the light up walls dramatically: small bulb-in-a-can floor-standing types are cheapest and can be hidden behind furniture or plants. Taller halogen models have a spindly elegance suited to contemporary décor. Clip-on spotlights and adjustable desk lamps can be beamed down on to work surfaces or up and away as the need requires.

As an alternative to a lot of rewiring, spotlights on tracks offer efficiency and flexibility, and are a good way of strengthening kitchen lighting. Another solution which is both practical and attractive is to adapt the idea of the dressing-room mirror and mount ordinary pearl light bulbs in a row (see picture). A wooden strip or decorative moulding running round the walls at just above counter height has outlets at regular intervals and a groove at the back for the wiring, obviating any need for cutting a channel in the plaster. It's an idea that combines decoration with task lighting, and could be used elsewhere.

Even with a whole range of light sources, there's always a time for candles as a source of instant atmosphere. Massed in a group or standing in a row in front of a mirror, they can make practically any occasion feel like something special.

Just as a mirror redoubles the effect of the candles, it will multiply plants or objects standing in front of it and suggest a generous profusion without taking up space. In fact it can be used to suggest more space. Large mirrors – perhaps from an old wardrobe – are among the most valuable instant-decorator's tools; little ones – such as individual mirror tiles – introduce sparkle in odd corners. As cover-ups, mirrors are particularly effective: whereas a picture or wall-hanging becomes an end in itself, mirrors open up extra dimensions as they play tricks with light and space.

Another way of mysteriously implying a spaciousness that is not really there is with screens. They can be deployed very effectively even in a small space, either literally screening something or more inventively creating a room within a room. A decorative screen wrapped round a worktable in a corner, for instance, or around the head of a bed, looks both grand and cosy. Antique screens can still be found in auctions and junkshops quite cheaply, especially when the covering is torn or missing. Re-covering is not difficult: use fabric, a collage of scraps, lavish wallpaper or marbled paper. Screen panels can serve a double purpose as a folding pinboard for cards, photographs and small pictures. It's essential to get a three-fold screen for stability, though four and five folds allow still more possibilities.

Painting the walls in your own sort of colour is the quickest way to make a major difference to a place. A fine colour on the walls makes a room look unified and finished, even before it acquires all its fabrics, furniture and accessories. The best paints for an emergency cover-up over ugly wallpaper or patchy wall surfaces are standard flat emulsions (latex) designed to cover in one or two coats: matt surfaces play down defects, and white or off-white is a good emergency strategy, which allows you time to consider what colour you really want. Special-purpose paints can cover up patterned tiles and a coloured glaze can make textured wallpaper look like stamped leather. An even more effective camouflage might be one of the easier decorative treatments – sponging, ragging and so on – which are flattering to uneven, rough, cracked or otherwise sub-standard walls, and create a glowing damask texture. They are relatively quick to do using paint straight from the can, and fun if you can rope in a helper. Experiment first on some old paper to see how much paint to use and the type of pattern you are creating. It's always better to go cautiously with colour at first and feel happy with the result, rather than get very carried away, mess it up and then lose all your confidence.

A safe colour scheme can make a subtle background to stencils in a contrast colour later on, or be given a further layer of ragging, spattering or whatever, perhaps with a tinted paint. If you aren't sure of the effect as you go along don't panic, try holding a picture against your wall – it often happens that the texture that seemed wild and chaotic when viewed unadorned and close up, settles back into lively painterliness of an attractive kind once you relegate it to the background.

Spattering coloured paint onto a surface produces a rain of coloured dots, random and sparse or dense

| | |
|---|---|
| COLOUR | 38 |
| SURFACE PREPARATION | 74–5 |
| PAINT | 96 |
| PAINT TYPES | 98 |
| PAINT FINISHES | 110 |

*Above: Never underestimate the dramatic potential of flowers. Use them generously, and they will do all the decorative work for you.*

*Far left: Painting furniture is easy and allows you to re-vamp what might otherwise be called junk.*

*Left: Narrow, awkward corridors can be corrected visually with careful use of colour. Here two blues serve to elongate the space.*

and even, depending on the implements and paint used and the distance at which the painter stands. A light spatter of white and black sharpens colours and gives a granite or porphyry effect. Spattering can be used on any surface but is particularly effective on furniture, giving it a lively texture which softens large areas or rigid shapes pleasantly. Spattering colours which pick up key colours in the décor will blend a piece in effectively. A painted line as a 'trimming' in the deepest tone used will also help to add definition to the entire effect.

It may be that in using painted texture to remedy unevenness, a room itself becomes amorphous. Borders delineating the walls give the necessary definition: stick on ceiling decorations or patterned wallpaper borders, or use stencils. Pre-cut stencils are available in a great range of designs and sizes, and can be used to paint attractive borders, spaced-out grid patterns, or even large-scale motifs with the minimum of effort or complication; or design and cut your own.

Walls are not the only surfaces to benefit from stencils or colour. Depending on the room and its shape, size and period, colouring up the woodwork, floor, ceiling or all of these can work wonders. It can add character, raising or lowering apparent ceiling height, fading out ugly features or emphasizing good ones, and substituting for non-existent carpet or rugs.

Ideally, all this type of painting work is best done with the room empty of furniture, but often it can be difficult to remove everything. With care and lots of plastic sheeting (or dust sheets), rooms can be painted around their contents so long as the surfaces are clear and the bulky items of furniture pushed to the centre, under cover.

Part 2

# THE INSPIRATION

As you plan your interior decoration you will gradually find you have one vital, indispensable ally: your own taste. You may perhaps have felt timid about this in the past, awed by the extravagance and imaginative range of the professional interior designers; but think of them as your resource, your bank of ideas and creativity on which you can draw. Concentrate first on fine-tuning your own reactions to interiors. Every time you walk into a room, even one you know well, ask yourself to identify the handful of things you like. Look through every book and magazine you can find, and be critical: note down the colours that continually seem to appeal to you, the little touches that seem to make all the difference, even the vague 'feel' that you find you like. You will find yourself gaining confidence in your own ideas, your own likes and dislikes.

This section looks at the less tangible, more subtle aspects of your interior decoration: the architectural shell itself and the part it can play, lighting, objects and collections used decoratively, and finally the soft furnishings. It is these elements that will in the end say the most about your taste and your style.

Whatever your circumstances, don't be afraid to pitch your ambitions high. Be inventive, creative, imaginative as you pore over books and magazines – then try to think of ways in which you adapt an idea you like so that it is both affordable and realizable.

*Make use of the ideas of the professional interior designers. Unusual side tables in glass are used to their maximum potential in this room, arranged to reflect light from the wall-lights above. These are not the only clever touches here: the translucent blinds, the warm wooden floor, the single sculpture in the corner, all combine to give a feeling of dramatic simplicity.*

# THE ARCHITECTURAL SHELL

Develop the knack of looking past the contents of any room you visit or see in a photograph. Undress it in your mind of all its furnishings and 'read' what's left in the shell of the room for style clues. The language of architectural style is clearest in the shapes of doors and windows, in the presence of structural features such as fireplaces, alcoves and beams and in detailing such as cornices and mouldings. But it also involves more general factors such as the size and proportion of rooms and the even vaguer qualities of atmosphere. Perhaps the best touchstone of atmosphere is your gut reaction to a room, whether it seems cosy or cluttered, elegant or austere – whether *you* would feel completely at home in it.

Try to interpret what it is you like about an interior that attracts you, and see what contribution the architecture makes to that effect. Magazines and catalogues offer a wealth of examples to help you get your eye in. Perhaps you like a particular room that seems light, airy, spacious and elegant. Analyze the ingredients that contribute to that effect. Does it owe those qualities to its sheer size, a large window, pale colours and plain surfaces, or to its lighting? Compare what you see and like with the shell of the room you have to work with. It's helpful if you can carry around with you as a sort of sixth sense an image of the amount of space you have at home. It may be possible to improve a small dark room in your home (with professional help) by dramatic measures such as inserting a larger window or knocking through a wall; even then, light-coloured paint and good lighting may never make it as bright as your ideal. It may be on a sunless side of the house, for example: aspect is the one factor you can never alter. It is sometimes better to go with what you've got and save both effort and

*'Architectural style' can be reinforced and added to (left), or used as a counterpoint (above): here an old house with some traditional features has been given a modern treatment that uses those features in a new and original way. But you might instead be looking for dominating shapes that speak for themselves (opposite). Here the building's shell is used to the full, making a bold, architectural statement echoed by the chair.*

disappointment. A small dark room may gain its character more readily in the direction of quiet cosiness than of airy elegance.

Making a room's architecture work for you need not entail drastic structural changes. The transformation can perhaps be cosmetic – disguise, camouflage, diverting attention to where you want it – and achieved by playing with lighting and display within the interior as well as by colouring and texturing the room's many different surfaces with paint, paper and fabrics.

## Starting points

Architecture includes the apparent absence of style in modern 'featureless' buildings as well as the distinct styles associated with particular periods and places. Both extremes of this spectrum are what you make of them. Modern interiors can be box-like and bland, but on the other hand they can offer a blank canvas on which to impose your own style. However, when introducing a major feature into a room, go easy on synthetic character – false beams, rustic fireplaces, new bow and bay windows can so easily just look out of place. More discreet details such as door accessories and mouldings, and in particular a cornice (crown moulding) of some description, give plain rooms a subtly finished look, upgrading them without creating spurious character.

Older properties of specific styles may seem to give less scope because they contain *too much* ready-made character in the way of ornamentation, stained glass and so on. If you are lucky this may be just what you want: many people, after all, go out of their way to choose a turn-of-the-century house (or a 1930s apartment or ranch-style bungalow) because they like its ambience. The tendency nowadays is to be sympathetic with the character of the building, and it is very fashionable in some circles for people to devote a great deal of time and energy to finding items of decoration that are exactly contemporary with the date of their property. You will find that many older properties have had a succession of so-called facelifts – it's not so long since anything considered old-fashioned was ripped out or covered up – and you inherit a muddle of out-of-date improvements that have themselves become period pieces. Have respect for these, if you can honestly say you like them, and don't be so adamant about re-creating a particular period or style that you throw good things out with bad. If you are lucky you may find features original to the house intact – fine cornices or crown mouldings under generations of paint, panelled doors hidden behind blank hardboard.

Features you feel are worth preserving or enhancing may give you the starting point for the style you evolve with your own things and your particular way of using the space. Restoration doesn't always

*Architectural details of all kinds can play a powerful role in your decorative schemes. One choice might be to restore the features and their surroundings to their former glory (right). Another option is to put them to use in a modern context (opposite). This chimney may still act as a flue, but now it has a decorative function that is almost as important – and very individual.*

entail slavish documentary accuracy. Museums and books show examples of period authenticity which may help you decide whether, say, to give a window an extravagant treatment of drapes and swags or a simple functional solution. You need not follow them to the letter, though: either of these options may look good interpreted in quite up-to-date fabric patterns. Both ornate town-house interiors and simple cottages can make a fitting background for hi-tech gadgetry and the clean lines of modern furniture, provided the proportional scale is right.

## Making the best of bad points

Features you don't like can be given less emphasis by the way you decorate them or, sometimes, by completely removing them – but *always* consult an architect, a qualified surveyor or an engineer about any structural alterations. Grand ideas, such as knocking down walls, should never be undertaken without professional advice, and that can quickly become expensive; so keep a rein on your ambitions when thinking about major changes.

Before committing yourself to any considerable expenditure, think about what you can do with canny disguise. Awkwardly positioned radiators, unsightly pipes and badly boxed-in utilities are common disfigurements in new buildings as well as old. You can camouflage such things with clever decoration – painting them so that they merge with the background and become an integral part of the scheme. Textured paint finishes can often make an effective disguise. The alternative is to dramatize them by a really striking treatment so that they make conversation pieces – using pronounced colour contrast is the simplest way of drawing attention to anything. (Contrast will emphasize shape, so it's worth using only on a shape that benefits from enhancement!) A shiny, brightly painted radiator can set the key for colour accents in a room. A defining line in a different colour at the join between walls and ceiling (a painted moulding or a flat border) flatters a well-proportioned room but confirms the box shape of a small square one, and is a constant reminder of an oddly-shaped room.

# Fireplaces

A bright fire burning in a grate is the most compelling focal point a room can have. People are drawn to a fire even when it no longer provides the room's main heating. When fires were the sole source of warmth, fireplaces were of major importance in a room. Not only did fires have to be efficient, but their special role was advertised by the surrounding framework of firefront and mantelpiece. This was partly practical necessity: space was needed for fuel, fire-irons and in some cases kettles, and the hearth gave protection from falling coals. Then the fire surround became a place to display ornaments and also a decorative object.

Whether or not a fireplace is used, it continues to exert a dominating effect on a room. For one thing, it tends to command a central position and is often set into a conspicuous chimneypiece. For another, a fireplace is by definition a sort of frame focusing attention on whatever it contains. When it is empty and the eye meets nothing in the centre of the surround, there's a sense of disappointment. If you use a fireplace irregularly, make it attractive with a pile of logs, plants, or dried flowers whenever no fire is lit.

A room *without* a fireplace is perfectly acceptable if its focus is centred on the layout of furniture or a display of objects – provided there is no sense of something missing. If the focal point of your room is in reality the television set, don't necessarily fight against that, but incorporate it into your scheme. Many houses are designed without fireplaces at all; many old houses benefited from the extra space when their mantelpieces were removed and the gap made good.

Perhaps the worst of both worlds is a dead-letter fireplace, one that is not a positive attraction (whether functional or not) but that uses up valuable space. Its very neutrality saps a room of character.

## Using the space

Once the structural considerations of blocking up a chimney are taken care of (see overleaf), you can deal with the opening in many different ways, depending on size (take advice on enlarging the opening). Use it for storage – try horizontal wine racks or vertical record racks; fill it with the television and video; make it into a mini-office with shelves and a pull-out desk top; fit it with doors and use it as a cupboard. In the kitchen it could become an alcove for the cooker or refrigerator. If, on the other hand, you want to leave it as a simple alcove or niche or install concealed lighting and display plants or a cherished possession, you move in the direction once again of creating a focal point in the room.

### Restoring and replacing

If you want to restore a house to its original style, installing an appropriate period fireplace is a major step towards creating the right atmosphere. Plenty of reproductions of both grates and fire surrounds are available nowadays, and there are books to help you pinpoint the subtle stylistic differences and choose one that is appropriate. Alternatively, you may simply want a fire, and in such a case a minimalist modern design is often a good solution, even in an older property – better by far than choosing some bastard style that is out of key, or something that is in keeping with the period of the house but the wrong scale. Gas-fired fake logs and coal can look good in a simple surround.

*Opposite, left: Traditional firefronts are easy to put in and often extremely elegant. They may call for a classic treatment.*

*Opposite, right: Hard modern lines are instantly softened when the fire gets going, providing a point of warmth and focus in potentially austere environments.*

*Right: Make unused fireplaces work hard for you decoratively.*

If you are lucky enough to unearth a covered-up fireplace at home, or if you find one second-hand, many minor alterations are easy to do. A fireplace with open brickwork may benefit from repointing – removing the old mortar and replacing with new. For this you will need a club hammer (small sledgehammer) and a 'plugging' chisel – with a groove along its blade – to chip out the old mortar, and a bricklayer's trowel to push in the new material. Use pre-mixed sand and lime or combine three parts sand to one part lime, for brickwork inside a hearth, as mortar can explode when exposed to heat.

To replace a firefront and lay a new hearth slab you will also need an electric drill and masonry bit, and a steel plasterer's float. Replacing tiles on the surround or hearth can make all the difference between a dreary fireplace and an exciting one.

## Practical precautions

Unless your course of action is of the purely cosmetic variety, remember that with a chimney and a fireplace

*The colour and practicality of bricks make them an ideal background for a real fire. They definitely justify the work of repointing and refurbishing.*

## REPOINTING

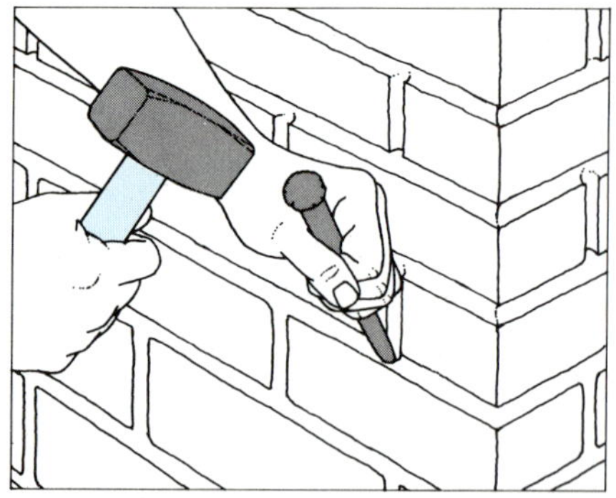

**1** Chip out the old mortar with a club hammer (small sledgehammer) and chisel to a depth of about 12mm (½in), and remove all the dust from the joints with a soft brush.

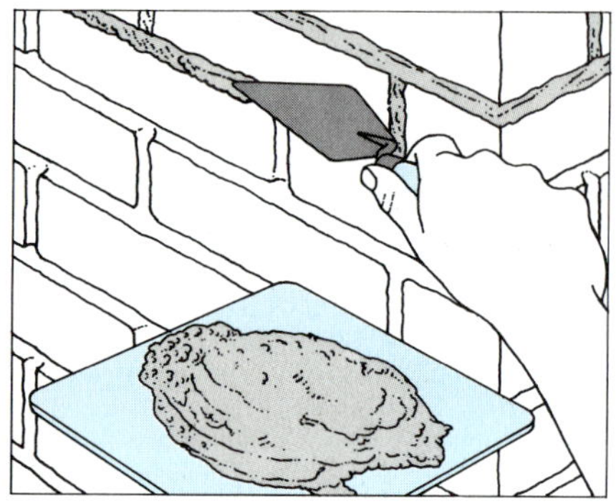

**2** Mix up a dryish sand/lime mixture to point about 1 sq m (10 sq ft). Wet the open joints with an old paintbrush, and then press in the new mixture with the point of a trowel.

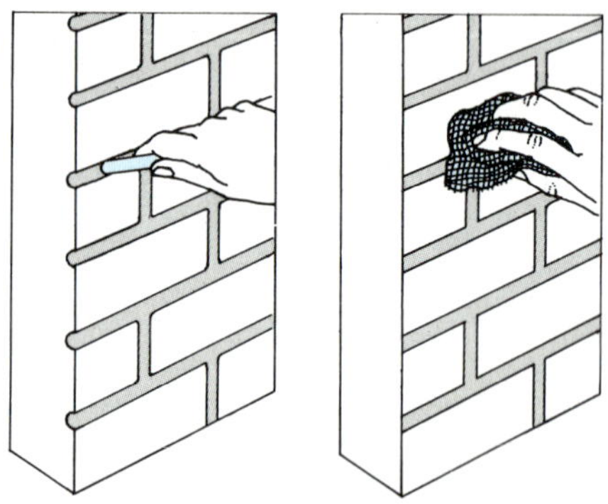

**3** For rounded (concave) joints (left), run a length of 12mm (½in) diameter wooden dowel along the mortar to leave flush joints (right), then rub the surface with sacking.

## LEVELLING A HEARTH

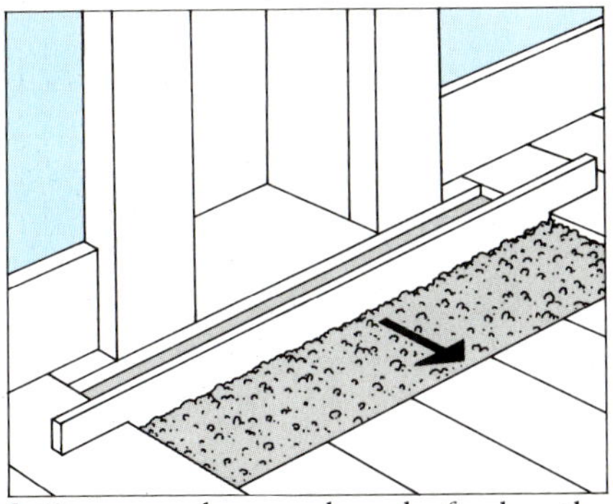

**1** Cut a notch at each end of a length of wood to the depth of the hearth-stone, and use this to level off a bed of crumbly mortar placed all over the hearth slab.

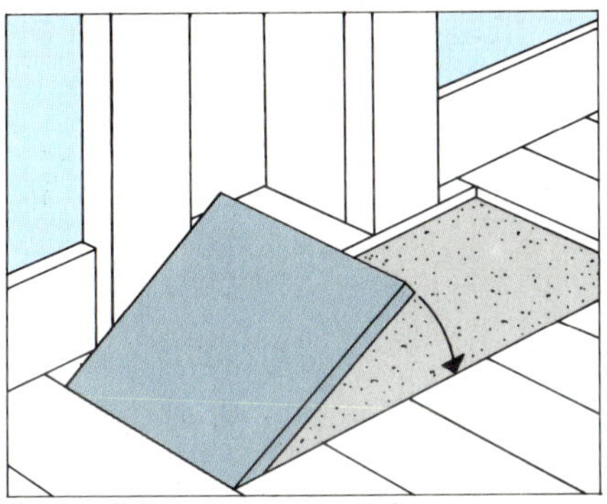

**2** Carefully lay one hearth-stone onto the mortar and tamp it down firmly with a wood block until it lies flush with the surrounding surface, then lay the other stone.

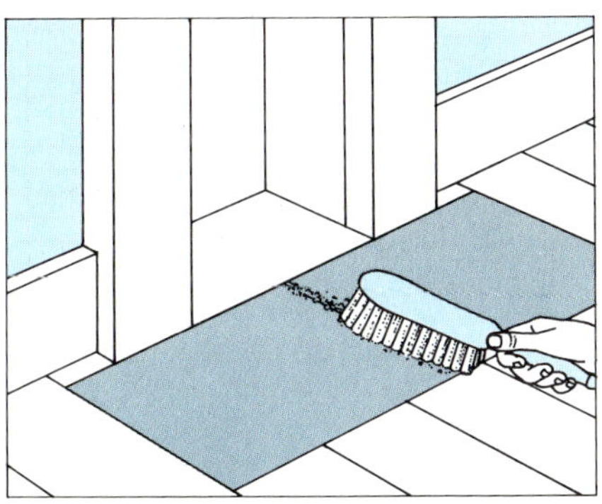

**3** Fill the joint between the two hearth-stones by brushing in a dryish mortar mixture with a stiff hand-brush so that the mortar is flush with the hearth-stones.

## ATTACHING A SURROUND

**1** Position the fire surround centrally in front of the chimney opening and chip away the plaster behind the fixing lugs. Drill holes in the brickwork to take plastic plugs.

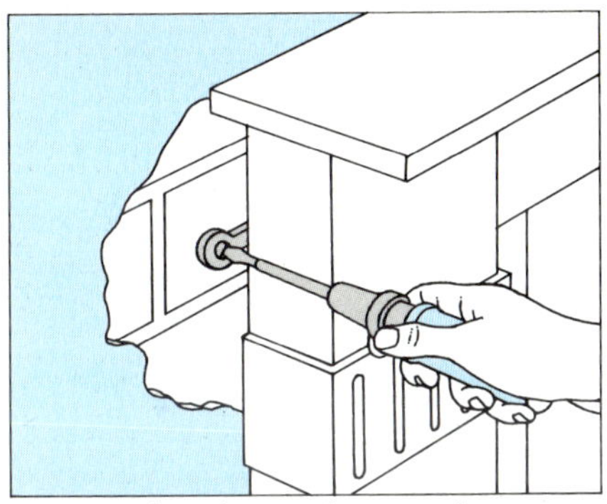

**2** Insert the plastic plugs, and screw the surround to the wall through both lugs with screws at least 38mm ($1\frac{1}{2}$in) long to ensure a strong, firm grip. Countersink below the surface.

**3** Mix up some one-coat plaster (page 82) to a pasty consistency and spread it over the lugs and brickwork with a laying-on trowel. Level it off flush with the surrounding plasterwork.

you are dealing with something structural. When a fireplace is blocked up or removed the chimney is often capped off at roof or loft level: if you are considering re-instating a fireplace, this process may need reversing. Either way, the state of the chimney and the degree to which the fireback and lining bricks are fireproof need professional assessment. First, call in a sweep who will give you valuable advice about the chimney condition, and then, unless you are extremely experienced at do-it-yourself, consult a builder about the best course of action. A professional will be able to advise you both about the structural aspects and the fireproofing. Remember that natural gas fires need adequate ventilation, and may use chimneys for flues.

### Cover-ups

Try masking a fireplace with a screen, either painted with a scene or fabric-covered to co-ordinate with curtains or upholstery. Hanging a fall of fabric from a high track or pole to hide the chimney completely is effective when it echoes window treatments. The easiest way of all is to stand something large in front of it – a table with masses of plants and accessories, dramatically lit to attract attention.

If the surround is itself striking, use it as a frame for a display of flowers, plants or statuary. Fill the gap with a sheet of mirror, which will double the effectiveness of the display, or a laminate that goes with the rest of the room.

If the surround is acceptable but the wrong colour, paint gives you the choice of picking it out in the colour of the woodwork so that it seems part of the room's framework. Brick surrounds can be painted, preferably with several coats of emulsion (latex) paint.

# Decorative Mouldings

Interiors in many European houses built before the 1920s were given finishing touches which might include mouldings or architraves around doors and windows; skirtings (baseboards), dados (chair rails) and picture rails around walls; and covings, cornices and ornamental mouldings around and on the ceiling. They were more or less elaborate and in excess made rooms seem cluttered, but perimeter ceiling mouldings, in particular, contribute a timeless elegance. The effort of restoring them subtly enhances the quality of a room's atmosphere, and different ways of decorating them helps to adjust proportions. Where conversion work or structural repairs have left a gap in the continuous line of these mouldings, it's vital to restore them to complete the room. Less ornate moulding designs are ideal for modern interiors to soften angles between walls and ceiling.

## Restoring

The original mouldings might have been moulded on site with wet plaster or applied later preformed with joins carefully concealed. Of the do-it-yourself replacements, the least expensive and lightest in weight is polystyrene, followed by fibreglass. Both of these look cheap and should be considered only if the ceiling will not take the weight of any other type. Better quality mouldings in fibrous plaster, GRP (glass reinforced plastic) or a resin-based material look more authentic.

**Cornices and crown mouldings** are elaborate sculpted bands of plasterwork often in a traditional pattern such as egg-and-dart, Greek-key or acanthus leaf. Layers of old paint, clogging up the moulding and making recognition difficult, must be painstakingly removed with a shavehook and small brush: warm

### FITTING PLASTER COVING

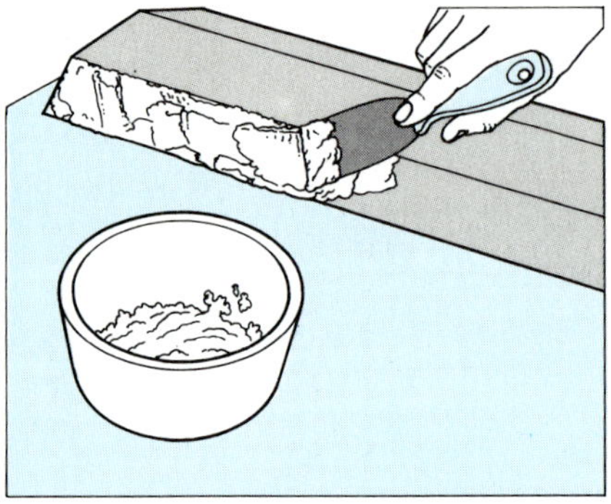

**1** After marking guidelines on the ceiling and wall and sanding the surface between them, mix the adhesive with water and butter it on to the back of the coving.

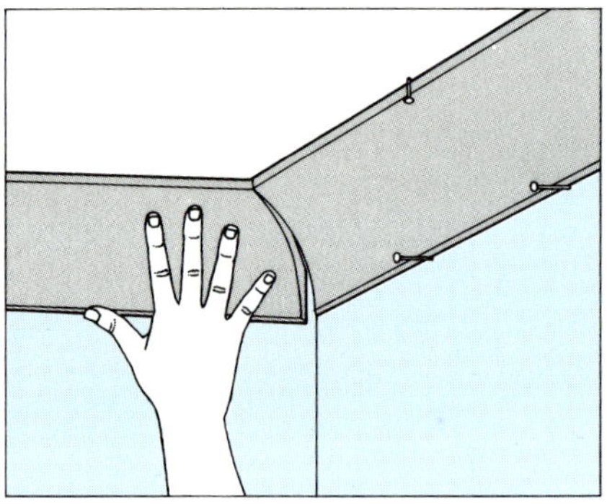

**2** Position the coving between the guidelines and temporarily support it with nails. Mitre the ends in corners with a fine-toothed saw using the cutting template usually supplied.

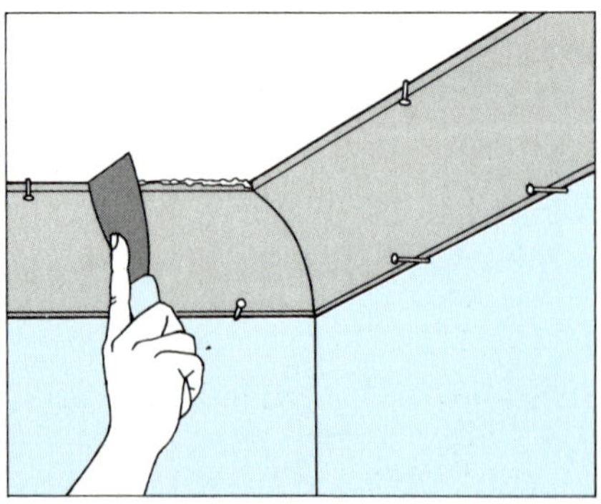

**3** Scrape off excess adhesive and use it to fill the joints between lengths, then brush over with a wet paintbrush. Remove the supporting nails after an hour and fill the holes.

### FITTING A CENTREPIECE

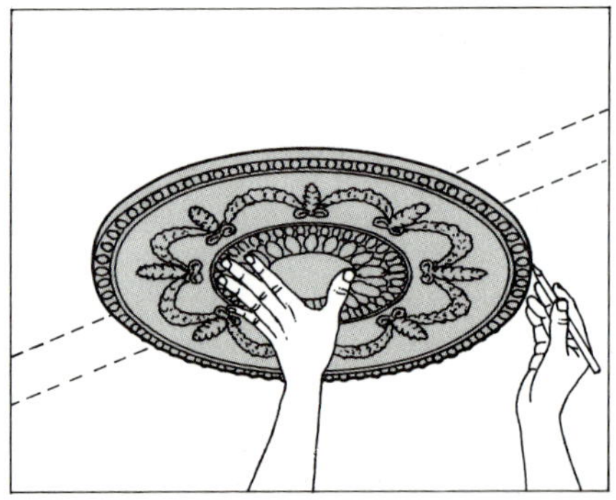

**1** Hold the centrepiece in position and mark right round it. Probe within the marked area with a bradawl to find the ceiling joists and mark their positions on the ceiling.

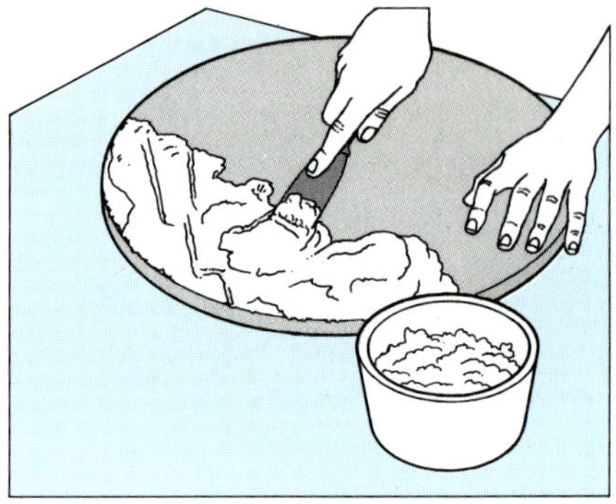

**2** Make two holes through the low flat areas of the centrepiece to take screws. Mix the adhesive and spread it 3mm ($\frac{1}{8}$in) thick all over the back of the centrepiece.

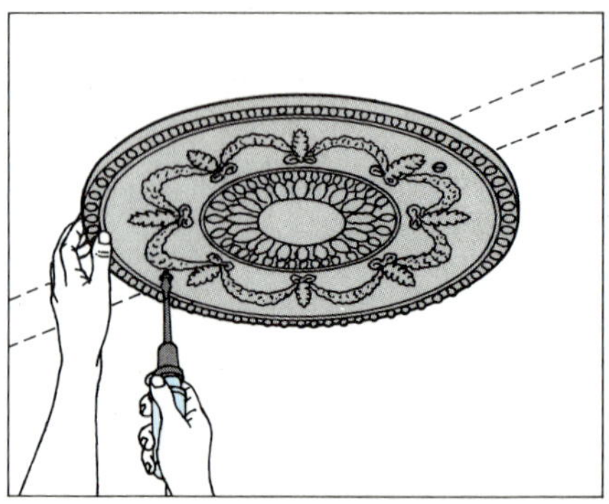

**3** Press the centrepiece onto the ceiling, with the holes below the joist, and secure it by screwing in 50mm (2in) No. 8 screws countersunk. Fill over the screwheads.

water will dissolve distemper, but use a proprietary paint remover and brush cleanser for other paints. To fill gaps or replace damaged sections you can buy lengths of the traditional patterns in different sizes. If yours is not a popular pattern, it is possible to get a matching length made up in fibrous plaster, and there are still some specialists around who will mould individual pieces to order. It is not difficult to slot a new piece into a gap (see right) and filling and painting will hide the join.

**Covings** are simpler in profile, effectively forming a curve between walls and ceilings. Where these were moulded in the original plaster it is sometimes difficult to decide where to stop decorating the walls and begin the ceiling (a wallpaper border sometimes helps to define this limit). Usually covings were added later, like cornices, and can be decorated in a similar way. Gaps in coving are not difficult to replace, and preformed coving is very easy to put up (see opposite).

**Ceiling centrepieces** that are original should have paint removed in the same way as cornices. Replacements are easy to attach and should be screwed directly into the joists (opposite). Tap with a hammer to locate the joists (the spaces between will sound hollow) and probe with a bradawl to confirm their positions.

## Painting

If the ceiling seems too high, paint the 'bed' (the flat part) a rich colour which echoes the floor in tonal value, and pick out the mouldings in a neutral or pale colour. This also draws attention to the ceiling mouldings. If you want to make them less obvious or give a greater impression of height, decorate the ceiling and walls in a pale, cool colour (blue, grey, green or lilac), and paint the mouldings slightly lighter or darker.

### REPAIRING PLASTER MOULDING

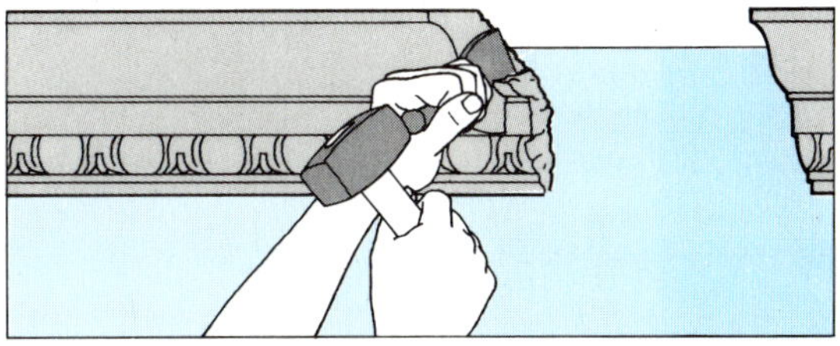

**1** Chip out the damaged cornice moulding with a wide chisel and club hammer (small sledgehammer), leaving the ends of the undamaged cornice flat and square.

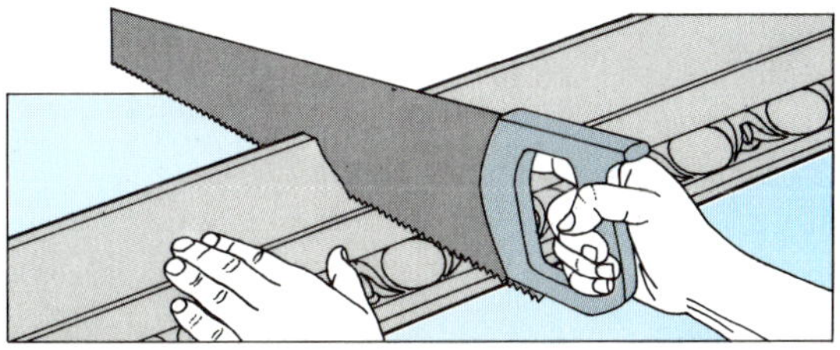

**2** Carefully measure the length of the gap to be filled and cut a piece of cornice 6mm ($\frac{1}{4}$in) less than this length, matching the pattern at the ends as accurately as possible.

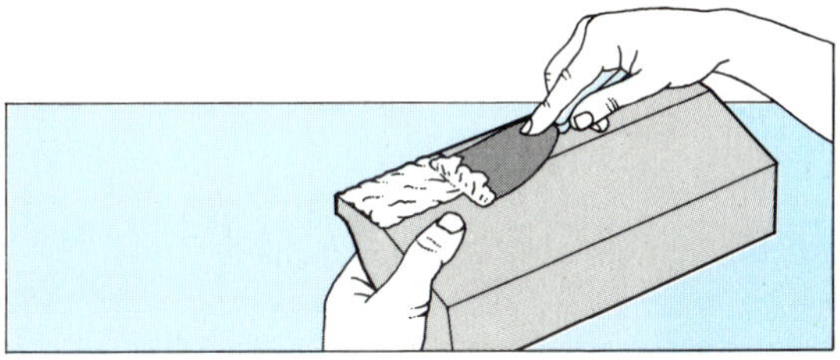

**3** Check the fit of the patch in the gap and adjust as necessary, then spread adhesive along the areas of the cornice which will be in direct contact with the wall and ceiling.

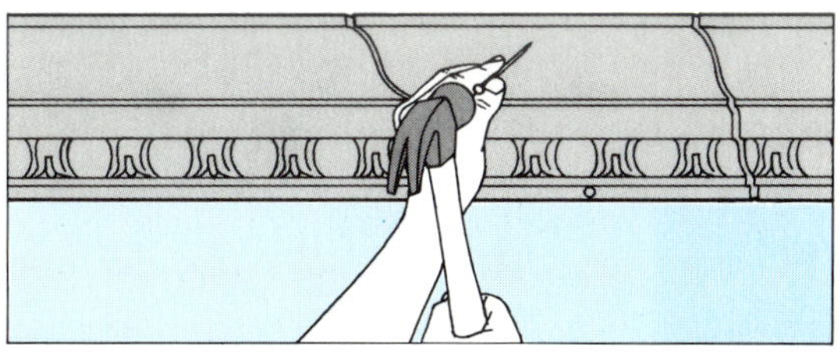

**4** Press the patch into the centre of the gap and ensure that the top and bottom edges align. Secure it to the wall and ceiling with galvanized nails punched below the surface.

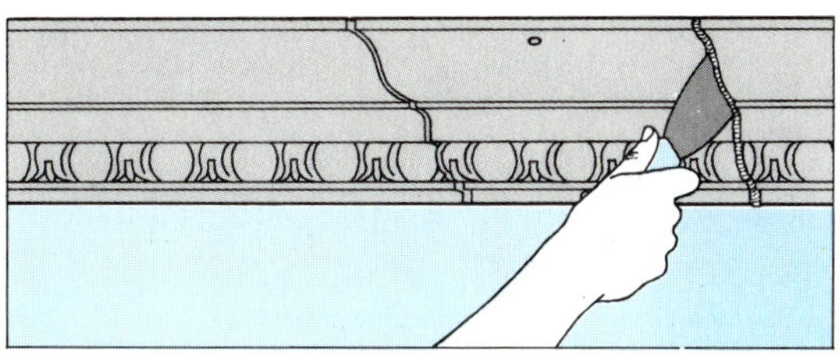

**5** Cut two pieces of scrim tape which are as long as the depth of the joints and then soak them well in a slurry of plaster. Push firmly into each joint, until just below the surface.

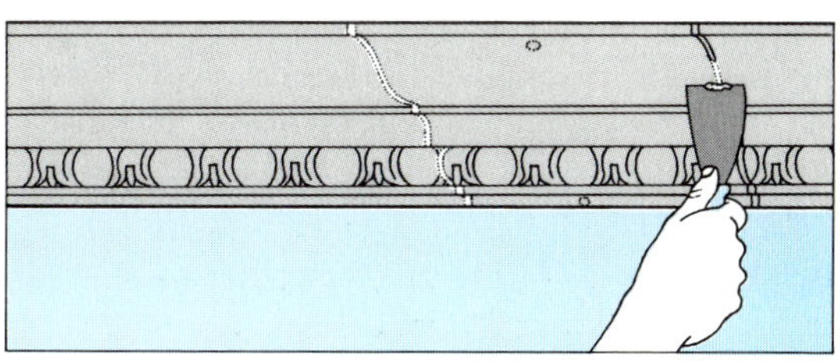

**6** With a creamy mix of plaster, fill over the scrim tape, pushing the plaster well into the joints. Fill over the nails and brush all over the repair with a damp paintbrush.

# WORKING WITH LIGHT

Change is the keyword for lighting. There is the obvious transformation when you flood a dark room with light at the flick of a switch, but between the two extremes of dark and light come infinite gradations. Light is a necessity, but its full potential may be harnessed to work in exactly the ways that suit you. A variety of appropriate fittings can keep pace with all the activities that every home must accommodate.

There are several different types of lighting used in the home.
*General lighting*, often created by a central pendant fitting, can be uninspired on its own but provides good, general visibility in a room.
*Task lighting* needs to be well positioned and directed. An angle-poise lamp can be placed on a desk, for example, to give light to read.
*Accent lighting*, often using spotlights, highlights objects, shelving and pictures, creating colour, texture and form.
*Information lighting* is the very utilitarian type which is needed for comfort and safety, such as the light by the garage door or on the stairs.

## Decorating with light

Because efficiency is the usual priority, the cosmetic value of light is often overlooked. Lighting quite literally changes the way you see things. You *can* paint with light, using it as a decorating tool to camouflage or enhance features. It is not a question of the fittings themselves so much as the character and positioning of the light source. Ordinary incandescent light bulbs diffuse a slightly warm-toned light all around, unless interrupted by a shade; most fluorescent tubes shed a colder light; spotlights and floodlights emit a brighter, often whiter, light in a particular direction. Soft-toned lamps in glowing shades seem to warm an atmosphere; powerful

white lamps directed at pale surfaces suggest the cool spaciousness of normal daylight.

You can exploit these effects to give an illusion of altering a room's dimensions. Low pools of light create an intimacy in a large high room where the ceiling is unlit, while a wash of light over a pale expanse of ceiling will make it seem larger and higher. By focusing light on more attractive areas you distract attention from imperfections in other parts of a room. A strong beam of light casts deep shadows: directed from one side, it throws textures and shapes into sharp relief; shining straight on, it flattens them, disguising the unevenness of a wall surface, for example.

Remember that light affects colour, and that you should view decorating samples in the room itself, and under *all* the lighting conditions that may be used. In turn, colour affects light, and low-toned matt surfaces are known to absorb more light than pale smooth ones.

## Flexibility

Use flexible lighting to make the same space work in different ways at different times. By illuminating a special area or putting on a particular kind of light, the flick of a switch can transform a kitchen into a dining room or a bedroom into a study. Even where rooms do not have to double up for such a variety of purposes, people have changing moods and pursuits, and the lighting in, say,

*Opposite:* Trompe l'oeil *needs a sympathetic lighting arrangement that will throw helpful shadows and enhance the total illusion. The pictures on this wall are not really hanging there, despite appearances: the frames and ribbons have been painted onto the wall itself, around prints stuck directly to the wall.*

**LIGHT FIXTURES**

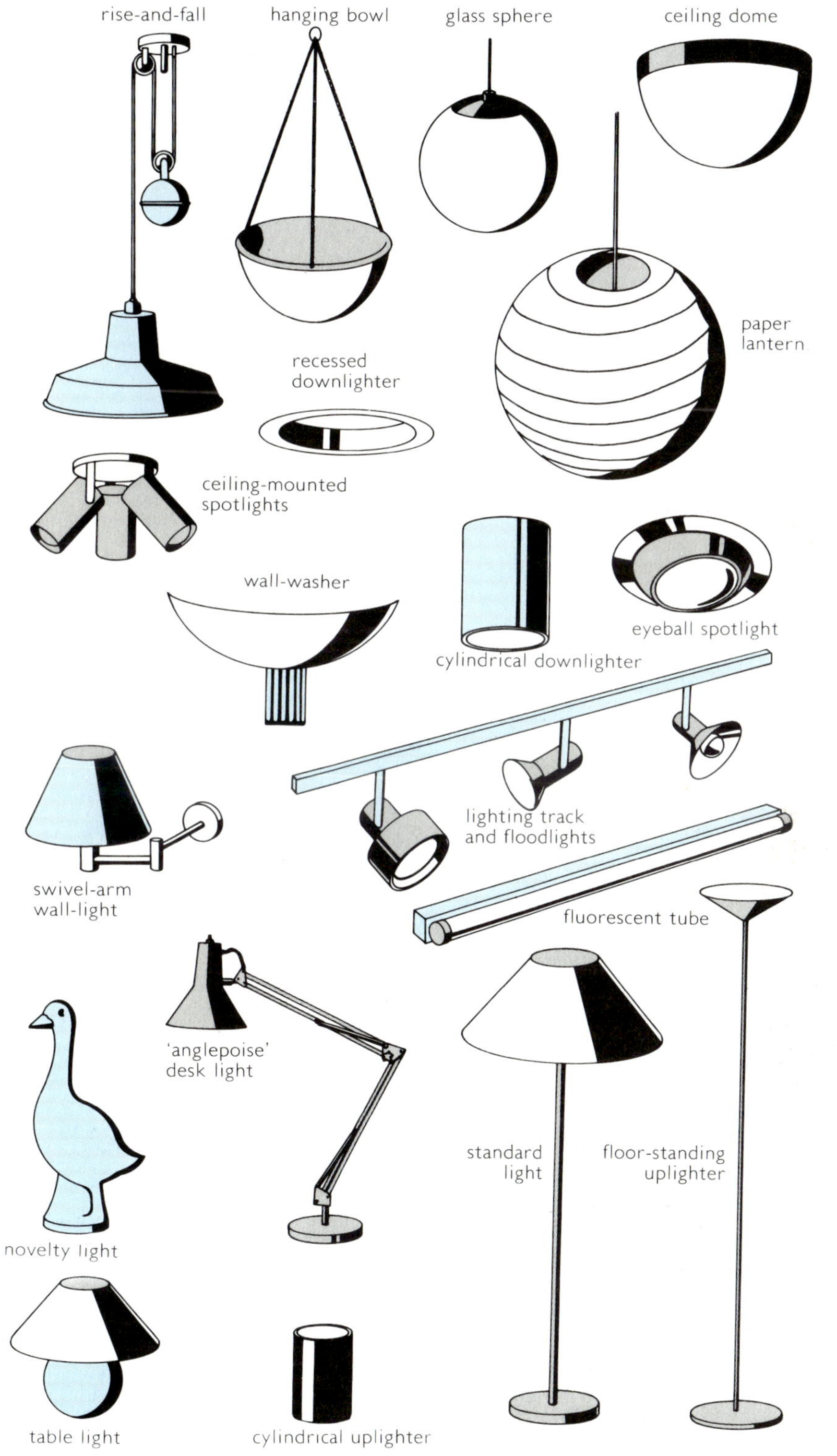

a living room can be varied to induce a mood of relaxation or to encourage industry. Sometimes a single fixture will serve more than one purpose, for instance an adjustable directional light can be beamed downwards on to a work surface or be turned upwards to bounce general light off a wall or ceiling. Desk lamps offer a good short-term solution and help you experiment with different effects and positions.

Another dimension of flexibility is in the use of dimmers, which permit one light source to provide bright general lighting or gentler background lighting as required.

Almost every room can use a combination of different types of lighting – and they need not all be used at once. To make it versatile, have the different items individually switched, but perhaps linked in two different circuits so that a whole set of lights can be put on at once.

## Planning

Plan what kind of light is needed for each room and how it will be used before deciding what style of fixtures will best achieve those results.

*Opposite: A bland decorative scheme will gain from fixtures arranged to create pools of light and areas of shadow. Deep shelving enhances the effect, for the light seems to be falling from shelf to shelf, creating interesting shapes in its passage. Highlighting a detail like a door handle draws the eye on and suggests a world – or at least a room – beyond this hallway.*

*Left: Mirrors and mirror glass produce all sorts of possibilities for interesting lighting effects. Recessed downlighters in the ceiling are good options for dining rooms, where it is often necessary to focus on the table rather than to light the entire room.*

**LIGHT PATTERNS**

Opposite page, left to right: flexible-arm desk light; ceiling-mounted spotlight; translucent uplighter; floor-mounted cylindrical uplighter; glass diffuser bowl for pendant; fabric-shaded pendant; balloon pendant. This page: a standing uplighter, a semi-directional standing floor light and a table light combine with each other to give atmospheric and accent lighting while still providing sufficient illumination for such activities as reading or writing.

One way is to begin room by room with the task or specific lighting and proceed outwards from there. Provide first for efficiency and safety on work surfaces and around steps. Next plan display lighting for pictures, objects or any key architectural feature that deserves attention. A certain amount of this specific lighting will bounce off adjacent surfaces, but some background lighting may be needed to supplement this localized lighting; and there may be a place for additional mood light sources.

Work through the house, planning what you need where.

**Kitchens** You need good direct task lighting for the night-time use of cooking and work surfaces; don't forget to place the lighting so that you don't work in your own shadow. Efficient ways of task-lighting kitchens include fluorescent strip (often harsh), spotlights on ceiling- or wall-mounted track, and concealed lighting under wall-mounted cupboards. An adjustable ceiling pendant works well over any dining area.

**Living rooms** Provide pools of light from table and standing lamps strategically positioned in relation to the furniture – but not to central heating thermostats. Display lighting can provide adequate background lighting; you could have light bounced off a wall from uplighters, create a soft glow with wall-washers or have lighting concealed behind a pelmet (cornice). Dimmers are one simple, flexible solution to a harsh central light fixture that has not been changed.

**Halls, stairs, landings** Safety is a priority here. Avoid dark corners and make sure treads and risers are clearly visible on stairs. Light bounced off the ceiling and walls may be sufficient, or you can light steps individually. Provide dual switching both upstairs and down.

**Bedrooms** Provide direct bedside lighting that will throw light on the page if people want to read in bed. Choose lights for the dressing table that shine on to the face, not into the mirror or the eyes. Light the inside of any deep cupboards, switched to come on as the door opens. Softer background lighting may be provided by concealed lighting, wall-washers or an attractive illuminated display. Have most lighting dual-switched from both bed and door.

**Bathrooms** Have lights around a mirror or as an integral part of a cabinet. You need general lighting and may also need task lighting in the shower and bath area. Always make sure it is *safe* for bathrooms, that fixtures are enclosed, and switched from outside or by pull-cord.

*Countertops in kitchen/dining rooms perform a useful dividing job between the two areas. Lighting the counter itself accentuates this.*

## WORK SURFACES

A fluorescent tube behind a baffle illuminates the work surface without causing unpleasant glare.

A wall-mounted adjustable spotlight gives concentrated illumination where it is most needed.

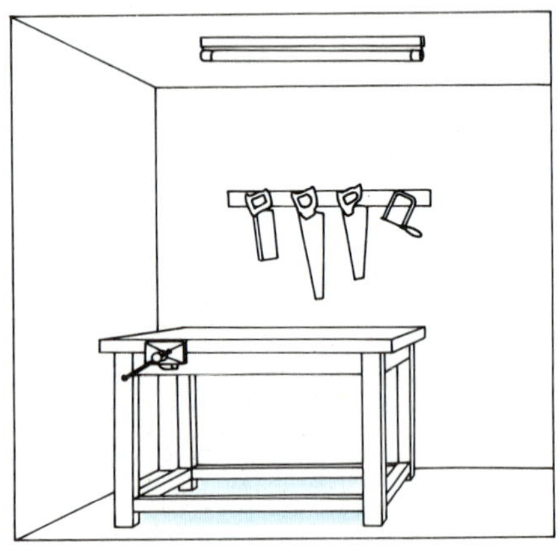

An open fluorescent tube and light-coloured walls provide shadow-free lighting over a wide work area.

## LIGHTING AREAS

**Stairs:** An overhead light behind the stairs creates enough shadow to define each tread clearly.

Recessed spotlights up the stairs highlight the treads and turn the stairs into an unusual feature.

**Dining room:** A low-level light should create a warm atmosphere without obstructing the view.

A downlighter creates a focal point on the table by highlighting a striking table decoration.

**Living room:** For general reading a standing floor lamp is ideal, as it can be moved to the required position.

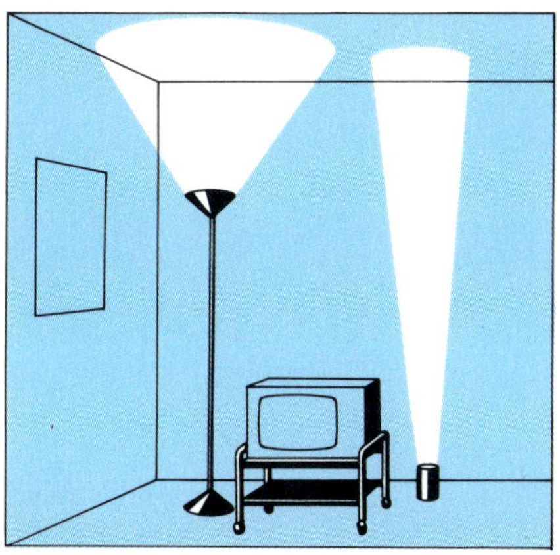

Uplighters can provide reflected general lighting as well as accent lighting, depending on the height.

## Fixtures

When buying the fixtures to implement your lighting scheme, you need to be satisfied with their appearance as well as with the light they produce. There is an initial choice between displaying the fixtures themselves – choosing them for their specific character and the way it matches that of the rest of the interior – and giving them a low profile, concealing them so you get the benefit of the light without having attention drawn to its source. Concealment can sometimes be done simply by placing an uplighter, for example, behind a piece of furniture or a plant. A striplight may be built in behind a baffle under a cupboard or shelf to conceal the tube.

One way of coming to terms with the wiring problem is to opt for one of the frankly 'hi-tech' systems using a number of lights on a track. This, with other sorts of spotlight, comes into a functional style category that looks remarkably good in older homes as well as modern ones, adding an unexpected touch to traditional surroundings; but this type of fixture will flatter almost any room.

Decorative lights and lamps chosen to echo or complement the room's style and colour should nevertheless do the task for which they are intended, and do it well. They are there to see by as well as to look at. A whole range of modern and traditional versions are available of table lamps, standing lamps, wall lamps, pendant lamps and directional desk lamps. Don't forget that shades, globes and even lamp bases can look quite different when illuminated – and that they should look good in both their daytime and night-time roles. Translucent shades contribute a distinct colour cast to their surroundings while opaque shades give localized pools of light rather than all-round illumination.

# WORKING WITH OBJECTS

An attractive display of interesting objects, whether plants, flowers, pictures or a favourite ornament, can be used to pull an entire scheme together and provide clever focal points and conversation pieces. Your own choice of accessories and the way you put them together give stock furniture and impersonal interiors the stamp of your individuality. Objects can provide just the right emphasis to complete a well-decorated room, and conversely they can also help to detract from an ugly architectural feature. Many different combinations will work and the accessories need not be expensive or exotic to create an interesting effect.

Without becoming too self-conscious, it helps to think in terms of 'composition' so that objects seem to belong where you have placed them and don't just happen to be lying around. Separating different arrangements with clear space and using accent lighting are devices that enhance this effect.

Trivial or ephemeral things gain importance by being together, so a number of them can rival a single more expensive or exotic item in creating an interesting display. Never be blinded by an object's normal purpose: things that you use every day and don't hide away – such as the fruit bowl, kitchen scales, even a pipe rack – do go to make up the visual impact of a room, so arrange them to your advantage. They can be enjoyed visually as well as for their proper function.

In a kitchen, try arranging pastas, pulses and herbs in clear glass jars; in a bathroom a large collection of potions, shampoos and creams can be shown off on a shelf instead of hidden in a cupboard as their jars are often colourful and pretty. Old-fashioned open cupboards are still one of the most pleasing ways to store your china, but when it comes

to glasses try to have some light shining through them somehow: shelves across a window reveal are one way; another is to light glass shelves from below with an uplighter; or from behind.

The keys to decorating with objects are to be bold and have fun with your ideas, and to remember that this is one of the easiest, cheapest and most dramatic ways to change the entire look and feel of a room. Play with scale: large vases can look good grouped with smaller ones, and a small room can be hung with large pictures or dominated by one large hanging. Move things around constantly, and don't ever feel you have 'finished': the most artful collection of things will look contrived and rigid to your eye in time.

## Grouping objects

A clever grouping of related objects will have a visual impact that in the end is greater than the sum of its parts. A collection of teapots, for example, could look extremely striking if they are well-displayed and well-lit, even if none of them is rare, expensive or without flaws. Pictures that are in themselves relatively uninteresting can look effective if framed and hung together, and they will always look better if hung over a piece of furniture. Try to

*The tops of cheese cartons and straw hats are unlikely things to use as a decorative focus, and derive a large part of their charm from that simple fact. They are both cheap and easy to find, and demonstrate the potential of amassing collections of everyday things. Here the collections have a strong personal touch, the cheese tops with their mount and frame that prevent them from becoming lost on the wall, the hats with their different shapes and colourful, varied ribbons.*

maintain one constant feature across the collection, so that if you have a mixture of shapes and sizes use matching frames, but if they are all the same shape try many different colours and types of frame to add visual interest.

Small items, such as postcards and photographs, will benefit from being mounted and framed together. Another option might be to frame them singly and create the illusion of pictures suspended vertically on a long ribbon. Choose a wide ribbon in a colour you like and that blends with the walls, turn over a small 'hem' at one end and attach with drawing pins to a picture rail or high up on the wall. Use a plumb-bob to ensure it hangs straight, and cover the place where you have secured it at the top with a bow. Next push picture hangers or pins through the ribbon and into the wall at the required vertical interval, and hang the pictures from them. Make sure you can see the ribbon between each picture. This treatment might work well on a stairwell, where you can stagger the lengths of the ribbons.

An unused fireplace is one place where you could make a little arrangement of objects, because you won't find yourself having to step over them to get somewhere. A piece of statuary might combine well with a basket or some china, and if you light the arrangement subtly you can make an extremely strong focal point.

## Single splendour

If you have a really spectacular object to show off, it will only detract from its style if you place it in a group, so display it on its own. An original piece of sculpture, a beautifully shaped piece of silver or glass or a classic oriental vase will all benefit from single treatment. A very special original painting positively needs to

| | |
|---|---|
| WALL FIXINGS | 42 |
| PAINT FINISHES | 110 |
| PICTURE RAILS | 166 |

*Opposite: If your budget constrains you to just a small collection of bowls and jars, look for a unifying colour and put the items into use: the total effect will be doubled.*

*Left: A jumble of jars and objects looks charming in any case, but the clever touch here is to hang a painting discreetly on the beams, which echoes the collection of jars, bottles and jams below.*

*Below: The effect of a single treasured object is enhanced with a suitable site and an illusionistic paint finish. Be as contrived as you dare.*

be placed on its own to give the maximum effect, and similarly a tapestry, wall-hanging or rug could well lose their impact if displayed as part of a group. Featured on a pale background a beautifully coloured rug, such as an Afghan rug, can look dramatic. These softer hangings can be attached by drawing pins or nails to a wooden strip, but you may have to sew some closely-woven reinforcing fabric round the edge first to prevent the fibres pulling apart. You might want to construct a frame by nailing some inexpensive wooden strips into a rectangle that fits the rug. Hang the strip or frame by means of picture wires from the picture rail if you have one, or from sturdy picture hangers or hooks. Rugs and fabrics can be very heavy, so choose your fasteners carefully: mirror hangers might be a sensible option on a wooden frame.

The area above a fireplace is always a good focal point to show off a single object. A large modern or traditional painting can really bring the space to life. Try hanging a mirror or displaying a clock to suit the proportions and style of the room; and don't feel constrained by a need to be symmetrical.

A lone object such as a beautiful vase or a carved mask from Africa will look stunning in an alcove, niche or featured on a stair landing with good accent lighting to show it off to advantage. To make the most of natural daylight stand it in the centre of a window, possibly on a glass shelf, but bear in mind night-time illumination as well, and the possibility of colours starting to fade in sunlight.

Special display shelves, and cabinets which incorporate integral lighting in their design, can also be used to feature single items, as well as for a complete collection. If you decide to treat several items as one, light them as such – a set of pot lids or

china plates, for example, grouped on one wall can be lit with spotlights mounted on the ceiling or wall. Or, alternatively, you could use one of the lights designed especially to illuminate pictures.

If you obtain a 'specimen' cabinet, or glass-topped table to house small, delicate items, lighting can be incorporated. When using a table, you might stand a table lamp on top. In some cases, this might well form an essential part of the grouping, and perform two separate functions: adding visual symmetry and providing illumination.

## Living displays

Finally, don't forget the potential of plants and dried flowers as display material in your home. Bring a designer's eye to bear on the plants themselves, and combine tall, striking foliage plants with small, variegated trailing varieties and seasonal flowering plants. They can also be combined with other interesting objects, such as a stunning piece of statuary, a jar of children's glass marbles, pebbles in water or even an interesting collection of large and small sea shells.

Dried flowers and grasses, even interestingly 'architectural' small branches and twigs, can be arranged in containers and used to brighten up a dull alcove or summer fireplace – anywhere, in fact, where a living plant might be starved of light or humidity. Bunches of dried grasses, herbs and flowers can also be hung upside down from suspended racks in kitchens to give a 'country' feel.

*Opposite: A collection of bowls, plates, jugs and cups as eclectic and as interesting as this should never be hidden away or made to look inaccessible. The decorative impact is immense, simply from the sheer number of objects.*

**LIGHTING PICTURES AND OBJECTS**

An inconspicuous eyeball fitting is a neat and effective way to light up glass display shelves.

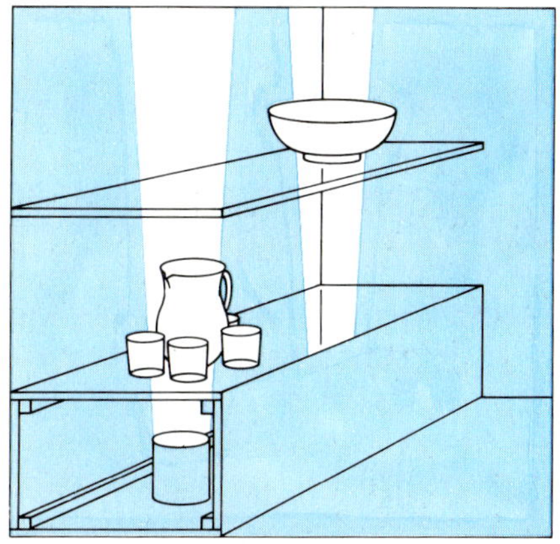

Cylindrical uplighters concealed below glass shelves pick out the objects placed above them.

Some framing spots have shutters which can be adjusted to light the area of a picture exactly.

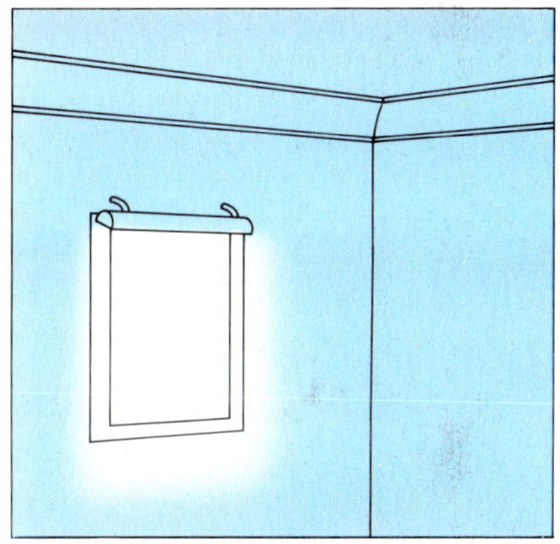

A wall striplight, the width of the picture and mounted directly above it, casts an even overall light.

Lighting a plant from above shows off its shape and really highlights the texture of all its leaves.

A hidden uplighter behind and below a plant creates an interesting mixture of light and shade.

# Shelves and Shelving

Shelving should be one of the most hard-working and attractive features in your home, for it can become the receptacle for all your most treasured possessions.

Non-adjustable shelves are the easiest of all to put up, whether within an alcove or along a wall. A shelf placed right along one wall at picture rail height can make a unifying touch, and you can then display tall items such as plates and bowls on it (you will need to attach a wooden strip to the shelf a short distance from the wall edge to stop them slipping). Simple too are brackets screwed into the wooden members of a window frame, supporting glass or wooden shelves and an interesting collection of glassware through which the light can shine.

For a shelving system, you can construct your own from quite inexpensive materials and a few woodworking tools, or from ready-made adjustable components: some build up into quite complex structures to which drawers and doors can be added for a wider range of options.

## Materials

Almost anything can be used for shelves, with a wide variation in price and the quality of the final effect. Most suppliers will cut your shelves to size for you. Chipboard (particle board), blockboard (lumbercore board) and plywood would all need to be painted to look good enough for display purposes, but are at least cheap and easy to handle. Plastic and laminates make good kitchen or bathroom shelves that are easy to clean.

To do justice to really treasured objects, wooden shelves are probably one of the best options. They would also stand up well to mini spotlights clipped to the edges, casting strong pools of light on the objects displayed.

| | |
|---|---|
| KITCHEN SHELVING | 10 |
| LIGHTING SHELVES | 31, 37 |
| WALL FIXINGS | 42 |
| MAKING SHELVES | 44 |

*Opposite and left: Kitchen clutter can be both decorative and functional. Open shelves the length and breadth of one wall is a simple, clean option, making life very easy for the cook – who now has everything within easy reach – and putting every inch of potential space to good use. Adjustable shelving is another very practical option: look for systems that fit in with the kitchen design – here modern in style and very functional.*

*Below left: Alcoves open up all sorts of possibilities for those who want to install their own shelves. These are supported on wooden strips screwed to the wall, and the shelves are shaped to accentuate the depth of the alcove itself. This would be best done by making a cardboard template and using that to cut all the shelves to the same shape.*

*Left: The space under a staircase can be opened out and used as a display area with very satisfactory results. Here glass shelves provide the horizontal ingredient, following the treads of the stairs, while metal strips with adjustable brackets provide the verticals. This staircase lacks a handrail, and is not suitable for anything other than very infrequent use: the shelving helps to enhance its decorative function.*

## LOAD-BEARING CAPACITIES OF SHELVING

Blockboard (lumbercore board), chipboard (particle board) – either plain, or faced with melamine or timber veneer – plywood and timber are the most common materials for shelving, although metal and plastic can be used. Glass is used for decorative or display purposes, and needs to be secured with special brackets. The size and weight of the load will determine the width, material and type of support – bear in mind that some materials weigh heavily even before a load is put on them. It is important to get the shelf span right and to have good supports firmly secured with screws of the right length.

*Maximum span between supports for medium to heavy loads*

| Material | Thickness | Maximum Span |
|---|---|---|
| BLOCKBOARD | 12mm ($\frac{1}{2}$in) | 45cm (18in) |
| (LUMBERCORE BOARD) | 19mm ($\frac{3}{4}$in) | 80cm (32in) |
| | 25mm (1in) | 100cm (39in) |
| FACED CHIPBOARD | 15mm ($\frac{5}{8}$in) | 50cm (20in) |
| (PARTICLE BOARD) | 19mm ($\frac{3}{4}$in) | 60cm (24in) |
| | 25mm (1in) | 75cm (30in) |
| PLYWOOD | 12mm ($\frac{1}{2}$in) | 45cm (18in) |
| | 19mm ($\frac{3}{4}$in) | 80cm (32in) |
| | 25mm (1in) | 100cm (39in) |
| TIMBER | 15mm ($\frac{5}{8}$in) | 50cm (20in) |
| | 22mm ($\frac{7}{8}$in) | 90cm (36in) |
| | 28mm (1$\frac{1}{8}$in) | 106cm (42in) |
| GLASS | Available in various thicknesses: 4mm ($\frac{5}{32}$in); 6mm ($\frac{1}{4}$in); 8mm ($\frac{5}{16}$in); 10mm ($\frac{3}{8}$in). The weight of all glass is considerable, and the shelf span must be estimated in conjunction with the weight of the load – your glass supplier will advise. A span of more than 50cm–60cm (20–24in) may not be recommended. | |

Metal shelving systems, intended for industrial and retail purposes, can be used domestically to good effect, particularly if yours is a hi-tech interior. They are very flexible and hard-wearing, and might make an interesting addition to a kitchen, putting on display all the normal cooking paraphernalia.

For transparent shelves, look for glass or acrylic sheet. Of these, glass is the best-looking but also the heaviest and the most fragile; but the alternative does scratch very easily. Transparent shelves can be very attractive across a window reveal.

You will need to use special brackets for glass shelves and the glass must be measured and ordered from a specialist or building supplier and cut to size. The edges should be polished smooth. If you want a particular shape, perhaps a curved edge, make an accurate template using stiff card or paper. Your supplier will then cut to fit.

### Load-bearing

Materials and fasteners are entirely dependent on how you decide to use the shelves eventually. Glass shelves, for example, would just not bear heavy books but are ideal for displaying china or small objects. Book shelves need to be sturdy and well made when you realize that 12 average-sized paperback books weigh about 2kg (4$\frac{1}{2}$lb), while the same number of hardbacks is at least twice as heavy. China, cast-iron cooking pots and pottery can be very heavy.

Supports must be attached securely to the wall with the right screws and brackets and be strong enough to suit the determined load. The front of a shelf should not project more than 25mm (1in) beyond the end of the bracket. Buy as many as needed, with one pair spare (see chart).

### Wall fixings

Most shelves, or their supports, are fastened to the wall by means of woodscrews, and the length and gauge number of the screw will be determined by the type of shelf and support, and how much you want the shelves to hold. As woodscrews will not grip satisfactorily in plasterboard (gypsum board) or masonry, you will first need to insert a wall-fixing device in these materials.

For most shelves, 50, 62 or 75mm long (2, 2$\frac{1}{2}$ or 3in) woodscrews will be suitable. In solid walls the screw must be long enough to pass through the support and at least 25mm (1in) plus the plaster depth into the masonry. In hollow partition walls, the length of screw will depend upon the type of wall fastening being used. Some come complete with screws. In all cases you will need to know the thickness of the support to choose the right length of screw. For

*Opposite: This confined area has been opened up with some cleverly-placed mirrors and put to good use with highly-finished and very original shelving, utilizing all the available space.*

| | |
|---|---|
| LIGHTING SHELVES | 33, 37 |
| WALL FIXINGS | 42 |

lightweight shelves, thin No. 6 gauge screws will be adequate, whereas for heavy loads you will need to use thicker No. 10 screws.

Exterior walls, whether of solid brickwork or with a cavity between two layers of masonry, will usually require the use of standard or heavy-duty plastic plugs, or expanding anchors for very heavy loads. The exception is breeze blocks which require a finned plastic plug or a collapsible rubber tube fixing to grip them properly. Breeze blocks can be identified by drilling a small pilot hole *using rotary action only* (ease of drilling distinguishes them from concrete blocks).

Interior walls may be built of solid or hollow bricks or blocks, or be stud partitions consisting of a wooden framework covered with lath and plaster or plasterboard (gypsum board). To determine the type of construction, tap the wall in various places: if it responds with a dull thud, it is solid; if it sounds hollow, it is a partition wall or built of hollow bricks or blocks. In either of the latter cases you should use cavity fixing devices. These are broadly of two types – collapsible anchors and toggles. Toggles are only suitable for stud partition walls, on which you may also be able to screw directly into the wooden framework (detectable by a duller thud). Plasterboard (dry wall) fixings

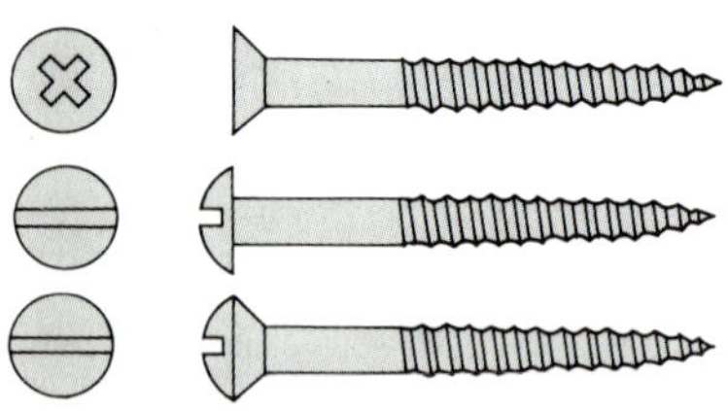

Screws are made in a wide range of sizes. Head shapes are countersunk (to lie flush), round (to secure flat metalwork), and raised (for securing architectural ware), and may be slotted or have a cross recess.

## FIXINGS FOR SOLID AND HOLLOW WALLS

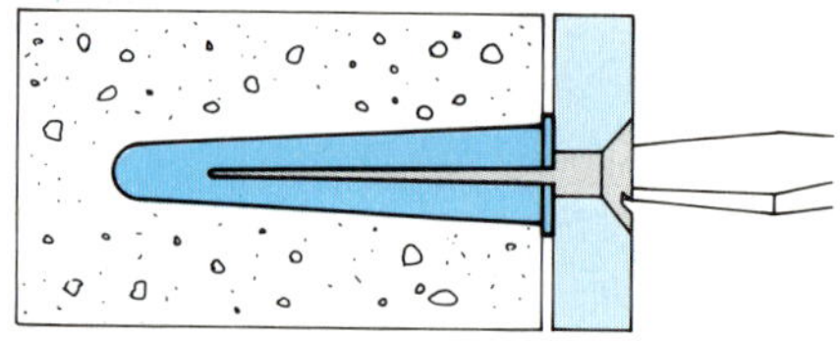

A general-purpose plastic plug, suitable for use in brick, high-density blocks, and concrete.

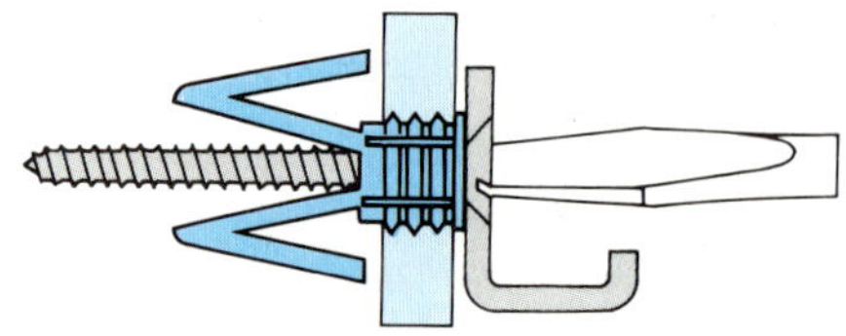

The barbs of a plasterboard (gypsum board) plug spread the load behind the board.

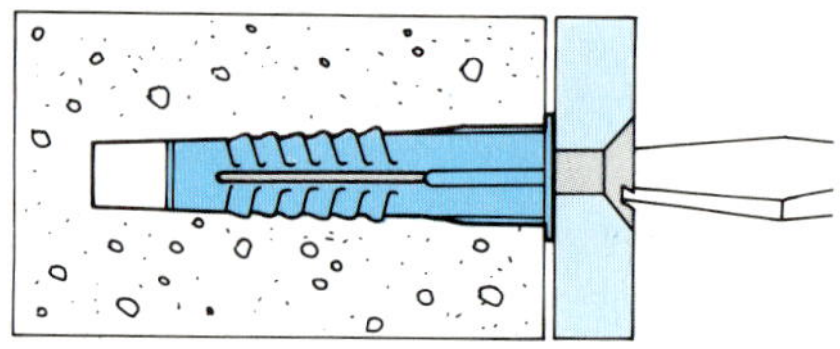

The ribs on a heavy-duty plug give it greater pull-out strength than the standard plug.

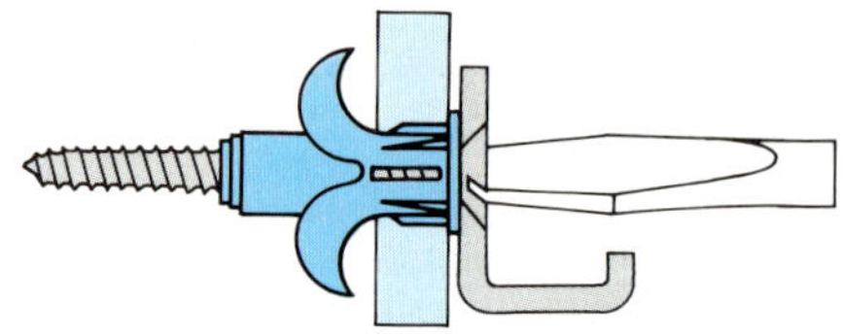

The hollow wall fastener has two 'wings' which open out behind the surface on tightening the screw.

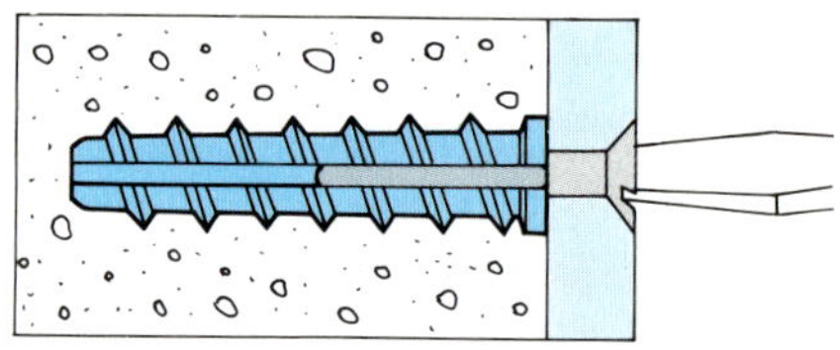

The lightweight cellular block plug has spiral ribs and is screwed into the drilled hole.

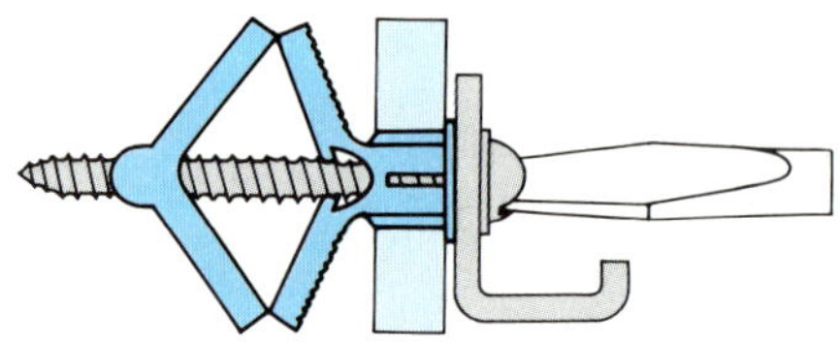

A collapsible plastic anchor is pulled up tightly behind the plasterboard (gypsum board).

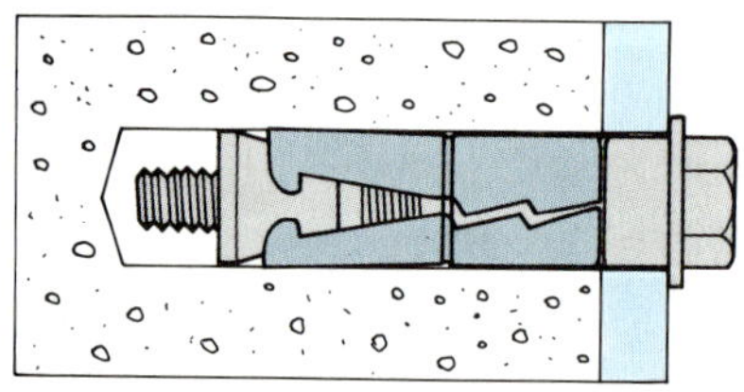

For securing heavy loads to masonry or concrete, use a masonry bolt (expansion anchor).

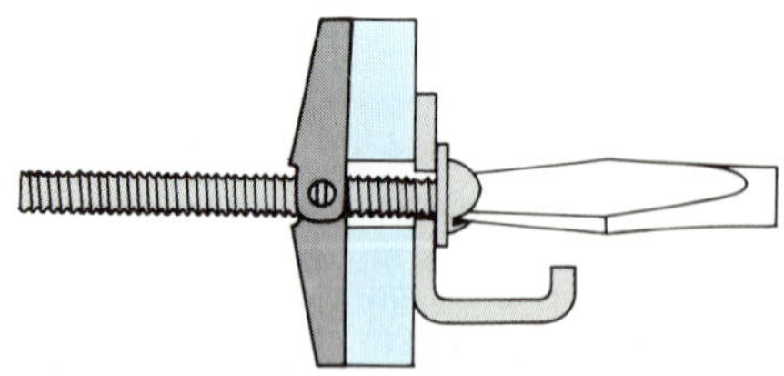

The bolt of a spring toggle must be fed through the fitting before pushing the toggles into the wall.

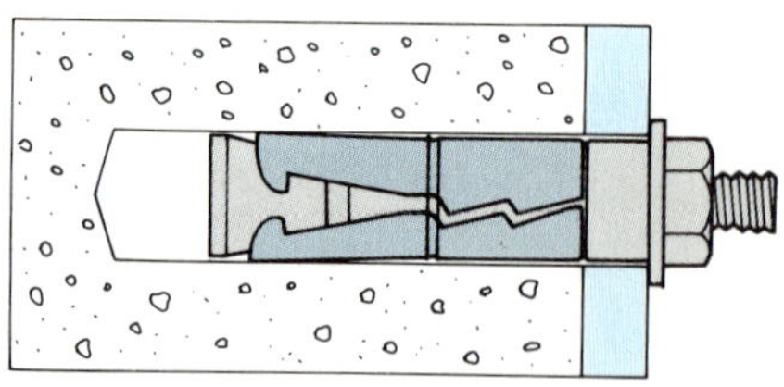

Another type of masonry bolt – here the bolt protrudes and the load is secured by a nut.

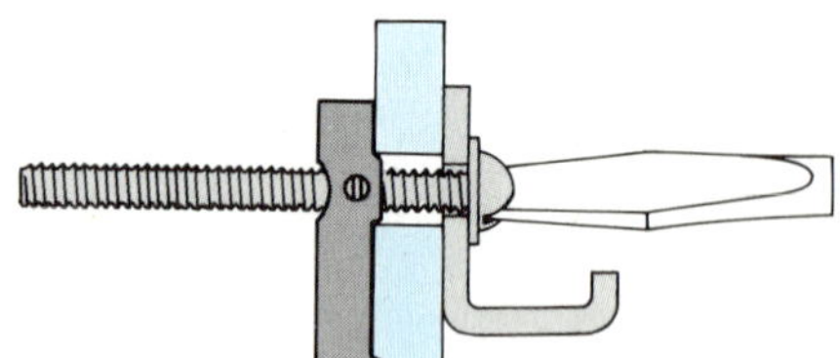

The gravity toggle falls into position behind the wall. Toggles are lost if the bolt is removed.

LOAD-BEARING 40
TOOLS AND EQUIPMENT 76, 160



will not support very heavy loads so always screw directly into the wooden framework.

The method of using wall fixings is basically the same for all types: mark the position for the hole, drill it with the correct size of bit, insert the plastic plug or other device, insert the screw through the shelf support, and screw it into the plug.

Take care not to drill directly above or below a plumbing or electrical fitting and, if you can, check the wall first with an electronic detector to indicate the presence of metal and live (hot) wires.

## Shelf supports

There is a wide variety of shelf supports available for home-made shelving. Simple L-shaped brackets come in different sizes and can be brass, steel or aluminium. A gallows bracket is made of wood and braced on diagonal members. Always use a spirit level to make sure the shelves are horizontal.

With adjustable shelving the top two screws in each upright are the most crucial, as these take nearly all the tensile (pulling) load. The uprights are slotted all the way down to take the necessary brackets, and you will of course need to line these up across the wall. First secure the left-hand upright at the top with one screw, and let it drop. Use a spirit level or plumb-bob to establish the vertical position and mark drilling positions on the wall through the holes in the upright. Swing the upright to one side, drill and plug the holes, then screw securely.

Slot a bracket into place and using a piece of shelving (on edge) and a spirit level, determine a level position for the shelf and mark the position of the next. Drill, plug and secure them with screws as before. When all the uprights are in place, slot in the brackets, add the shelves

### OPEN-WALL SHELVING

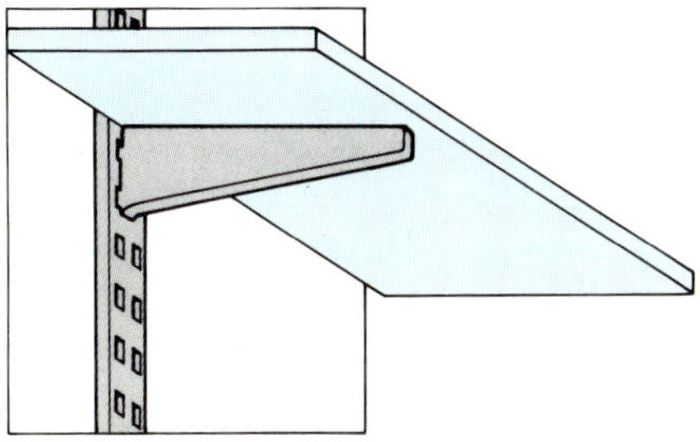

Support brackets for adjustable shelving slot into different positions in uprights screwed to the wall.

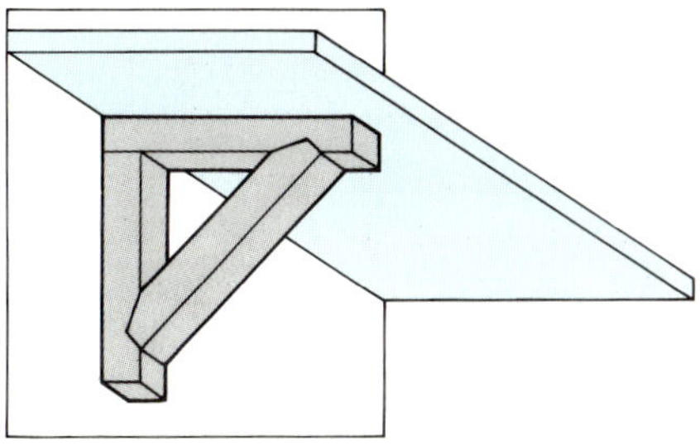

An easy-to-make gallows bracket. The angled brace must be set into notches in the other members.

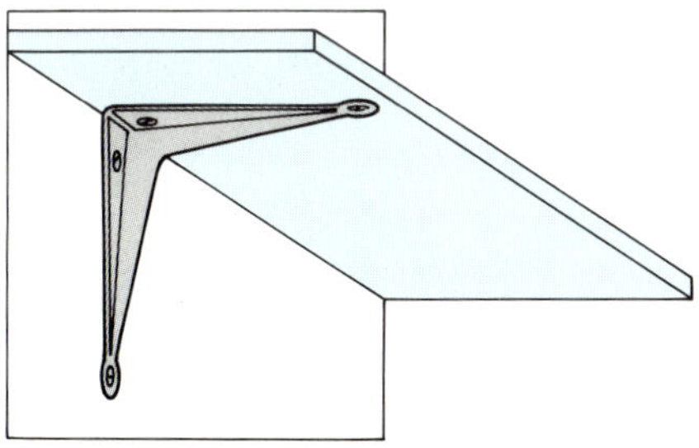

Pressed steel angle brackets, in a wide range of colours, will support very heavy loads.

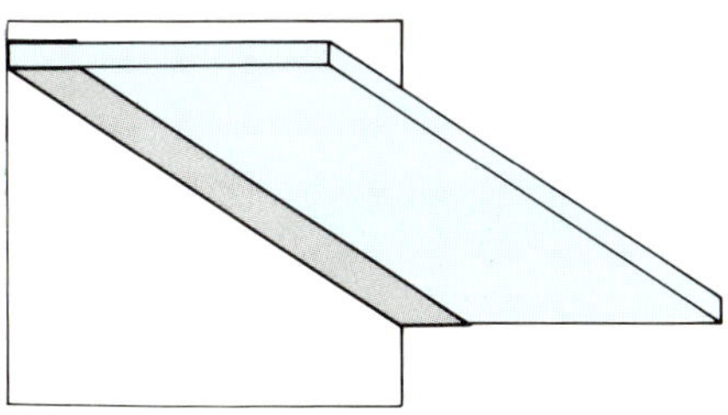

Cantilever shelving is simply pushed into a U-shaped channel screwed to the wall.

### ALCOVE SHELVING

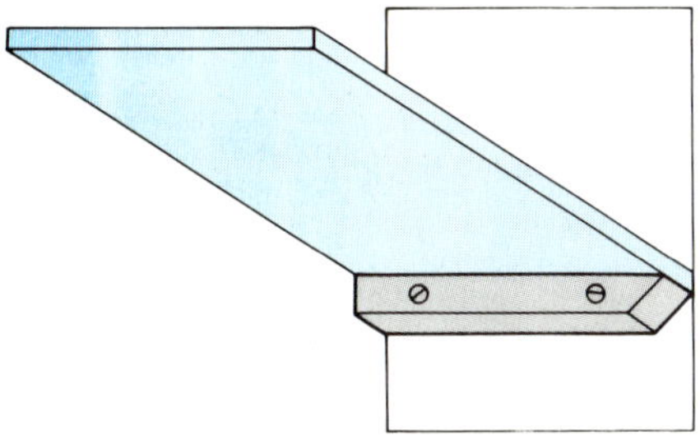

The simplest shelving of all, supported on a wooden strip which is screwed to each side wall.

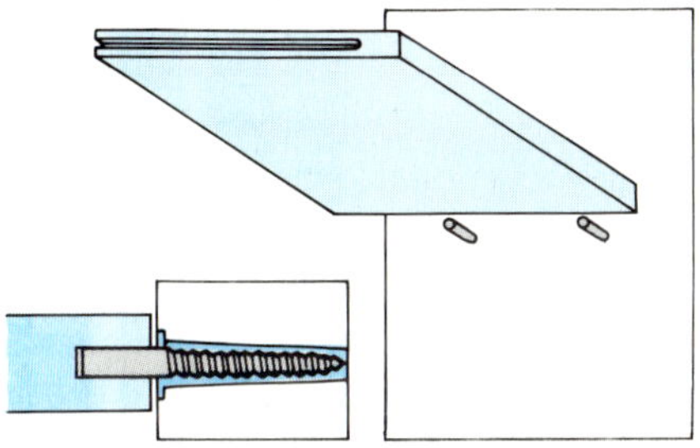

Groove the ends of light display shelves and slide them on to screws with sawn-off heads.

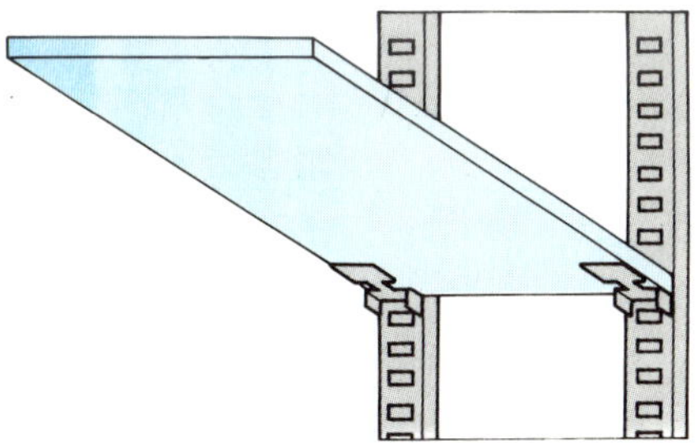

The support clips of bookcase strips slot into the four uprights (two at each end of the shelves).

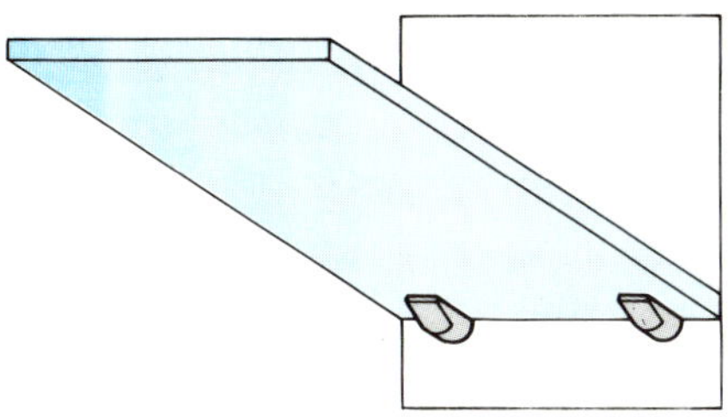

Shelf support studs fit into plastic 'bushes' which are then set into the sides of a cabinet.

and secure them to the brackets.

If you are fitting shelves into an alcove, you can use wooden strips, metal angles, triangular brackets, or one of the strut-and-bracket methods illustrated.

When you have marked the wall and attached the supports, you may find the walls are not absolutely true, in which case each shelf will have to be a slightly different size, and cut to shape along the back edge and each end. If necessary, make a template for each shelf and get them cut to shape by the supplier.

## Making shelves

A wall-mounted set of interlocking shelves (right) is excellent for display purposes. Look for real timber that can be waxed to show off its natural colour, or paint it to fit in with your particular scheme. Any appropriate width of timber will do: the notches should be cut to half the width of the timber, and as wide as the timber is thick. Adapt the design for a larger number of shelves if you need them – it might make a good spice rack, for example.

If you are in rented accommodation, or likely to move fairly frequently, it may be better to think about buying or building free-standing shelves with a supporting frame, rather than attaching shelves to the wall. Free-standing shelving is much more flexible – you can add to it or subtract, or move it around when you want to replan a room. If you have really heavy books to support, a firm, free-standing structure may end up being more practical than a wall-mounted one.

A simple floor-standing bookcase in wood (opposite) is not difficult to make, and is a good simple structure to start with. The shelves sit on a series of 'rungs' down each side, rather like some types of industrial shelving that are available.

**INTERLOCKING DISPLAY SHELVING**

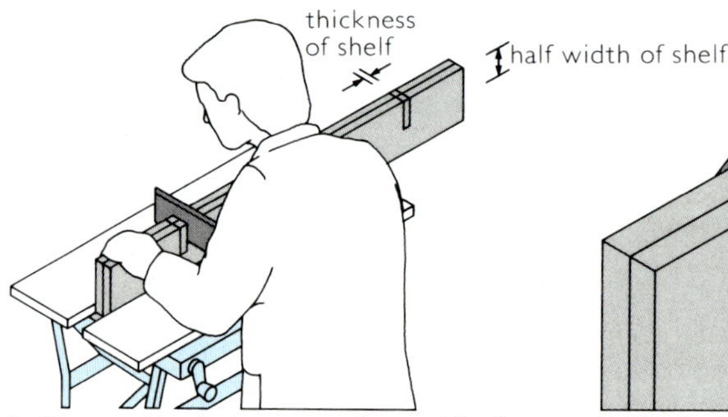


**1** Clamp the shelves together with the ends flush, and mark out the notches: they should be as wide as the timber and the depth of half the timber's width. Cut down the sides of the notches with a tenon saw (backsaw).

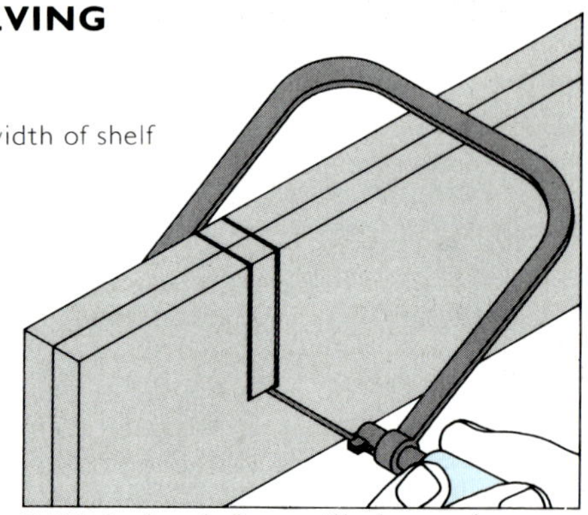

**2** With the shelves still clamped together, cut across the bottom of the notches with a coping saw, setting the blade at an angle to the frame. Cut notches in both the uprights in exactly the same way.

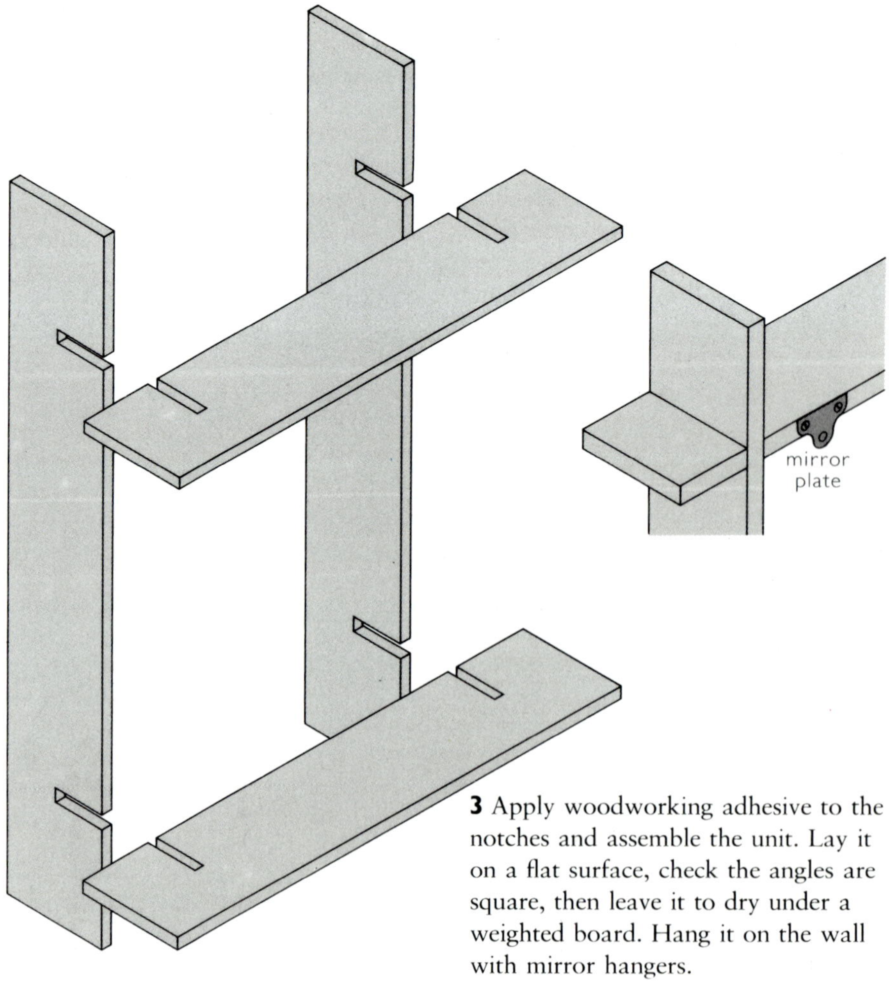


**3** Apply woodworking adhesive to the notches and assemble the unit. Lay it on a flat surface, check the angles are square, then leave it to dry under a weighted board. Hang it on the wall with mirror hangers.

| | |
|---|---|
| LOAD-BEARING | 40 |
| WALL FIXINGS | 42 |
| WOOD | 156 |
| TOOLS | 76, 160 |



## FREE-STANDING SHELF UNIT

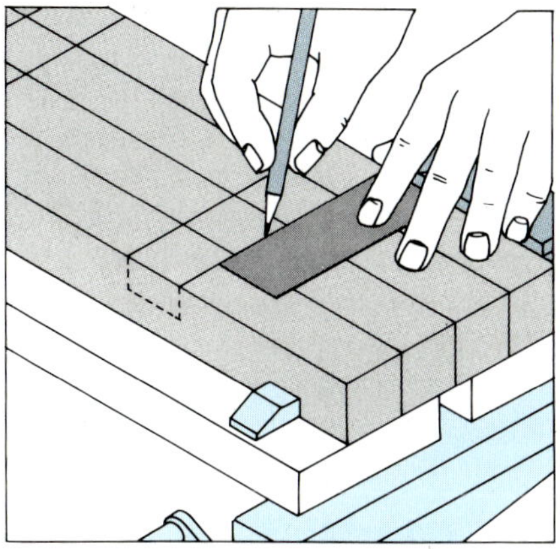

**1** Cut the uprights and clamp them together, ends flush. Mark on the positions of the shelf bearers and square the marks across. The notch depth is half the bearer thickness.

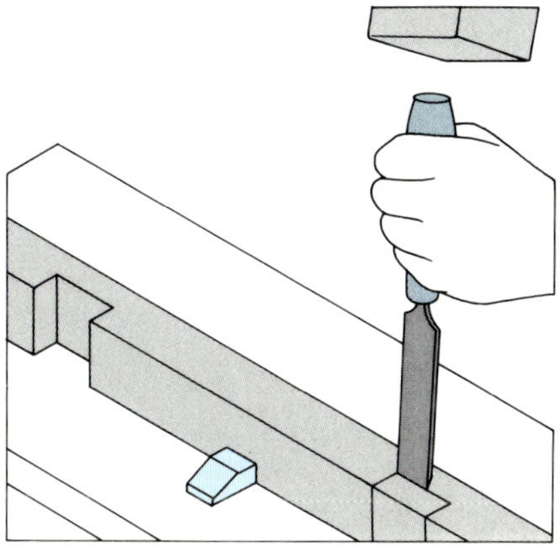

**2** Saw down the sides of each of the notches with a tenon saw (backsaw). Clamp the upright on its side and chisel out the waste, with the angled face of the chisel towards the waste.

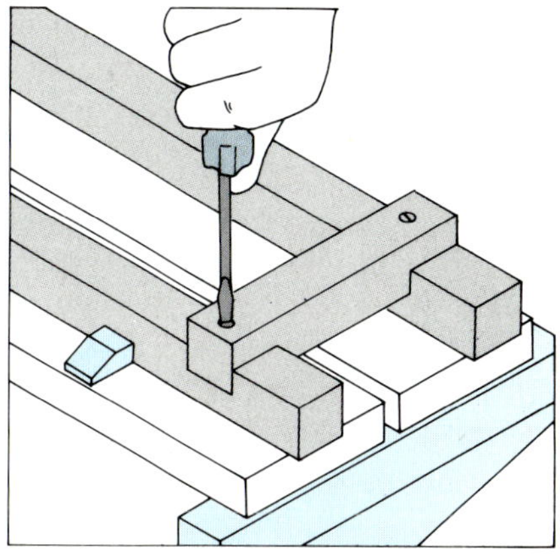

**3** Cut the bearers, and drill and countersink the fixing holes. Glue and screw them in the notches of the uprights with the ends flush to form two 'ladders'.

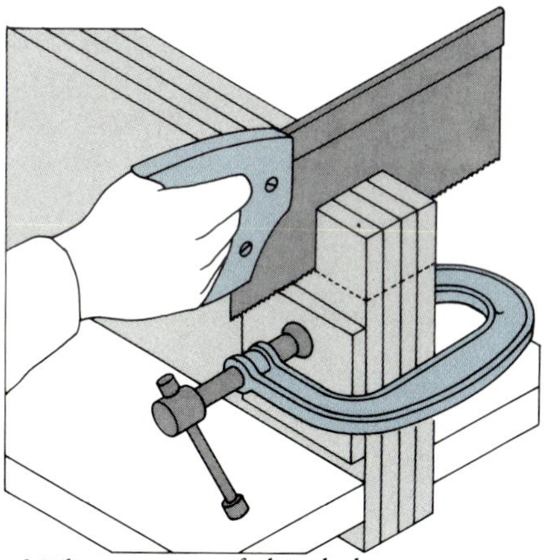

**4** The corners of the shelves are notched round the uprights. Cut the shelves and clamp them together, ends flush. Mark the notches and cut them out with a tenon saw (backsaw).

The shelves of this unit are supported on a ladder section at each end, with the 'rungs' spaced at the desired distances. Because the unit is free-standing, a brace is needed to strengthen and keep it from leaning sideways. This is set into the back edges of the shelves and one of the uprights.

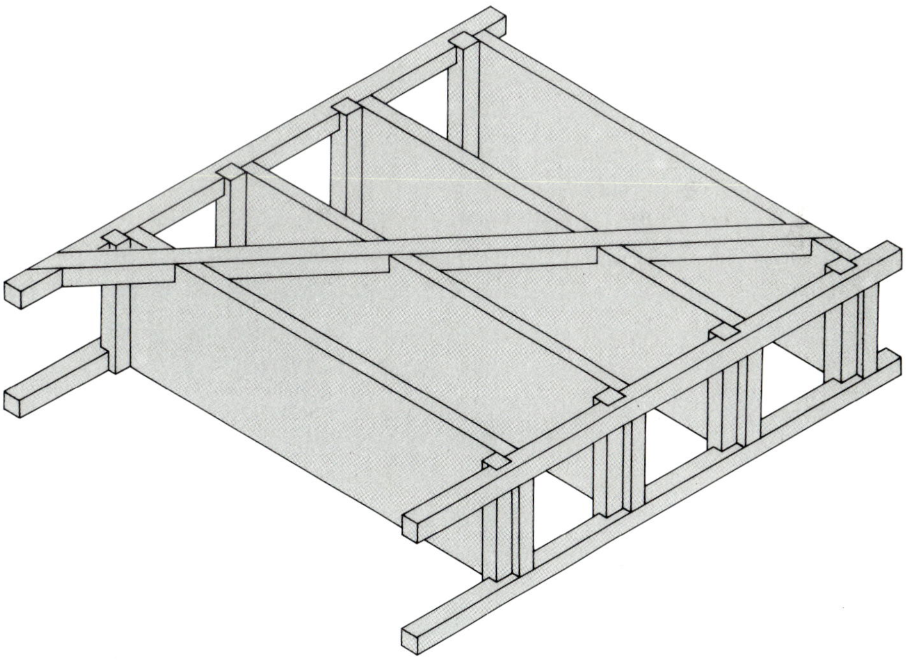

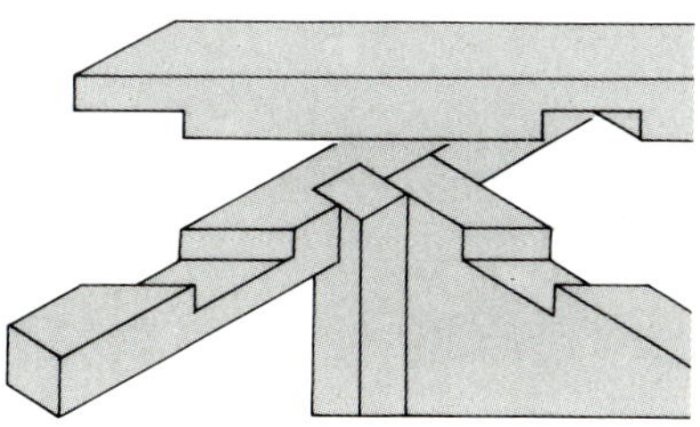

**5** Put the shelves and bearers together and lay the brace across to mark the notch positions. Cut out the notches in the brace and the backs of the shelves (they will be half the thickness of the brace and at an angle to the shelves), then glue and screw together.

# WORKING WITH FABRIC

Good interior design is as much to do with soft furnishings as with the more obvious forms of decorating. They should be planned, discussed, thought about during the very earliest stages of designing the decoration of your home, for you will continually be using them as a source of colours, as accents, and for that confident flourish that makes your home a pleasant place to live in.

Fabric is used in many parts of a living room, for example. It is needed for curtains, blinds or shades at the windows, for lampshades, for cushions and tailored or loose covers for furniture. Carpets and rugs are also textile products and should be considered in the scheme of things. Fabric is so versatile it can be used dramatically, to divide rooms, tent ceilings or to drape walls and hide any poor plasterwork or ugly features. Most importantly, it will bring a feeling of rich, perhaps colourful, luxury to your rooms.

The choice of fabric, the colour, pattern and texture, is very much down to individual taste. It is often dictated by the style you are aiming at. Pretty floral cottons, mini-prints and checked gingham look good in cottage-style rooms. Velvets, brocades, silks, satins, moires all suit a room which is more formal or opulent. Bold geometrics and heavily-textured weaves can look superb in a modern room, especially accompanied by suitable furniture. But don't feel constrained by do's and don'ts: an unexpected choice may score from just that simple fact.

If you want to create a period feel in a room, there are many original patterns produced on different fabrics which will give a ready-made authentic look. There are the floral patterns designed by William Morris and the abstract patterns of the English Bloomsbury Group, for example, not to mention the many co-ordinated collections of today.

| | |
|---|---|
| FABRIC THROW-OVERS | 10 |
| COLOUR | 58 |

*Left: Fabric is allowed to make a strong visual statement in this room. Very simple loose covers on the sofa and armchairs are enlivened by a truly gorgeous quilt and cushions. They echo the colours of the plates displayed above the fireplace, and invite the visitor to sit down and relax in comfort.*

*Opposite: Curtains needn't be confined to windows. Fabric can be a colourful divider between the sitting and dining areas of a room, allowing you to pick out an existing colour or theme – here the yellow and the black of the rug and furniture – and to emphasize it in another medium.*

The soft furnishing style needs to suit the type of fabric, as well as being right for the room. Fabrics which pleat up crisply are ideal to use for Roman blinds, tailored covers or pleated valances. Materials which drape softly can be made into festoon or Austrian blinds (balloon shades) or used to line walls with extravagant fabric 'curtains'. With the exception of fabric for decorative cushions, always use a proper furnishing fabric. Other types simply will not stand up to the wear and tear, and will not be resistant to sun, condensation, stains or fire. Always use a suitable upholstery fabric for loose and tailored covers too.

Some fabrics are very versatile and can be used for more than one function. Sheeting, for example, can be used for tenting and draping as well as more normally for bed linens. Ticking is another versatile fabric which is very cheap to buy as it is normally used to cover mattresses or chairs. It is cotton and only comes in certain colourways, but if they match your design scheme you can re-cover furniture at a very reasonable price.

## Cushions and covers

Removable covers on upholstered furniture are a practical way to change the look of a room and to give new life to furniture. Bright, colourful covers can be put on for spring and summer, and then taken off to expose a warmer type of upholstery fabric for winter. A new cover will revitalize an old sofa.

If you want to use a boldly patterned fabric, make sure the design will work well on the furniture and not look mismatched across the seat, back and arms.

Classic loose covers are not too difficult to make yourself, provided you are confident with a sewing machine. You can also have them custom-made or buy instant covers, if you are lucky enough to have furniture which is the right shape. For an instant furniture transformation you can make throw-over covers, using old sheets which have been dyed or patterned using fabric paint. Wool shawls, blankets, dhurries can all be used as throw-overs, to hide tired upholstery.

A simple single bed can be made to look like a sofa during the day – or

COLOUR 58
FABRIC AS WALLCOVERING 125

permanently – if it has a neat cover and bolster cushions at each end.

If you are having tailored or loose fabric covers, make sure the fabric is strong and easy to clean. The traditional loose cover material is a linen/cotton mixture, but there are many other suitable materials.

Cushions come in assorted shapes and sizes, and with a range of different fillings. Good-quality bed pillows, for example, are made from down, or a feather/down mixture, and these retain their shape. Polyester filling is very good to use and is completely washable. Foam chippings are sometimes used, but they lose their shape very quickly; other fillings include cotton waste, and kapok, which can become lumpy.

Most cushions can be bought covered in a plain or patterned fabric. They can also be bought with just a plain lining to cover yourself. Alternatively, you can start from the beginning and either cover a slab of foam or make up a lining. Always buy the best-quality filling you can afford and make sure the main cover can be easily removed for cleaning.

Try to make a variety of cushions in different textures and trim them to suit the fabric style. Piping is a popular trim for cushions. With a bright, modern pattern make the piping to match one of the featured colours. Or with a stripy material, choose piping in the dominant colour. The choice is endless, and you will be surprised at the effect a few generous throw cushions will have on your scheme.

*Opposite and above left: Fabric brings an element of luxury, if you use it lavishly. Cloths for tables look extravagant if they hang right down to the floor; loose covers can have tucks, gathers and bows added to liven them up; a second-hand screen can be easily renovated with fabric attached by ties at top and bottom. Alternatively, choose bold designs that make a dramatic statement on their own (opposite).*

*Above right: To a beginner's eye, 'tenting' ceilings and draping four-poster beds can look very complicated and off-putting. But an effect like this, using an inexpensive, very lightweight fabric, would be simple to achieve with a relatively flimsy wooden structure.*

# Window Treatments

Whether you intend to make your own curtains, blinds or sheers, have them made for you, or buy them ready-made, the starting point is always the same: consider the size and shape of the window, its aspect, and its position in the wall. Don't go against the prevailing architectural style or the overall decorating scheme, but help to emphasize it. Look at the view from the window and decide if you want to be able to see as much of it as possible or whether it needs screening because of an ugly view or inquisitive passers by. If the window is itself beautifully shaped, think about not covering it up at all, or at least 'dressing' it so that its form is shown off to maximum advantage. Conversely, it is easy and effective to disguise an ugly window shape with a clever treatment.

Whatever the type of treatment you choose, it will have to suit the decorative theme of the entire room. Traditional settings can take opulent window dressings, such as full-length drapes, swags and tails, extravagant pelmets and valances. Very often, however, you will be looking for something simpler and less overpowering, perhaps mounted on poles rather than tracks and with no trimmings at the top.

## Tracks and poles

How to suspend your chosen window treatment will depend on the type you have chosen and the window. Semi-circular bow and angled bay windows require track that bends or special poles which are curved. If you want to show off the curtain headings, then the track or pole will be part of the decorative treatment. Metal track is sturdier and is recommended for very heavy drapes. Valances need a special track that is fixed above the curtain track itself, while a pelmet (cornice) is rigid and fixed over a board. Sheers

### FITTING CURTAIN POLES

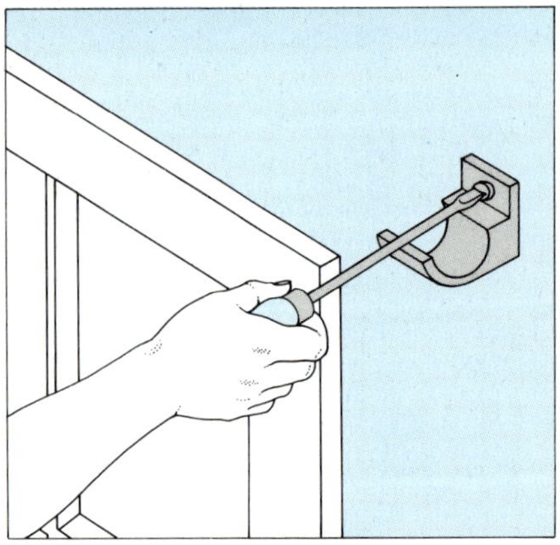

**1** Drill, plug and screw a bracket to one side of the window. Remember the curtains stop at the bracket.

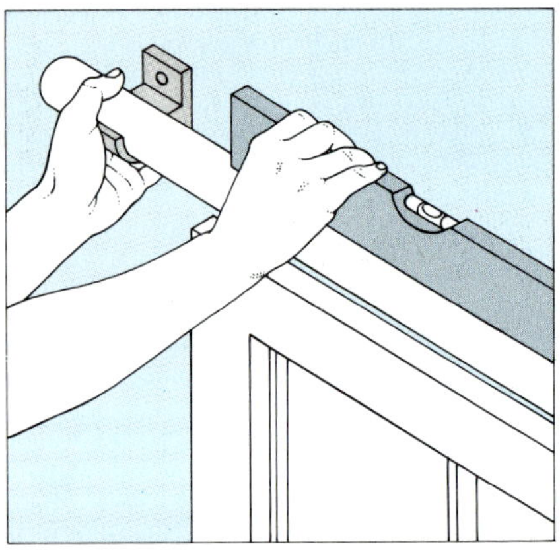

**2** Rest the pole in the first bracket and place the second in position using a spirit level.

**3** Slip the curtain rings on to the rod, fit the decorative end pieces and rest the pole on the brackets.

### FITTING CURTAIN TRACK

**1** Brackets for track are secured to a wooden strip screwed to the wall or timber frame studs.

**2** After screwing on the two end brackets, stretch string between them to align the others.

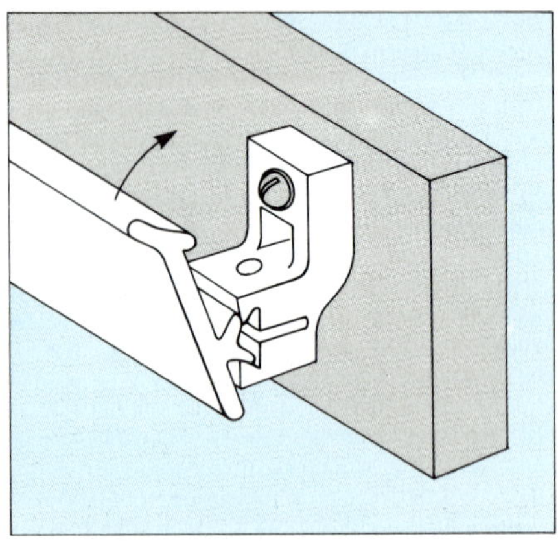

**3** Slip the curtain rings onto the rod, the end stops, and then snap the track into the brackets.

| | |
|---|---|
| SIMPLE SHEERS | 8 |
| WALL FIXINGS | 42 |
| TOOLS AND EQUIPMENT | 76 |

*Left: Any austerity in the simple pole and neutral-coloured fabric in these curtains is subtly overcome by the extravagance of their length. Their gentle folds give a feeling of luxury and simplicity to a beamed cottage interior, with a fresh touch that is assured and pleasing.*

*Below left: Distract attention from an uninteresting window with no view with an unusual curtain such as this. Beads add interesting texture and colour to a plain wall, creating all sorts of decorative possibilities.*

*Below right: The awkward shape of a dormer window demands novel and imaginative solutions. These curtains are gathered onto hinged curtain rods that swing back against the window at night. Because the actual area is small the treatment of the fabric needs to be bolder than usual, and frills are a good solution: here they help to soften a hard-edged architectural shape.*

can be headed with special tape and suspended like ordinary curtains; they can have wires slotted through casings sewn into the tops, or be hung from rods by means of fabric loops. Sheers can be mounted directly on to a window casement.

Roof windows that slant away towards the floor need special treatments. One method is to have two sets of poles, one at the top of the curtains and one to hold them back across the angle of the slope. Some windows, with curved or arched tops, may have to have the fabric stapled or pinned to the frame permanently, following the curve, with the curtains held open during the day with tie-backs. This does, however, cut out some daylight.

If you plan to use at least two layers at the window, with a blind or shade under the full-length drapes, you will need to choose a suitable blind to work well with the curtains.

Roller blinds (shades) work on a simple ratchet and roller system, which means you only have simple brackets to screw to the window reveal, or top of the frame, to support them. Venetian blinds come with their own header brackets, and are positioned in a similar way. Festoon blinds (balloon shades) have headings like curtains, and need track to support them. Attach Roman blinds (shades) to wooden strips screwed to the wall.

## Headings

The type of treatment you decide on for your curtains will determine the headings you use to pleat the fabric into luxurious folds. Some headings pleat up fabric much more tightly than others and use rather more material. This is a point worth thinking about if you are working to a restricted budget.

If you plan to hide the curtain tops under a pelmet (cornice) or valance,

## CURTAIN HEADINGS

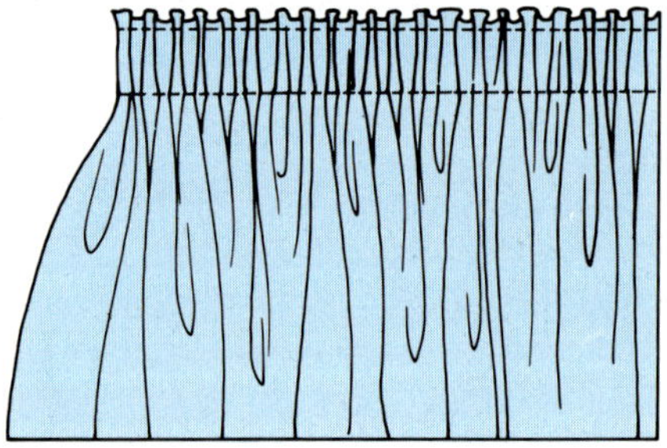

**Standard** – the simplest tape, it just gathers the fabric. Allow for $1\frac{1}{2}$ times the track length.

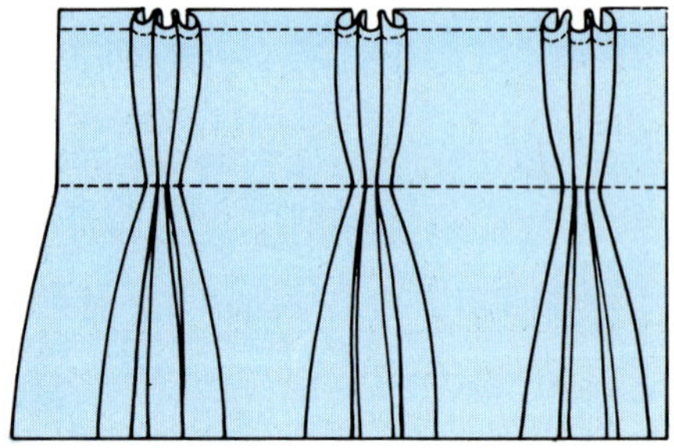

**Box** – pulls up into even box pleats. Match pleats across curtains; allow for $2\frac{1}{2}$ times the track length.

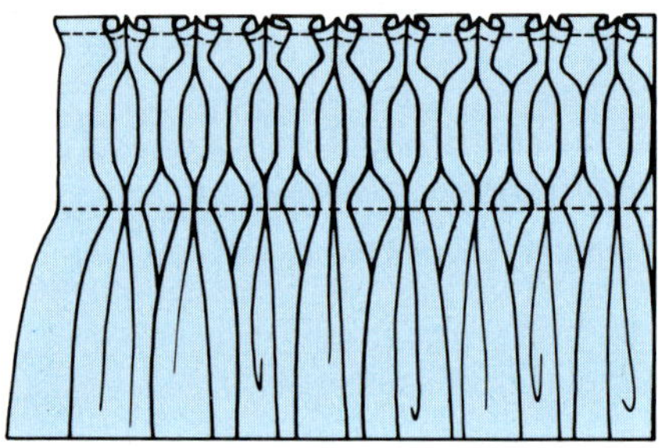

**Triple** – allow for twice the track length. Make sure the pleats will match across adjoining curtains.

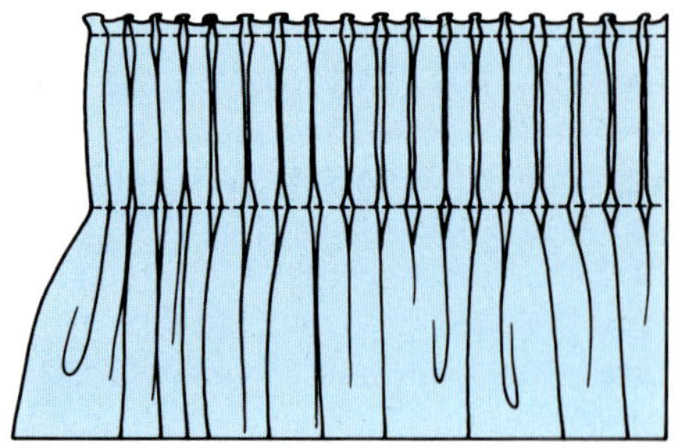

**Cartridge** – pulls into even rounded pleats. Match across curtains. Allow for $2\frac{1}{2}$ times the track length.

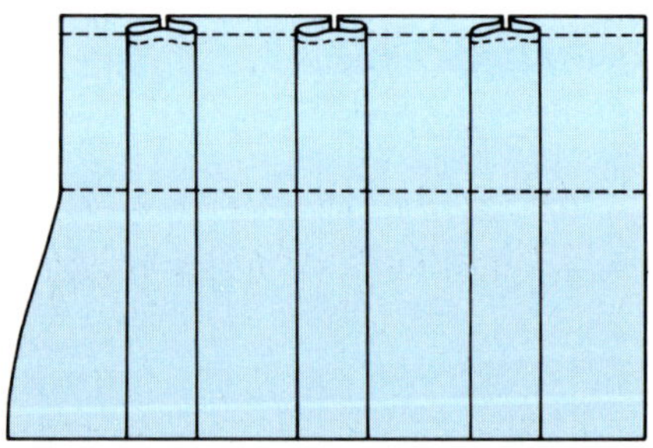

**Smocked** – one of the decorative tapes – looks good with sheers. Allow for twice the track length.

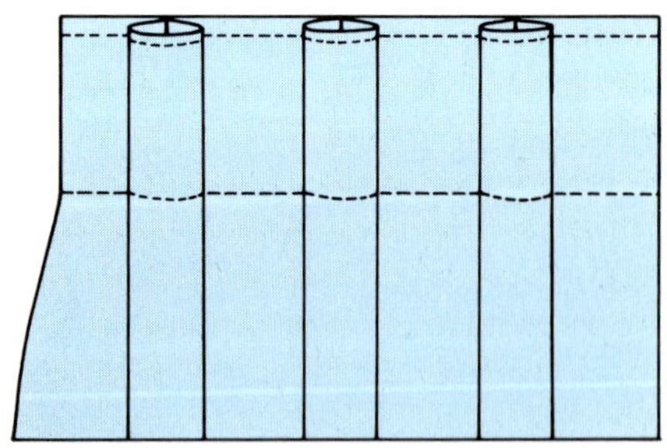

**Loops** – straight loops inserted between straight curtain and facing. Allow for pole length plus turnings.

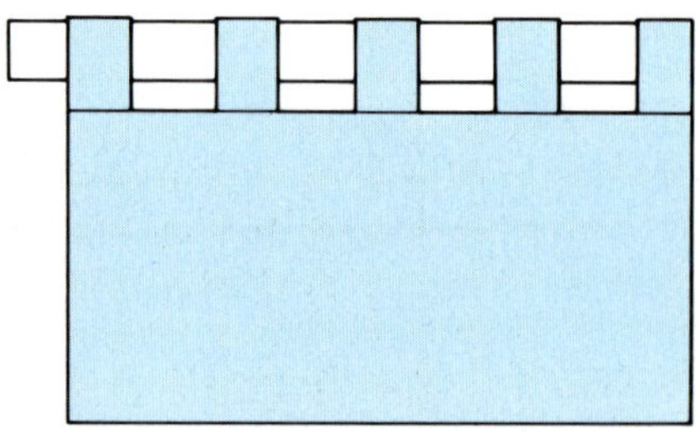

**Pencil** – a popular tape that pulls up to form even pencil pleats. Allow for $2\frac{1}{4}$–$2\frac{1}{2}$ times the track length.

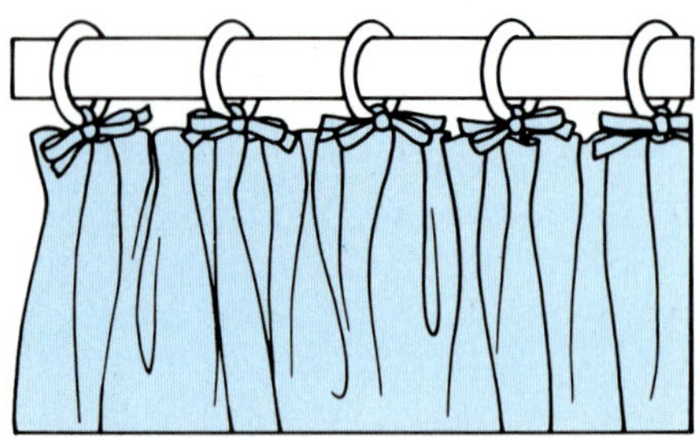

**Ties** – insert ribbon lengths between curtain and facing: tie through rings. Allow for twice the pole length.

the heading can just be a simple, gathered one. If you want to leave the headings so they can be seen, whether on a track or a pole, you may want the heading itself to be more decorative: pinch or pencil pleated, or shirred, goblet headed, smocked or trellised (see opposite). These effects are easy to achieve using special curtain-heading tapes, which are sewn to the top of the curtain. All these tapes can also be used to pleat up fabric valances and 'skirts' for tables.

## Pelmets (cornices) and valances

These cover the tops of the curtains and can be more elaborate to look at than pleated headings. Some pelmets (cornices) are made from wood, laminate or another rigid material, and can be stained, painted, papered or have fabric stuck on to them. This type can look clean, geometric and quite simple, but they can also be shaped – scalloped, castellated or gently curved – in whatever style suits the shape of the window and style of the curtains. Other types are made from fabric, which is then stiffened with buckram or Vilene, or frilled and pleated to make valances using any of the curtain headings opposite. Some very opulent fabric valances are combined with elaborate 'swags and tails' – extravagant draperies, that loop and fall luxuriously over a curtain pole.

There are also some special pelmet 'formers', which help with style as well as stiffening. All pelmets (cornices) and valances can be trimmed with fringe, lace, braid or frills to suit your taste and design.

Designing your own pelmet (cornice) is not difficult and there are various ways to work out just how it will eventually look, without having to cut and shape any materials. Pin up the fabric to simulate the finished curtains – or use sheeting. Cut out

### PELMETS (CORNICES) AND VALANCES

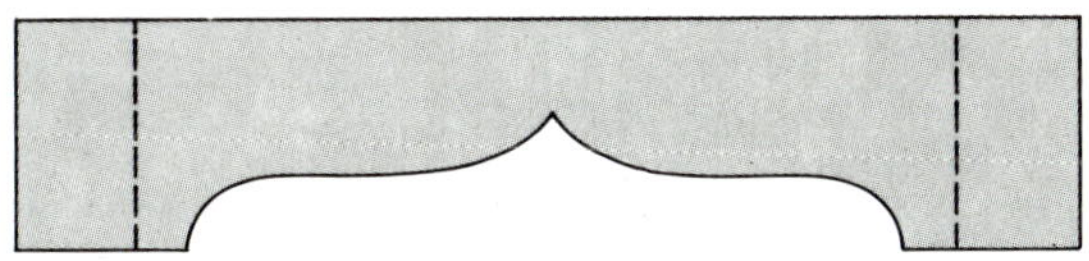

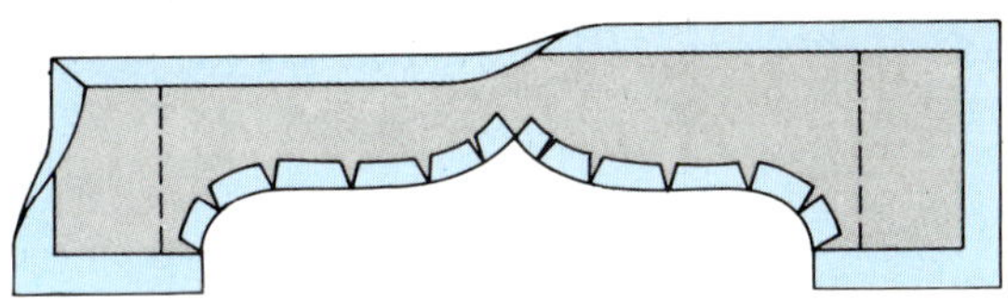

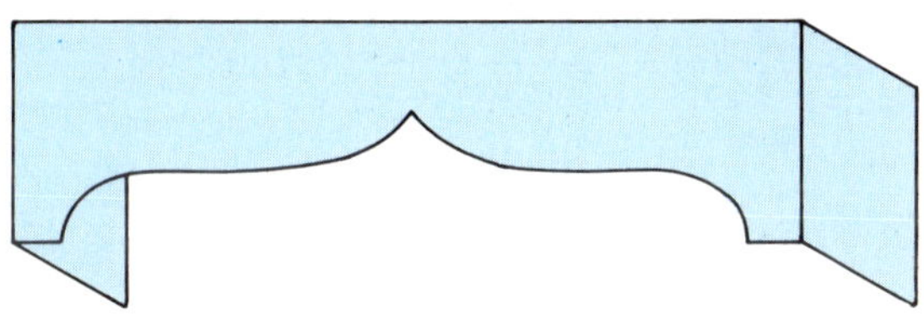

Make a pelmet (cornice) board from a 100mm (4in) wide piece of 12mm ($\frac{1}{2}$in) thick plywood, 50–80mm (2–3in) longer than the curtain track. Attach board to brackets 50–80mm (2–3in) above the curtain track. Add a square of plywood to each side at right angles. Cut adhesive stiffener to board length plus side pieces, cutting a decorative edge. Peel off backing from one side of the stiffener and stick centrally to wrong side of fabric, trimming to leave a 20mm ($\frac{3}{4}$in) border. Peel off backing from the upper side and stick down turnings, notching into curves. Stitch lining fabric to wrong side. Attach to board with touch-and-close spots.

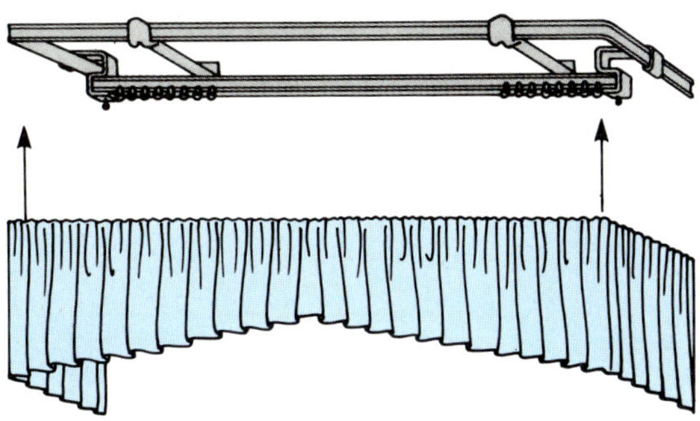

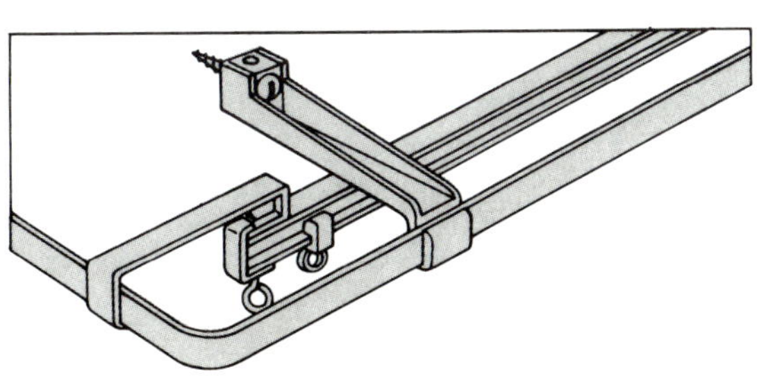

Locate the valance rail above and in front of the curtain track on special brackets following instructions. It will screw to both the wall and ceiling. Make up the fabric valance in the same way as a curtain – choosing a heading tape compatible with the curtains that will be hanging underneath. Stitch together as many fabric widths as necessary, shaping the base edge if desired. 'Bag out' with a lining. Add heading tape and hang on the valance rail using curtain hooks.

possible shapes in paper, pin to the top of the window, and adjust until you are happy with the result. Another way is to take a photograph of the window wall, and sketch on various effects. There are various aids to making pelmets available from curtain-making specialists and soft furnishings suppliers.

## Pattern and colour

When it comes to choosing fabric for the main window treatment, the scale of the pattern is very important. A fabric with a large repeat will not show its design off to any real advantage if used on a very small area, and the pattern itself may look out of scale with the size of the actual window. When it comes to colour, the only rules are those you want to make for yourself. A particularly dominating colour, such as a strong red, may be best used in a small area, since its impact will be great in any case. White or cream curtains falling to the floor can be deliciously cool and elegant, while lavish, extravagant, boldly patterned full-length curtains could be striking.

With co-ordinating fabric and wallcovering, make sure that the design matches across both. If your curtains are already made, hang them just to see where the pattern repeat falls, then paper the walls to match; otherwise hang the paper and match the fabric to that.

## Linings

You will get a much more professional effect to your curtains, and they will hang better, if you line them; they will also keep more light out and more heat in. Loose-lining means that the lining fabric has a special tape sewn to it. Hooks are then put through this tape and the curtain tape for hanging purposes – the bottom edges are hemmed separately. Sometimes the lining fabric

### MEASURING WINDOWS

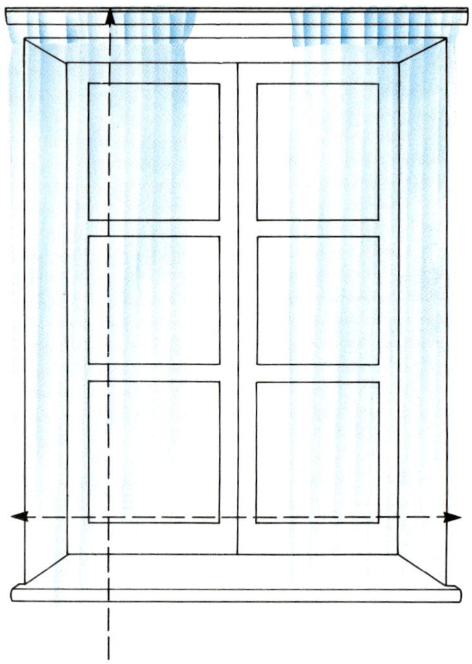

Before you make a pair of curtains, fix your track or pole above the window. For curtain length, measure from the top of the track or the bottom of the pole to the sill, above the radiator or to the floor. Take away 15mm (½in) from this so the curtains will clear the floor, radiator or sill, then add on hem and top turnings. For the width, measure the track and divide by the number of curtains. Estimate fabric by multiplying as required by the type of heading chosen, then add on for side hems.

For cross-over sheers, attach the pole or wire above or to the window frame. Measure for the sheers in the same way as curtains, but measure diagonally to make sure the curtains will reach across from corner to corner when they are swept back.

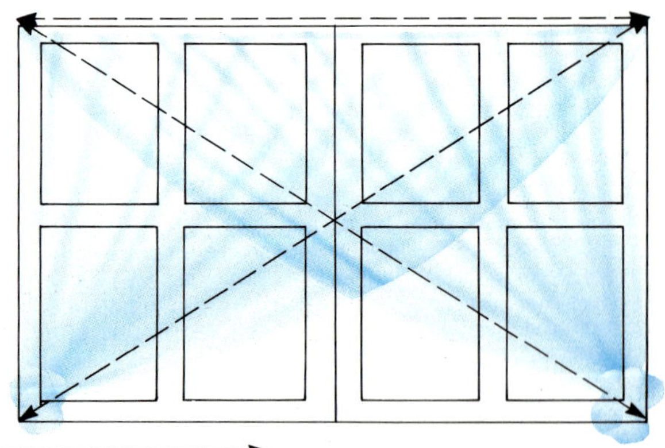

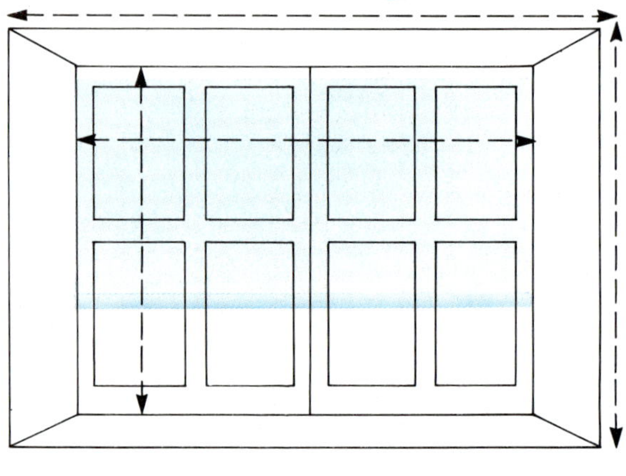

Position blinds or shades inside or outside a recess. For one inside, measure horizontally, and deduct 10–15mm (⅜–⅝in) from each side for blind mechanism. Position roller 3cm (1¼in) from top. Measure from top of roller for length of blind. With no recess, extend blind width beyond window edges for 40–60mm (1½–2½in).

will be stitched to the main curtain all round (locked linings) but this method means that the lining and curtain cannot be detached and must be washed or cleaned together.

If that is not what you want, look for a system that allows the lining to be detached. Some tracks enable you to put separate curtain hooks into heading tape on the lining, which are then clipped into specially-designed runners on the track.

## Sheers

Sheer curtains are often an essential part of window treatments for privacy and for diffusing light. Many different styles are available, and don't feel you must use traditional fabric: very lightweight cotton can be deliciously cool and simple. Lace is another option. Modern lace is based on old patterns and can be charming. If you have a casement or french window, one option is to put the lace, ungathered, on to curtain wires along the top and bottom of the actual window, so that you can see the delicate tracery of the lace itself. Traditional old lace can be hunted down in antique and junk shops, and used for sheer curtains.

*Blinds and shades come in all shapes and sizes. Festoon blinds (balloon shades) are mounted on track, like curtains, and add a touch of luxury to a room (top left). If yours is a window with a radiator beneath, you can use a simple roller blind to do the job of keeping the dark night out and tie the curtains back permanently (bottom left). You may want to hide the track and roller at the top with a pelmet (cornice). Blinds can also be a very sensible alternative in kitchens or bathrooms, where you don't want a great deal of fabric to get in the way (above).*

Part 3

# THE PLANNING

Planning a decorative scheme with an unlimited budget and a completely free hand is both easy and enjoyable; the reality, however, is rarely like that. You will inevitably have pieces of furniture, for example, or existing decoration in some rooms that you cannot afford to abandon completely – or perhaps you don't want to. The art of clever planning is to incorporate these limitations without letting them spoil what you are trying to do. As far as possible try to treat your existing furniture as a positive item. If you have a built-in wardrobe that you don't like, don't just decorate around it and allow it to stand outside your overall scheme: you are only drawing attention to its unwantedness. Look for ways of 'dissolving' it with paint finishes, or facing it with mirrors to make it disappear visually. Cleverly planned camouflage will distract attention from things you don't like and allow them to continue being useful.

As you plan your schemes look around for new materials, new gadgets, new styles that you may not have known existed. The planning stage can, however, be a very protracted one: don't be afraid to follow your instincts and commit yourself to a colour or a scheme if that is what you know you want.

Finally, think in terms of the whole house, flat or apartment. Look at each colour in relation to the others you want to use, remembering that when the doors are open you will be able to see through to the colours in other rooms. A red room, for example, is not a separate entity but part of an overall scheme.

*A kitchen can be squeezed into a relatively small area, but natural light is a desirable commodity. This area is indeed small, but it makes good and unusual use of a skylight, while the dining area is close by. Colour has been used with sensitivity and restraint, so that no diner could feel jarred by bold colours.*

# COLOUR SCHEMES

Colour helps to create atmosphere, and a careful choice for your room will give it the right mood and ambience. You will find you can use colour to make a large room look smaller and more intimate, or a small room larger and more spacious. By subtle use of colour you can help to warm up a cold north-facing room, or tone down a very sunny room.

The patterns you select for the walls, ceiling and floor will set the style of the room. Fabrics will give the room a certain look, whether it be modern or traditional. The type of furniture and accessories you buy will also help to set the style.

## Colour matching

Unless you are starting right from the beginning, most rooms have to be planned round an existing item such as a bathroom or upholstery suite, flooring or kitchen cabinets, which have to be incorporated into the new colour scheme. Try and take a sample of any existing features with you when you look for items to build up the scheme. If you cannot take actual samples, match up pieces of wool, fabric and yarns, or manufacturers' paint shade cards.

If you have no fixed items to worry about, then you can start with the room itself, and make the colour scheme work for you to enhance or improve the existing structure.

Never rely on a photograph or leaflet as a correct guide to the colour of an article you are going to buy. Collect actual samples of paints, papers and fabrics from shops and then take them home. Check the samples in the room where they will be used, in both natural and artificial light – always look at samples in the right place. Check flooring on the floor or wallpaper against the wall and take into account light and shadow. Curtain fabric needs to be gathered and looked at with light behind

*Opposite, above: Sunshine yellow is a recurring colour in the pictures and accessories, picked out to stunning effect in the walls.*

*Opposite below: Strong colours are best used in small areas, such as on the woodwork in a room.*

*Above: White is a positive colour, just like any other. A totally white room lit by natural light will have an interplay of light and shadow, of white shading through to grey, that no interior designer could ever achieve artificially.*

and in front of it, as it will eventually hang at a window in normal daylight and at night-time.

## Characteristics of colour

Use the characteristics of the various groups of colours to create the mood you are seeking. Use colour to create the feeling of space. Pale, receding colours such as greens, blues, lilacs, greys and white will do this. The most spacious effect of all is created by using tones of one colour – a monochromatic scheme. Cool colours also work well in warm west- or south-facing rooms. The lighter the value of a pale, cool colour, the larger the room will appear.

Use warm, advancing colours to add intimacy to a room or make a large area seem smaller. Red, pink, orange, gold, terracotta, yellow, apricot, burgundy, brown or rich cream are the sort of strong colours you could choose.

Use sunshine colours – yellow, gold, apricot or peach – to brighten up a dull and dark area. Use colour to create a restful atmosphere in a room. The pale, quiet ones will do this, particularly the soft neutrals such as cream, beige or soft dove grey. Pure white can be harsh and uncompromising or clean and fresh, depending on the room's aspect. White can be as positive a colour as a red or yellow, so choose an off-white if a soothing look is what you're trying to achieve.

If you want to create an exciting atmosphere where people just pass through, such as a hallway, use bright, primary or 'jazzy' colours. The contrasting colours – red and green, blue and orange, lilac and yellow – will all create a stimulating room, particularly if the colours are then combined with some bold geometric patterning.

One secret of the interior designer's art is to add some colour contrasts to a scheme to give it life. Try painting the decorative wooden mouldings in a warm colour to give a really striking effect to a cool, pale room. Add some cold, pale touches to a rich, warm setting or some bright, primary colours like red or blue to a neutral scheme.

### Instant success

If you find colour-scheming and matching difficult, there is an easier way of working up a successful scheme. Choose a multi-coloured, patterned item for one of the surface treatments, either a wallcovering, a carpet or other flooring, or an upholstery or curtain fabric. If the pattern is on the walls pick out one colour for the ceiling and woodwork, a second for the furniture, another for the flooring and so on. Alternatively, choose one colour for picking out all the wooden details, for the curtains and for such things as rugs: you may find you need this unifying element to create harmony. Whichever way you do it, you will still need to set about collecting samples, for you will be amazed at how many variations there can be of a sky blue, for example.

*Three room treatments using one colour demonstrate firstly the variations in that colour, and secondly the ways in which you can put colour to work for you. Boldly-patterned fabrics (opposite) will compete for attention with anything you use on the walls, so pick out a single, restrained, colour and use that. A single flat colour can be a good way of accentuating an object or accent in a contrasting*

*colour (left). Use accents like this to intensify the colour of the walls and dramatize the entire room. The rich blue in this collection of glass and ceramics (above) would only be weakened by any attempt to pick it out elsewhere: much better to let the objects speak for themselves.*

## THE ORDER OF WORK

**1** Decide on the overall design scheme, measure up rooms accurately. Work it out on paper with room-by-room scale plans, and plan lighting effects carefully. Sort out any necessary structural work and agree a realistic budget. Choose colours and select surface/ window treatments, incorporating existing items where necessary
**2** Get estimates for any structural, electrical or plumbing work. Organize floor laying, and estimate quantities and costs for do-it-yourself jobs
**3** Order furniture and materials
**4** Have all building, plumbing, electrical and structural work done first
**5** If you are doing a house, start with the functional areas – bathroom, kitchen, etc. Then work from the top down, leaving stairs and hallway till last
**6** Plan for decorations: take furniture out of the room, or push it into the centre and cover with dust sheets. Take up floorcoverings or tape down newspaper and polyethylene dust sheets. Cover built-in furniture with dust sheets. Take down shelves and other wall-hung items and remove curtains and tracks or poles. Switch off electricity and remove light fixtures (employ an electrician if you are at all uncertain). Take off door hardware, but leave the spindle and a spare handle
**7** Secure loose floorboards, replace worn sash cords and do any necessary maintenance. Have the chimney swept where necessary
**8** Check tools, obtain special ones if necessary. Check all materials, making sure you have enough to complete the job, and that paint or wallcoverings come from the same batch number and are identical in colour
**9** Clean down the room, starting with washing ceiling, then walls and woodwork. Wash walls from the bottom working upwards; dust down woodwork, then wash
**10** Proper preparation should be done next, in the following sequence:
- strip off paper from ceiling and any wallcoverings;
- rake out cracks and holes in plaster prior to filling;
- wash and sand walls again to remove old size and paste;
- repair plaster and fill cracks and holes;
- scrape, burn or strip defective or unwanted paint from wood or metal;
- rub down, fill cracks in wood, sand down and prime as necessary

**11** The order of decorating will depend on your materials:

**For painted ceiling and walls**
Line ceiling and walls as necessary.
Paint ceiling then walls.
Prime bare woodwork, apply first undercoat, sand down lightly and apply second undercoat. Sand again and apply top coat.

**For papered ceiling and walls**
Paper ceiling.
Prime bare woodwork, apply undercoat, sand down lightly, apply second undercoat. Sand lightly and paint top coat. Line walls, if necessary, and hang wallcovering.

**For painted ceiling and papered walls**
Line and paint ceiling as necessary.
Prime bare wood, apply first undercoat to wood, sand down, apply second undercoat. Sand lightly and paint top coat. Line walls, if necessary, and hang wallcovering.

**12** Lay floorcovering
**13** Replace all curtain tracks, door hardware and shelving
**14** Hang curtains or window treatments
**15** Replace or install light fixtures
**16** Bring in the furniture
**17** Add accents, accessories, plants and other finishing touches to your scheme.

Opposite: There is today a bewildering array of materials available to the home decorator, as you will find as you set out armed with catalogues and a calculator to plan your schemes. Gauge carefully the potential usefulness of each new gadget or design you find, and don't be lured by novelty alone.

Below and opposite are just some points to remember as you plan your decoration room by room.

**1 Hallways, stairs and landings**
Practicality is at a premium here. Look for floorings that will wear well and will show as little dirt as possible. Carpets are the most common choice for stairs, but paint can be fresh and appealing. Look for good day- and night-time illumination, and a wall treatment that will be easy to clean. This might be a good area to experiment with a paint technique, as mistakes will draw less attention: protect it against knocks and dirt with one or two coats of varnish.

**2 Sitting and dining rooms**
These will probably be your showcase rooms, where you mainly entertain guests, but they must also be decorated to suit your own needs for relaxation and conversation. Look for floorcoverings that reflect the composition of your family: a very pale carpet, for example, will be a constant source of anxiety

## YOUR OPTIONS, ROOM BY ROOM

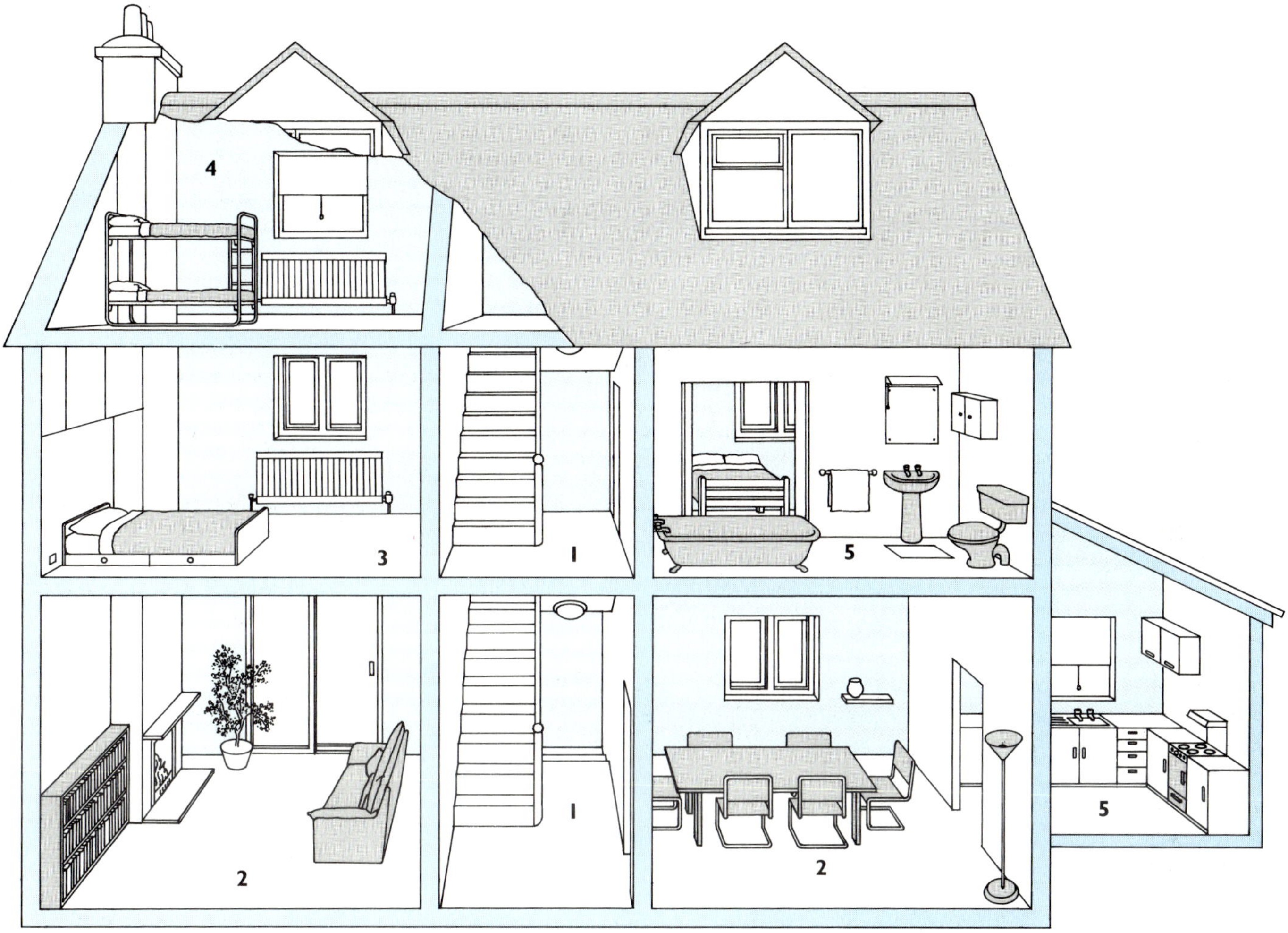


if you have small children, and a collection of rugs will be a problem for elderly people with sticks or walking frames. Since these are both rooms for sitting in, give some thought to how you light them. Avoid harsh overhead lighting and make use of wall-lights, uplighters and spots to give areas of shadow. Look for warm colours for the walls, or let the walls retreat and allow strong colours to be carried on the soft furnishings. In a dining room, the table will always be the focal point, so make the most of it and light it with sensitivity.

**3 Bedrooms**
One objective of planning a bedroom scheme is to provide plenty of storage space for clothes. A floorcovering is probably not subject to heavy wear in these rooms, so you could opt for a luxurious carpet; or brighten up bare floorboards with inviting rugs. Colours and designs should on the whole reflect the fact that this is a room for relaxation.

**4 Children's bedrooms**
To a child, a bedroom has to be much more than somewhere to sleep: it is also his or her territory. With very young children you can have fun with jolly wallpaper and fabric designs that you yourself like, but as the child gets older you may have to leave more scope for the child to do what he or she wants. That probably means a wall treatment that can perhaps be drawn on or stencilled, and a floorcovering that you don't mind being spoiled. But in these rooms the choice of furniture is probably more important than the background decoration. Children need space for their toys and hobbies, and are often excited by the idea of bunkbeds or playhouses.

**5 Kitchens, bathrooms**
See pages 66–67.

# FIXTURES AND FURNITURE

When you first start to think about planning your home, always consider the 'working parts' of the house or apartment first, that is, the kitchen and bathroom. Are they as functional and convenient as they should be? Decide exactly what purpose and function each room should fulfil – which will often mean designing each room to suit more than one purpose. Always try to maintain a flexible approach to your home.

If you have a large house, a room leading directly into a garden might be better as a child's bedroom/playroom, with another downstairs room made into a family living room. If you have a small house, plan carefully to avoid a cluttered feeling.

In a one-bedroom apartment, the use of space is going to be critical. Planning a sofa bed into your living room scheme allows you to have people to stay. Some flats and apartments have a large hall area which can often be transformed into a dining area. You may need to think about a dining table and chairs that can be neatly folded away so that they do not intrude on useful space when not in use.

One-room living is becoming much more common and planning the space carefully is essential for happy living. As one room will easily become untidy, storage is an important consideration. If you can, create 'zones' with furniture. Give privacy to the bedroom area by screening it off with attractive roller blinds (shades) or concertina screens during the day. A dining table that can slide out of sight when not in use can also work very well in this type of living arrangement, where space is at a premium.

*The very square shape of this open studio has dictated the rectangular arrangement and style of the furniture; the table and sofas have been placed carefully in the centre of the room allowing people adequate space to walk around them without cutting across conversations.*

## Planning on paper

To get your requirements right, plan your home to scale on paper and work out furniture positions, lighting and electrical work, plumbing and structural alterations in relation to the fixtures. Do this before you buy anything or redecorate.

First, you need to measure up accurately, using a metal tape or wooden rule. Use these measurements to draw out the shape of the room, to scale, on squared paper, or use the charts available in many catalogues. A helpful scale might be 1cm on paper to 25cm of floor, or $\frac{1}{2}$in to one foot. Mark in doors and windows, including the way they open, and any recesses and projections that appear.

On a separate piece of squared paper, draw out the shapes of your proposed furniture and appliances in the same scale as the room plan, and colour them. Cut out the shapes and move them about on your plan to establish practical positions. Think three-dimensionally, so that you are able to fit items under window sills and also under and above countertops.

First of all you will need to work out the traffic flow, and make allowances for people to move around the furniture in comfort. In a dining room, remember that chairs, for example, will need to be pushed well away from dining tables; and you will not want people continually walking across sitting or eating areas to get to other rooms. Try to 'zone' the area with furniture for flexibility:

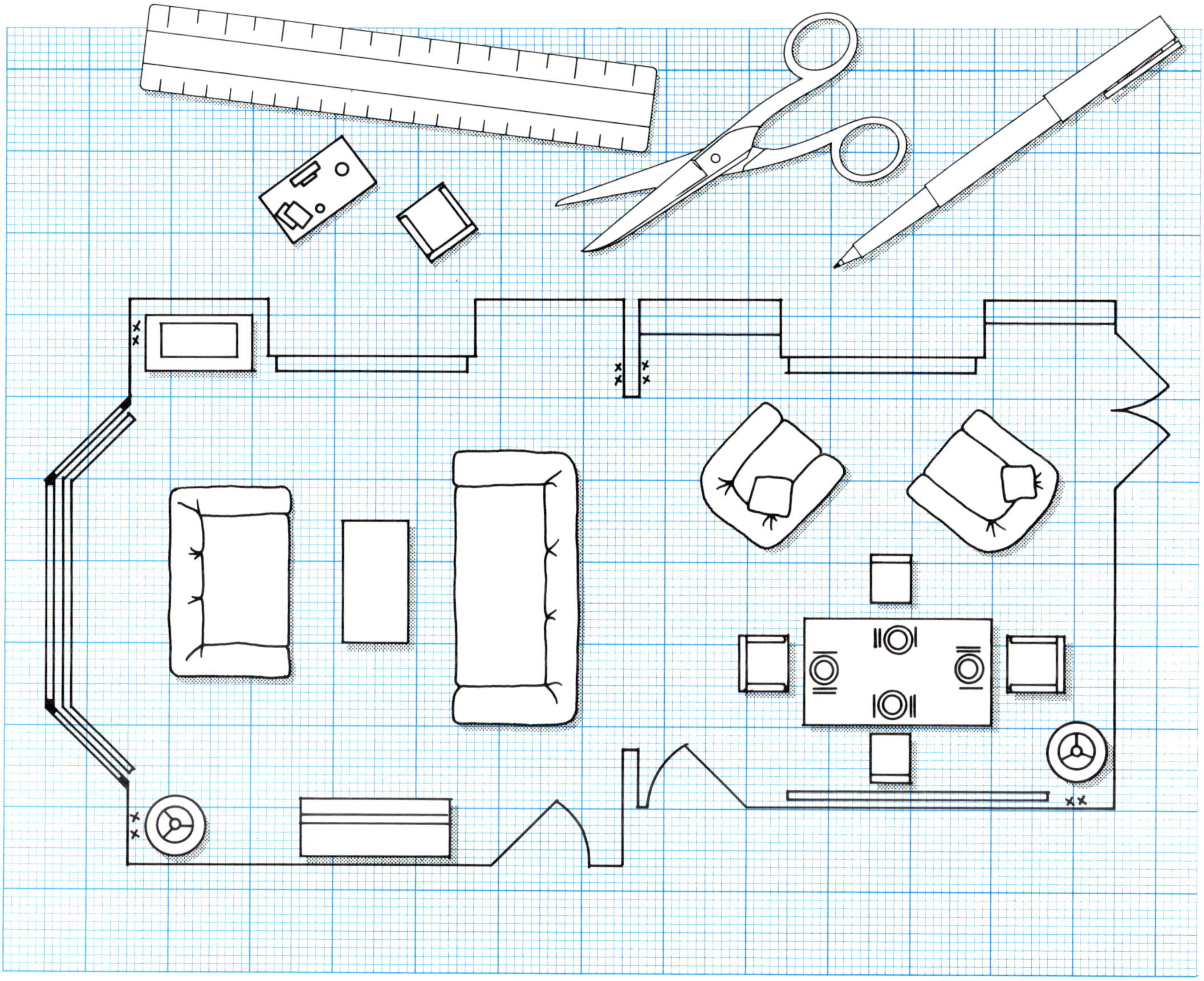

you can position sofas at right angles to a fireplace wall, facing each other across a coffee table, and back the sofa which faces the dining area with a serving table. Once you are happy with the final layout, stick the furniture and equipment shapes down on the scale plan.

Plumbing is the next thing to consider, including the water supply and runs of pipes to service baths, showers and basins as well as external plumbing. Sometimes – probably often – compromise may be necessary, as what you think is the ideal position for a bath, for example, might just not be practical from the plumbing point of view.

Plan lighting carefully and work through the house room by room, working out what you need where, now and in the future.

In a bedroom you will want good, direct lighting for the dressing table/make-up area, lighting for the interiors of cupboards, and for reading in bed. Some softer, background lighting can be provided by concealed lighting or wall-washers. Try to have dual-switch lighting from both bed and door.

In the kitchen task lighting is necessary for the cooking area, work surfaces and sink.

If your living room doubles as a living/dining area, you will need good, direct light over the dining table while enjoying a meal, perhaps from a pull-down pendant. The rest of the room may well be lit by just a soft background glow. Dimmers can be used to lower the light intensity of central lighting.

*Draw a floor plan on graph paper including doors, windows, power outlets and radiators, and position scaled cut-outs of your furniture.*

## Organizing the essentials

The bathroom and the kitchen are the two areas which need the most careful thought and planning. The obvious problems are fitting all the necessary equipment into what is often a very restricted and awkwardly shaped space, but safety should also play a very important part in both rooms.

### In the bathroom

- Choose a non-slip flooring material or carpet and make sure any medicine cabinet is placed out of reach of children and is lockable.
- Good lighting is essential and safe electrical items – shuttered shaver supply units, no power outlets and totally enclosed electrical fittings – must be used. In many countries you will need to control fixtures with pull-cord switches or switch them from outside the door.
- Fit hand-grips next to the bath, shower or toilet if you have elderly residents or visitors.
- Think three-dimensionally – position a basin so there is space to stand or bend over it comfortably, with enough elbow room (53cm or 1ft 9in) each side of the centre point. The shower and bath should be easy to get in and out of, and there should be enough space to stand next to the bath or the shower cubicle. Also allow enough space for somebody to be able to bath a child (you need about 70cm or 2ft 3in).
- The toilet and bidet are a fixed height from the floor, but adequate access (80cm or 2ft 7in) is needed. If the two are sited side-by-side you may well be able to reduce the overall width.

### In the kitchen

*Do not*

- place the sink and cooking area opposite each other in a confined space as there will not be enough space for two people to work.
- position a cooking surface under a window as you may burn your clothes when you lean over to open the window.
- place a cooker (range) near to a door, where pan handles could be knocked when the door is opened.
- arrange power outlets so that cords trail across the sink and come into contact with water.

*Do*

- consider the heights of various appliances and kitchen units and try to think three-dimensionally when planning (see opposite).
- have adequate lighting and a non-slip flooring.

All the necessary kitchen equipment can be arranged into a 'work triangle', which is made by the food storage and preparation area, the cooking area and the serving/cleaning up area.

## Plans of vertical surfaces

As well as using your scale floor plans to help fit everything in, you might find it useful to think vertically, and make a wall plan. Try to construct these vertical layouts with the objective of reducing any unneccessary bending and stretching.

Use the same principle as described on page 64 to draw up a scale plan on squared paper. Allow for the depth of skirting boards (baseboards), removing them if necessary to get appliances in flush, the door and window frames, the position of pipes and items such as power points. Measure the width and height of all appliances, cut out same-scale shapes, and fit onto the elevated wall plan. The standard height of kitchen cupboards is 90cm (3ft), but some appliances are slightly taller so countertops may need adjusting to

**WORK TRIANGLES**

**It is important that a kitchen should be arranged so that the food storage, preparation and cooking areas are conveniently placed in relation to each other.**

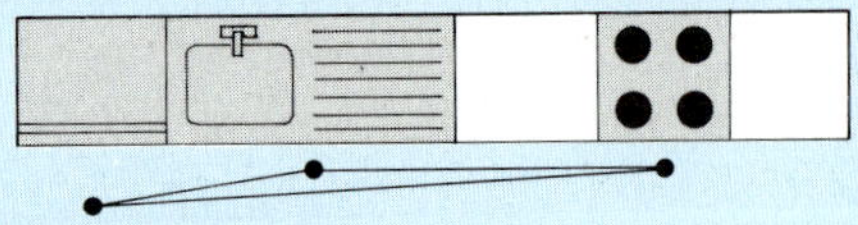

Single-wall layout

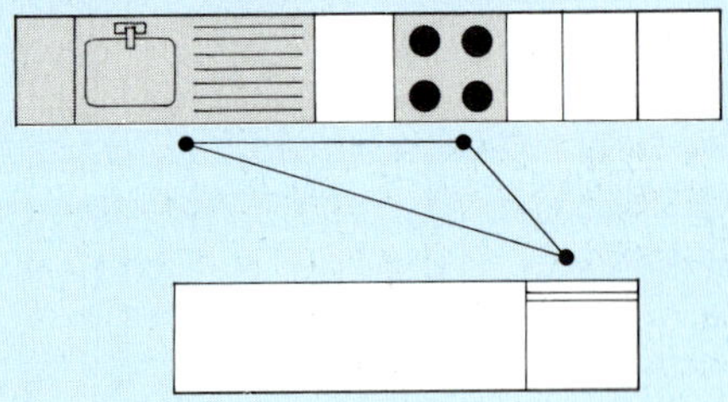

Galley or corridor

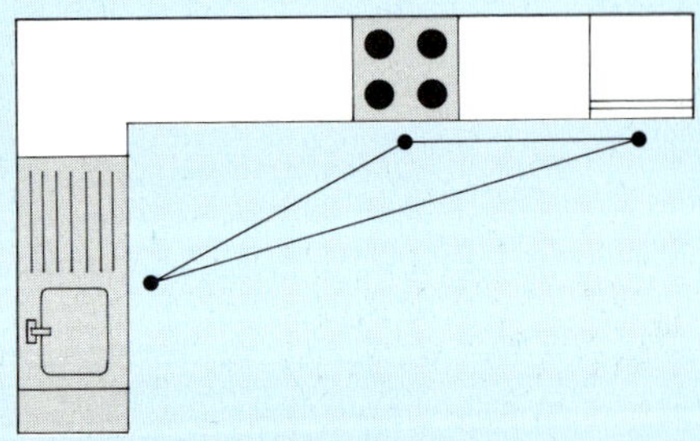

L-shape

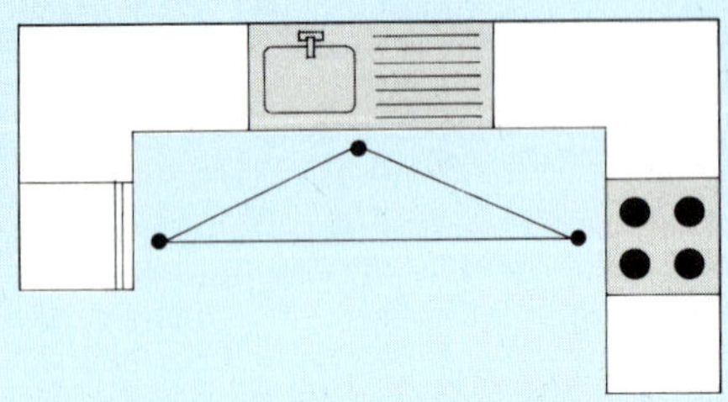

Island unit

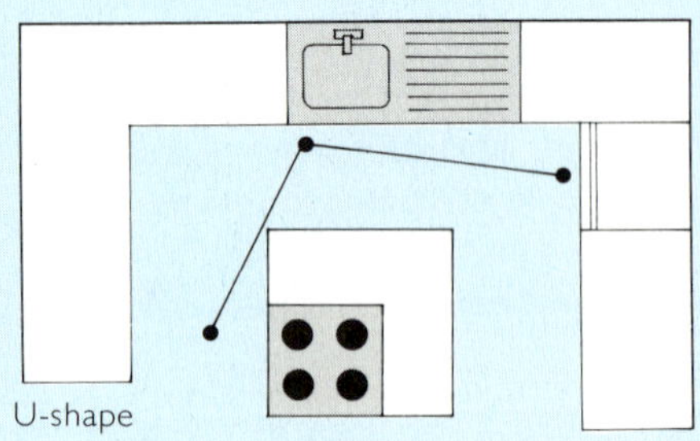

U-shape

## KITCHEN CABINETS

Kitchen base units come in a standard height of 90cm (3ft), but it is possible to adjust this height by increasing the depth of the base at the bottom. When your kitchen is installed it should be possible for the cabinets to be raised up on a plinth or strip of wood – but if you need this flexibility, perhaps because you are unusually tall or have non-standard kitchen appliances that you would like to fit underneath a countertop, ask your supplier at the time of ordering. Wall cupboards can be of varying heights, depending on what you want to store in them and the access you need, and should be sited 60cm (24in) above the countertops.

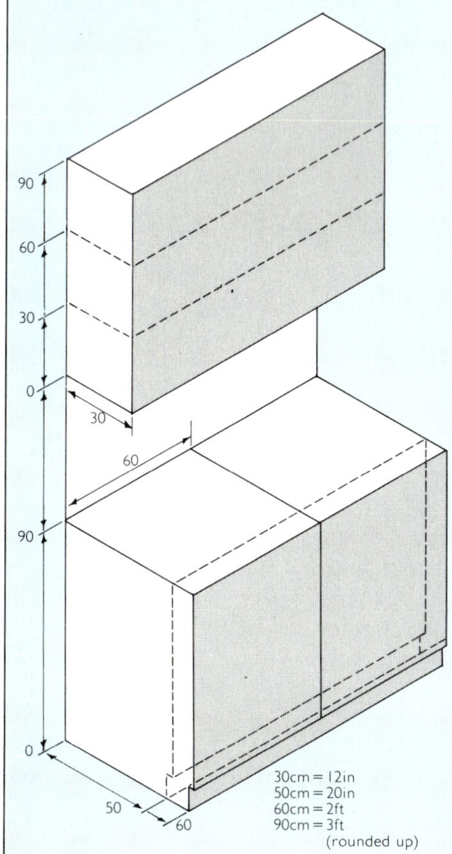

form a flush work surface. Do not build a kitchen around old appliances, as this might cause problems when replacing them with modern sizes which now conform to a standard measurement.

Site wall cupboards or open shelves at least 60cm (20in) above countertops, but do not place them too high if one of the people who will be cooking is short.

Some items may be stacked on top of each other. Matching washing machines and tumble dryers or refrigerators and freezers come complete with stacking fittings – follow the instructions carefully about which appliance goes at the bottom. A small dishwasher with a drop-down door can fit on a countertop.

If you are planning a new kitchen and are thinking about buying cabinets from a well-known kitchen supplier they will often do a kitchen layout plan for you. This will either be free or a nominal charge will be made and then deducted from the price of the cabinets.

*A corner in a kitchen very often becomes 'dead' space, perhaps taken up with bits and pieces that you can't easily reach. It is, however, a very neat place for the cooking area.*

# STORAGE

Careful planning for storage is needed from the moment you move into your new home. It needs to complement the proposed style and fit within any budgetary constraints. Think about what you want now, but also allow for the future. There is no point in only including a few book shelves when you know you love books and will acquire many more. You also need to consider the accessibility of your possessions. Some lend themselves to ornate display, while you will want others to be hidden away for just occasional use. There would be absolutely no point, for example, in hiding away in a cupboard your favourite records that you play all the time.

Consider storage when making your room plans and choosing new furniture and fixtures. Think about how rooms might change over the years. A child's room, for example, will start out as a nursery with only very basic furniture or storage space, but a child's needs soon change as he or she grows and provision will need to be made for books, games and toys. In the teenage years a computer, records and players and items such as sports equipment will be called for. Try to plan a room which can respond to change.

In the kitchen you may begin with only the basic equipment but as time goes on and your skills as a cook grow you will need much more. Allow for the necessary room when planning your kitchen cabinets. In the dining area, initially you might only need to store a limited amount of china, but in time you will acquire a full dinner service, several sets of glasses plus everyday china, cutlery, glasses, linen and mats. Some items can be stored in the kitchen, but the rest will need to be kept as close as possible to the dining table. A sideboard to match your dining table can be one solution, or possibly a built-in unit with storage at the bottom and glass shelves on top. Shelving is often a particularly important component of the living room, for books, records, cassettes and treasured possessions. If you like collecting china ornaments, allow enough space for the collection to grow in years to come.

In bedrooms you will need to store clothes, cosmetics, personal effects and possibly spare linen. You will also need somewhere to keep items which are not used so often, such as luggage, items for infrequent hobbies and miscellaneous sports equipment. If the rooms are dual-purpose or multi-functional they will need to incorporate a large amount of flexible storage.

Many homes have built-in cupboards under the stairs. These can be used to house coats and jackets at the front or items like vacuum cleaners and ironing boards. Little-used items can be stored right at the back, but arrange them in a neat order or the area can all too quickly become very untidy and cluttered.

## Storage style

Storage can often be very utilitarian in appearance, but looks extremely effective in the right setting. Industrial shelving systems, stacked wire baskets and wall racks and other basic storage can suit a domestic situation surprisingly well. They might be appropriate for a workshop, a garage, or a teenager's room when an elegant shelving system is perhaps not required.

*Opposite: The ceiling isn't the most obvious place for storing things, but in a small room it can make a very decorative and space-saving solution.*

*Left: Ample shelves combined with colourful roller blinds (shades) contrive to make a highly decorative alternative to bedroom cupboards, without their inflexibility. The blinds can be changed with your whims, depending on whether you want to pick out a colour in a bedspread or decide to continue the colour scheme of the walls.*

## STORAGE ZONES

Frequently used items on shelving (right) should lie within an arc formed by fully stretching an arm above the head and moving it, still fully stretched, to hang by the side. This area can be extended for lighter items to the height of the hand when standing with the trunk half bent (centre). Shelves in front of a desk should be easily reached (far right). Other areas should hold only seldom-used items.

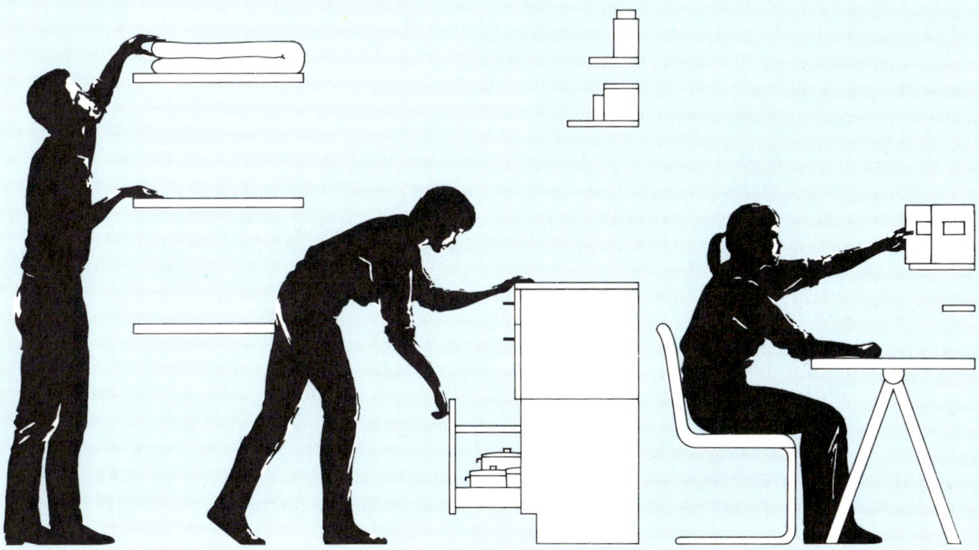

In other cases, storage systems need to be camouflaged so that they do not stand out too much against the design scheme. If you are using wall-mounted struts and brackets for shelves, colour these to match the wall which supports them, so they blend in. A contrasting colour can be used, however, if a more dramatic effect is wanted. Coloured strips for uprights and push-on shelf edges are available.

Built-in furniture can be decorated to suit the room scheme, perhaps so that it matches the background. You can also do this even if you have bought an old wardrobe or a chest of drawers for storage purposes. You might try using paint finish, such as rag-rolling, sponging, marbling or wood graining. Another way of hiding big, bulky built-in units is to face the doors with mirrors, but ensure that the existing doors and hinges are strong enough to take the considerable weight of the glass. This works very well in the bedroom as it is useful for dressing and makes the cupboards disappear into the background. Mirrors can also bring reflected light into a dark area like a hallway and help to magnify the size of a small room.

## Simple storage

You can often begin with very basic storage and add to it, or alter it, as you go along. Plastic-coated wire baskets which pull out of cupboards and units are very versatile and can be used in bedrooms and kitchens. A wicker or wooden blanket chest which doubles up as a coffee or bedside table will store essential items now and can be up-dated with more sophisticated storage equipment to suit your room design later.

In a bedroom, recesses on each side of a fireplace can be ideal to convert to simple storage with adjustable shelves, hanging rails or hooks. They can be cleverly concealed behind a pull-down blind or shade. Doors or even fitted units can be added at a future date. A long dress rail can also be used to hang clothes and be covered by a floor-to-ceiling curtain on a ceiling track.

In a hall or bedroom an attractive hatstand can become a decorative storage item for storing hats, scarves or jewellery such as necklaces.

## Utilizing space

Look at all the areas of your home for available space, for it is sometimes possible to wall-mount cupboards

*Above: The ideal – and stylish – solution to storage problems in one-room living. Hollow, sliding panels screen a bedroom area during the day while providing valuable shelf and hanging space for clothes. In the evening they can be slid back to reveal the sleeping area behind.*

*Opposite: Any wall space, no matter how narrow, can be fitted with shelves and pushed into service. This example is visually satisfying because the cassettes are in scale with the size of the wall space – the records on the other wall would not have looked as pleasing.*

and shelves in blank corners that you had not originally considered. There is often plenty of space under the bed to add a drawer unit to house toys, linen, towels or other items. If the drawer is on wheels or castors access will be easier. The area around the bath can be filled with tailored shelves or pull-out racks to store cosmetics. A bed or a bath can also be raised on a platform to create extra storage space underneath.

Apart from making the best use of recesses and blank walls, always make maximum use of the space available in cupboards. They can be fitted with pull-out rails for flexible hanging storage, perhaps shoe, tie and scarf racks. Deep and corner kitchen cupboards are suitable for a carousel, and this idea can be adapted for other inaccessible corners. The carousel has two or three shelves and swings out when the door is opened, making it easy to reach the stored goods. Spice or lid racks can also be added to the inside of doors on kitchen cabinets where space is at a premium.

## The broad view

As always, think three-dimensionally when working out storage facilities and apply the same principles as you would in kitchen and bathroom planning. Try to think ergonomically, and position items so that any bending or stretching is kept to a minimum. Access is also important, for you do not want to be forever unpacking cupboards to find everyday items: put articles which are rarely used, such as the Christmas turkey dish and tree lights, skiing gear or barbecue equipment, right at the back of cupboards. Store items in a way appropriate to each one. Always place items such as household tools, for example, in a safe, dry place, for if they are stored in a damp area they will quickly rust.

Part 4

# THE PREPARATION

It is always stressed, and with good reason, that a well-prepared surface will make all the difference between a spectacular finish and a disappointing one. It is a waste of your time and effort to paint or paper a wall in the expectation of achieving what you can see in one of these pictures, if in the end your wall is just not up to it. Preparation is hard and often rather alarming work, as you turn your rooms into chaos and commit yourself to major redecoration; but try to think of it as the first step towards a brand new, personalized, home. As you rip out other people's ideas, you are creating a blank canvas on to which you can project your own.

Choose a finish for your rooms that is appropriate to the existing state of the walls. With a very damaged, uneven plaster, you are only asking for trouble if you choose a silk- or gloss-textured paint, for it will simply show up all the problems. Look for a paint finish that will distract instead, or a paper that will hide the surface.

A good deal of mess is inevitable, so keep your morale up either by preparing and decorating each room in turn, or, if stripping everything at the same time seems appropriate, by preparing and decorating one room first, as perfectly as you can: it will give you confidence and encouragement as you get down to the rest, not to mention providing you with somewhere to relax at the end of a hard day.

*An effect as clean and simple as this does require careful work at the preparation stage. Flat painted walls will show up any bumps or cracks unless you have sorted out the faults beforehand, and a tiled floor is most unsatisfactory if the tiles aren't lying completely flat. The whole effect relies on sensitive use of the materials themselves, from the stripped wood of the chairs and table to the plants in the conservatory.*

# Surface Preparation

When sanding a surface, use a fine-grade abrasive paper and aim for a smooth finish. When keying, use a coarser grade to scuff it. Wash surfaces down with warm water, adding a little household detergent if the surface is very dirty.

## WALLS, CEILINGS

| Previous treatment | New treatment | Preparation | Comments |
|---|---|---|---|
| DISTEMPER | Paint – oil-based or emulsion (latex) | Wash off all old distemper; or wash down and use lining paper | To test for distemper, wipe over the surface with a damp rag – if a powdery substance comes off on the rag the paint is distemper. You cannot paint over distemper except with more distemper, as it will break through the new painted surface, causing it to flake off. If lining prior to painting make sure any paste is removed from the front before painting |
| | Wallcovering (paper, vinyl) | Wash down and key with abrasive paper; size or use stabilizing primer if necessary | |
| | Tiles | Wash down, make sure surface is sound | |
| | Wood cladding (siding); fabric | Clean thoroughly. No other preparation necessary if fabric or cladding to be fixed on wooden strips; cross-line the walls if fabric is to be stuck | |
| OIL-BASED PAINT (gloss or eggshell/ lustre) | Paint – oil-based or emulsion (latex) | Wash down, key lightly. Use the appropriate undercoat for oil-based paint | |
| | Wallcovering (paper, vinyl) | Wash down, key lightly | |
| | Tiles | Wash down and key | |
| | Wood cladding (siding); fabric | Wash down; key if fabric to be pasted on | |
| EMULSION (LATEX) PAINT (water-based) | Paint – oil-based or emulsion (latex) | Wash down; key a silk vinyl. Matt emulsion (latex) can be an undercoat for oil-based paint | |
| | Wallcovering (paper, vinyl) | Wash down | |
| | Tiles | Wash down; key a silk vinyl | |
| WALLCOVERING Paper Vinyl Special wallcoverings | Paint – all types | Check to see if colour-fast; if so, paper or vinyl can be painted over. Make sure covering is adhering firmly to the wall; slash and restick bubbles or peeling seams; wipe any adhesive off front; prime any metallic inks | If wallpaper is hand-printed and not colour-fast it will smudge; it will have to be stripped, or the wall lined. Sand down other papers to hide any obvious joins and to remove old adhesive from the front before painting. |
| | New wallcoverings | Strip off old wallcovering, fill and smooth walls; if necessary size. If using special wallcovering, cross-line first | Always make sure any old wallpaper adhesive is completely removed with water and a scraper before painting or re-papering; walls can again be sanded smooth if necessary |
| | Tiles | Strip, fill and key | |
| | Wood cladding (siding); fabric | Clean thoroughly. No other preparation necessary if fabric or cladding to be fixed on wooden strips; cross-line walls for fabric | |
| TILES (ceramic) | Paint (use special ceramic tile paint only) | Wash down; make sure grouting is sound, and is flush with or below the surface; sand if necessary | Make sure the tiles are secured firmly to the wall; if not they will have to be removed and the wall treated as new. Remove all old adhesive by chipping and scraping, and fill all holes. |
| | Wallcovering | Wash down | Contoured vinyl is really the only recommended type |
| | Tiles | Wash down | Old tiles can be covered with slim 'universal' tiles |
| | Wood cladding (siding) | Wash down | |
| | Fabric | Not recommended unless attached to wooden strips | |

| **Previous treatment** | **New treatment** | **Preparation** | **Comments** |
|---|---|---|---|
| TILES Ceiling (Polystyrene) | Paint – emulsion (latex) only<br>Wallcovering<br>Wood cladding (siding); fabric | No preparation necessary if tiles are adhering firmly<br>Not recommended<br>Remove tiles, clean ceiling and use wooden strips | *Never* paint ceiling tiles with oil-based paint as they become flammable. Make sure the tiles are firmly fixed. If not, remove and treat ceiling as new |
| NEWLY PLASTERED WALLS (must be completely dried out) | Paint – emulsion (latex)<br>Wallcovering – use paper, *not* vinyl<br>Tiles<br>Wood cladding (siding); fabric | Sand lightly, use thinned-down coat as an undercoat<br>Must be left for six months; apply coat of size<br>Key to provide grip for adhesive<br>Attach wooden strips to completely dry walls. Do not paste fabric on | Newly plastered walls may show signs of shrinkage, cracks or efflorescence during drying, and painting is usually recommended. Do not use vinyl wallcovering as it will not let the wall breathe |
| **WOODWORK** *Doors, shutters, mouldings and window frames* | | | |
| PAINT (oil-based) | Paint – oil-based, gloss or eggshell/lustre | Wash down, scrape or burn off flaking or blistered paintwork. Sand down, fill cracks and holes and sand smooth. Treat knots with knotting and prime bare wood; undercoat | Always use the manufacturer's recommended undercoat to match the top coat |
| | Polyurethane varnish or oil | Strip off previous treatment, wash down, fill, sand and prime; treat any knots and apply varnish or oil. The first coat forms an undercoat | If sealing or oiling wood to show off the natural beauty, all old paint or stain will have to be completely removed. It is worth considering having doors or shutters stripped professionally |
| STAIN | Paint – all oil-based types | Wash and sand down, remove as much old stain as possible. Fill holes or cracks and sand smooth. Treat knots, prime – use aluminium primer if applying a lighter colour – and undercoat | |
| POLYURETHANE VARNISH | Paint – all oil based types | Remove varnish with chemical stripper, sand, prime and undercoat. If varnish is in good condition, sand and paint over | |
| | Stain | Remove varnish with chemical stripper, and sand | |
| | Polyurethane varnish or oil | As described for previously painted wood | A darker varnish can be applied over a keyed, varnished surface |
| NEW WOOD | Paint – all oil-based types<br>Stain | Sand, fill cracks and prime<br>Sand; where necessary sand before sealing | |
| **METAL** *Radiators, windows and pipes* | | | |
| PAINT | Paint – all oil-based types | Rub down with wire brush to remove any rust or flaking paint, or apply a rust remover or convertor. Strip off perished paint, fill cracks, prime and undercoat | Interior metalwork does not become rusty as a rule, so wire-brushing is more likely to be necessary on exterior metalwork |
| NEW METAL | Paint – oil-based or enamel | None needed with enamel. Prime and undercoat for oil-based paint. Some radiators come ready primed; use metal primer on damaged areas | |

# Essential Tools

Whichever type of finish you finally decide to use on walls, ceilings, floor or woodwork, it will only look good if the surface underneath is sound. Preparatory work can be boring and take a long time but it is always worth doing properly.

## The necessary tools

The right tools for the job will make the whole process of stripping and decorating much easier. Try to keep them in pristine condition: always clean them after use, oil or sharpen as needed and store carefully in a dry place so that they do not rust.

Build up your basic tool kit (opposite) gradually, adding tools as you need them. Aim for a sensible selection of tools, which you know you will need to use, and buy the best quality you can possibly afford – they will not break as easily as cheap versions and will last longer. Many tools can be hired or rented at minimum cost from local decorating or do-it-yourself centres, so it often makes sense to do this for specialist items or ones where storage would be difficult, such as ladders.

Items which have more than one purpose will often justify the expense of buying them. A portable workbench, for example, is an extremely versatile accessory which can be used for woodwork and many other different decorating and do-it-yourself jobs. The decorator's wallpaper pasting table is another good item to have, as apart from being used for wallpapering, it folds down flat and becomes an ideal surface on which to cut fabric.

Always read the manufacturer's instructions for handling a tool, and always remember to follow the standard safety measures.

## Simple remedies

It is not always necessary to strip right back to the basic surface. If there are no rusty or perished areas on metal or woodwork they may only need washing with a proprietary cleanser, and then 'keyed' with abrasive paper to provide a good matt surface for the new paint. If only a small area is in bad condition you can repair just that section, but make sure it is smooth and blends with the surrounding area.

If wallpaper is in good condition and sticking firmly to the wall, you may be able just to repaint it. Most wallcoverings will take emulsion (latex) paint although a very strong colour or pattern might need three or four coats to cover it properly. Be careful with some handprinted papers; these may need sealing to prevent them from smudging or 'bleeding' and spoiling the new paint. Do not worry if you paint over paper and bubbles appear – this is normal and they will usually dry back completely flat.

If the surface is previously painted smooth plaster or a textured paper, you may be able to paint over it with a new colour and very little preparation. All you will need to do is wash the walls or ceiling down first with some detergent and warm water – a greasy kitchen wall will need to be washed down with a stronger mixture, such as a washing soda solution – and rinsed off with clean water. You must determine, however, what type of paint was used previously: old-fashioned distemper, for example, has to be completely removed or lined as other paints will not adhere to it. Some of the wallcoverings which are easy to strip, such as vinyl, have a backing which stays on the wall when the front layer is peeled away. If this is smooth, you may be able to use this as a lining paper and simply paper over the top; otherwise soak and strip. Dry strippable wallcoverings are designed to be easily removed.

### PORTABLE WORKBENCHES

**A portable workbench combines a sturdy work surface, which folds flat when not in use, with the facility to clamp items securely in the room where you are working. The simplest model folds out to a height of 58cm (23in) – ideal as a saw-horse – and the 61cm (24in) jaws open up to 100mm (4in) apart. Wide boards can be clamped by inserting plastic stops into holes in the top of the jaws. The jaws can also be closed up out-of-parallel to grip irregularly-shaped items. Despite its weight of only 8kg (18lb), it will support a load of 250kg ($\frac{1}{4}$ton). Larger models with two working heights have jaws up to 120cm ($30\frac{1}{2}$in) long. On one model, the back jaw may be swivelled through 90° to clamp downwards – ideal for glueing. Another accepts a table top for power saws and routers.**

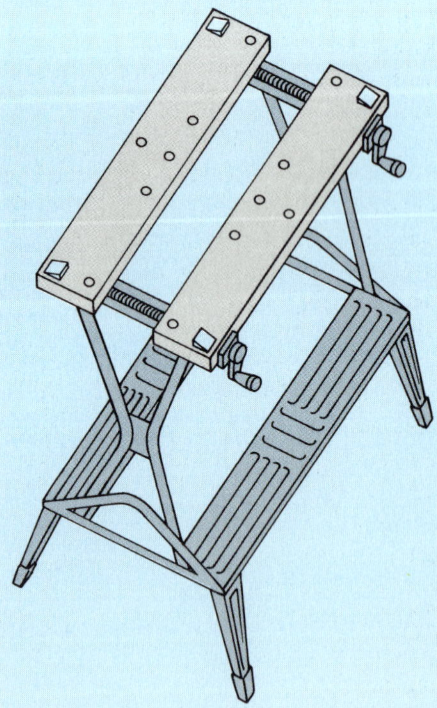

| | |
|---|---|
| SURFACE PREPARATION | 74 |
| WORKING SAFELY | 78 |
| STRIPPING SURFACES | 80 |
| TOOLKITS | 100, 126 143, 160 |




## BASIC AND PREPARATION TOOLS

**1** Try-square for right angles; **2** Spirit level checks horizontals and verticals; **3** Adjustable spanner (wrench) for turning nuts; **4** Medium-size screwdriver with interchangeable blades; **5** Claw hammer pulls out nails too; **6** Bradawl marks and starts screwholes; **7** Plumb-line and bob for vertical lines; **8** Handyman's knife cuts and marks out; **9** Steel tape-measure, with or without clamp; **10** Wire brush removes rust and scores washable wallpaper; **11** Hot-air paint stripper burns off oil-based paints; **12** Blowlamp (propane torch) requires more care than 11; **13** Serrated scraper scores washable wallpaper; **14** Self-levelling scraper removes wallpaper without damaging plaster; **15** Filling knife for filling cracks and small holes; **16** Wood chisel for general chiselling; **17** Abrasive papers and cork block for sanding wood and plaster; **18** Pliers grip, and cut wire; **19** Bolster (wide) chisel chips out plaster or masonry; **20** Shavehook scrapes paint from flat and curved surfaces; **21** Tenon saw (backsaw) for accurate cuts in wood; **22** Two-speed electric drill for wood or masonry; **23** Twist bits (for drilling wood and metal) and masonry bits.

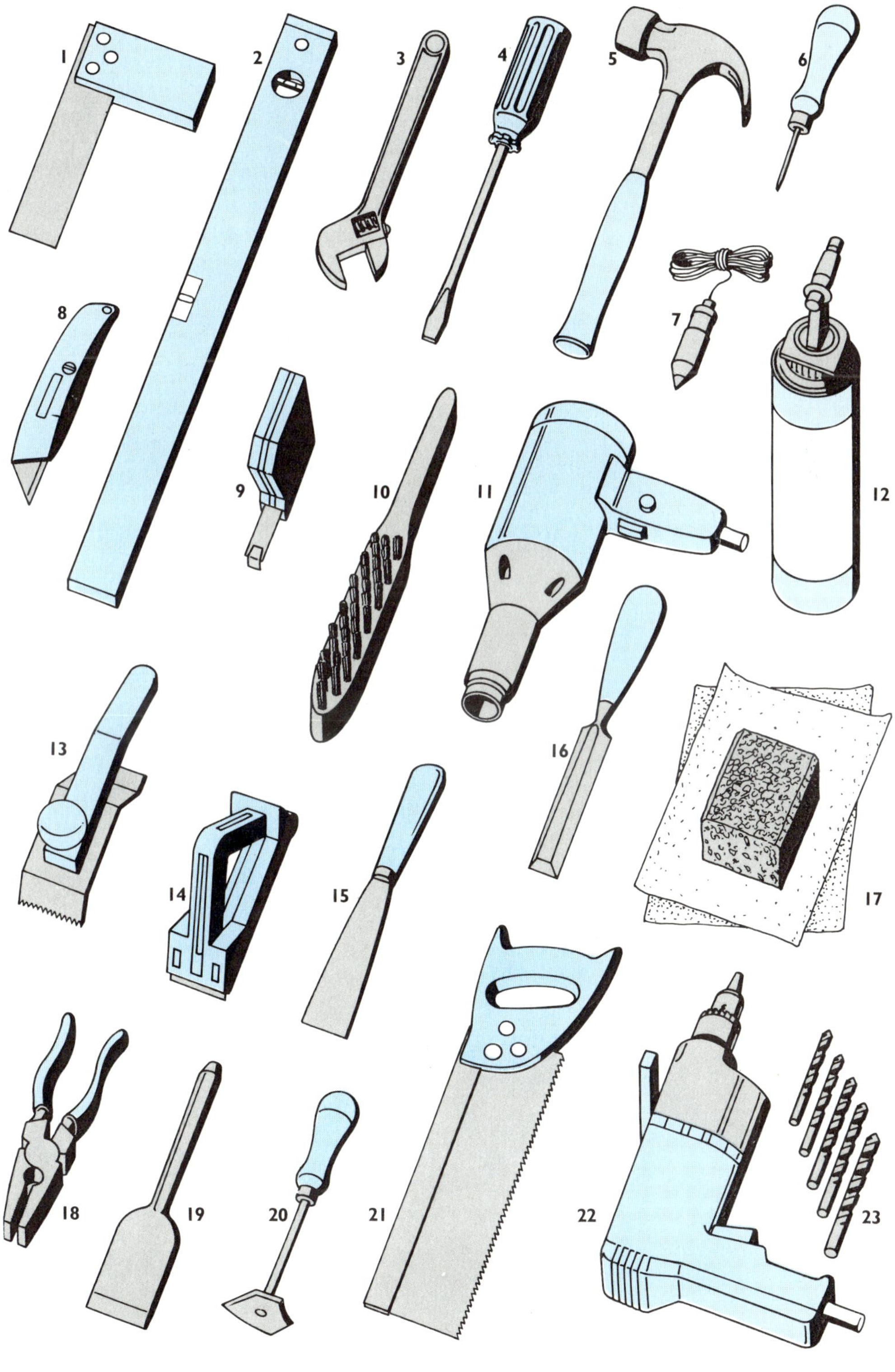

# Working Safely

Always keep your do-it-yourself tools and equipment in a garage, shed or cupboard that can be locked. Never leave paint strippers, cleansers, paste or paint out, especially if there are children around.

One obvious hazard is working with ladders, tower platforms or scaffolding, both inside and out. Balance is always a problem, especially when you are trying to hold tools or decorating materials: remember that you can topple off a ladder when you are just a short way off the floor just as easily as you can from a height.

Before you begin work, and especially if you are using an old ladder, lay it down flat on the ground and check all the rungs to make sure they are firm. Always set step-ladders squarely and fully extended, so they lock and cannot fold up on you. Have a ladder hook or shelf to hold the paint or tools.

If you are working with a large extending ladder out of doors, set it up at the correct angle to the wall and follow the basic rule of 1 to 4: if the top of the ladder is 4m (4yds) above the ground, the bottom should be 1m (1yd) out from the base of the wall. Leave three rungs overlapping in the centre on extension ladders. If necessary wedge or secure the bottom of the ladder so that it cannot slip and attach a ladder stay at the top, or at the very least make sure it is firmly secured.

If constructing scaffolding, clamp the boards securely to their support. If you are balancing them between two ladders, whether inside or out, ensure that these are of the same height, and that enough board protrudes each side.

Do not stretch out too far when on any ladder or platform and wear thick, non-slip shoes. If you have any doubts about using ladders, hire (rent) a tower platform for bigger jobs, which is a much safer structure.

**2 & 5** Combination ladder for use as extension ladder or steps, and particularly on unequal levels.

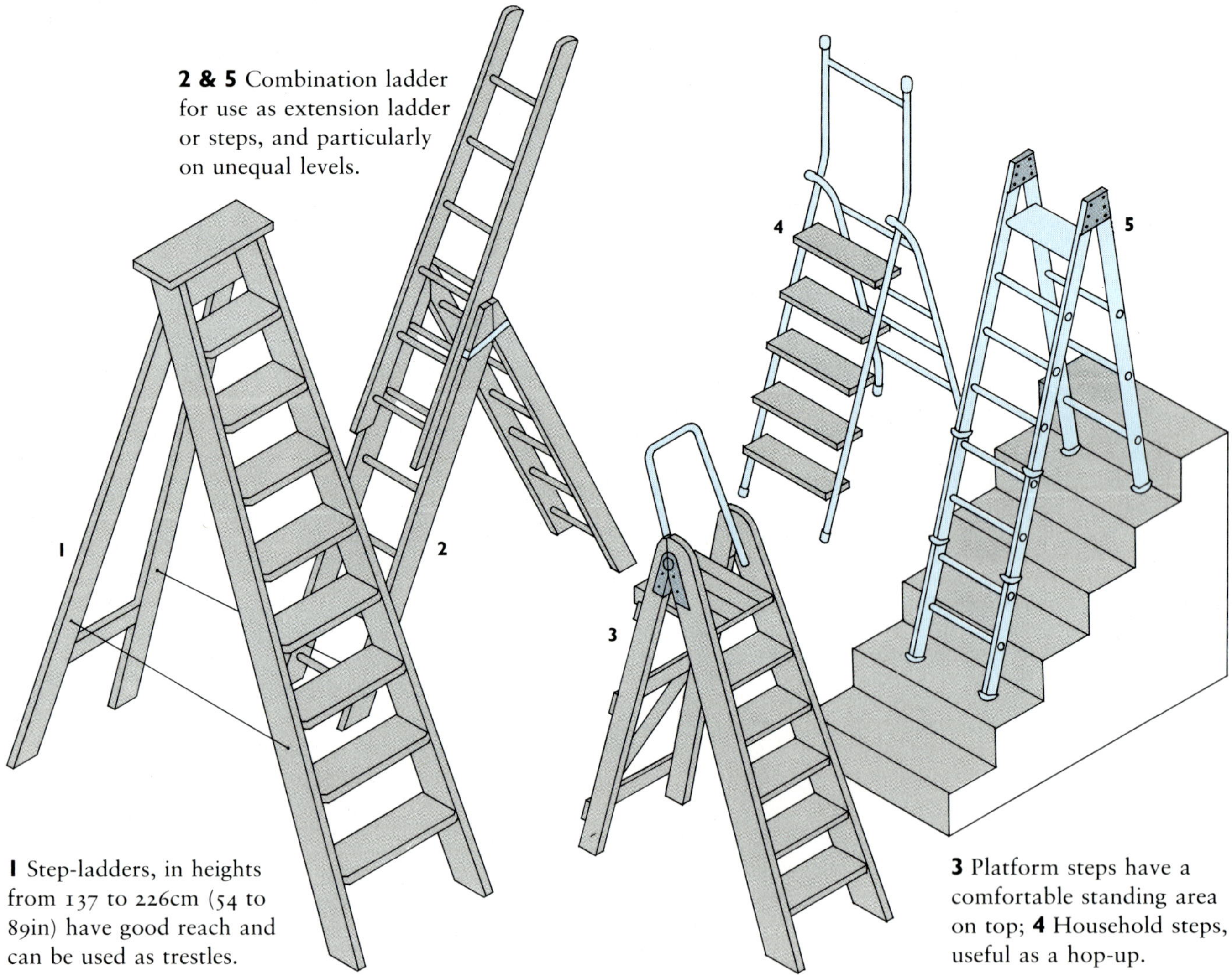


**1** Step-ladders, in heights from 137 to 226cm (54 to 89in) have good reach and can be used as trestles.

**3** Platform steps have a comfortable standing area on top; **4** Household steps, useful as a hop-up.

## WORK PLATFORMS

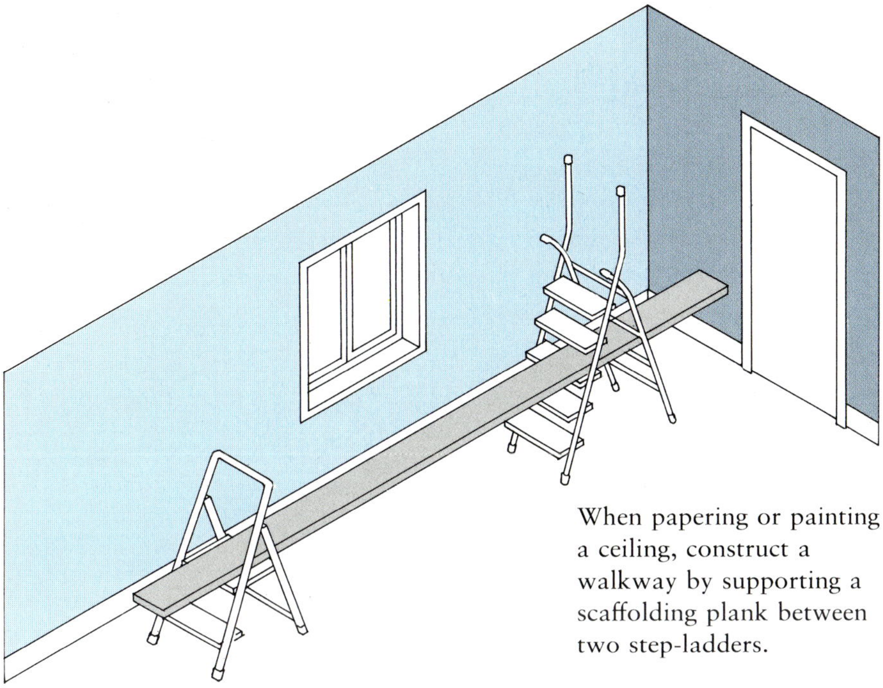

When papering or painting a ceiling, construct a walkway by supporting a scaffolding plank between two step-ladders.

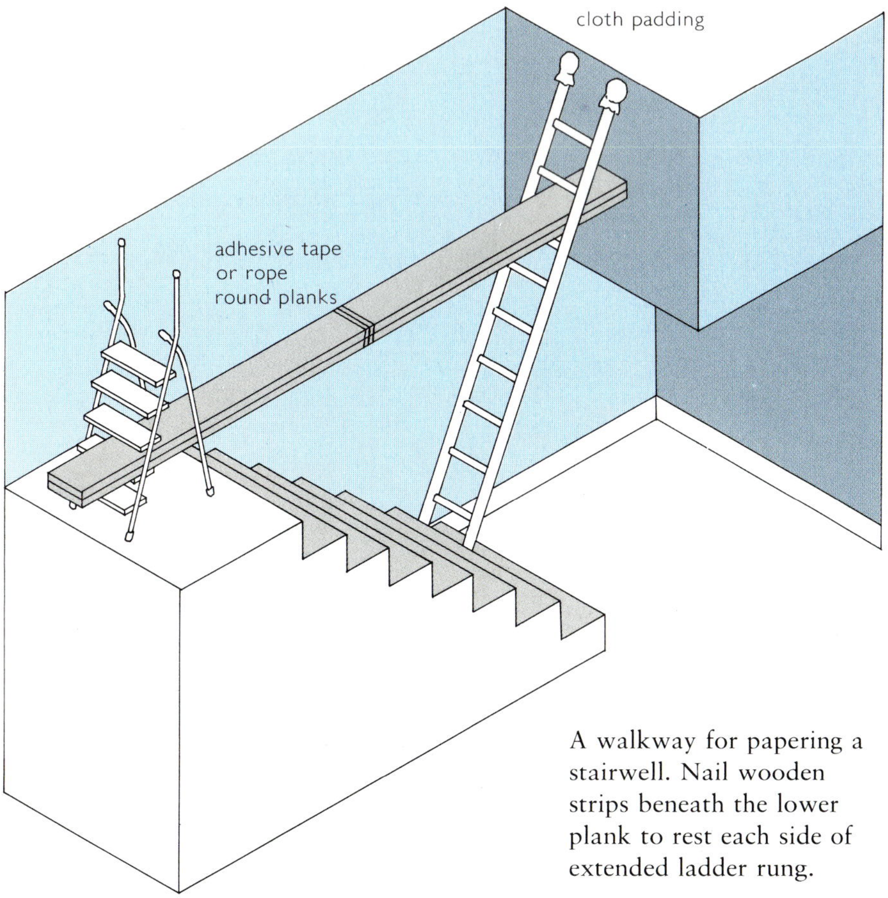


A walkway for papering a stairwell. Nail wooden strips beneath the lower plank to rest each side of extended ladder rung.

### Safety tips

*Do*

- try and work in daylight if possible, or fix up a good source of electric light.
- work in a logical sequence and clear up as you go along.
- make sure you understand how to operate power tools and check that they have a long enough lead (cord), or use an extension. Disconnect from the power supply before changing blades or bits. Use a special circuit breaker for protection.
- always keep your fingers *behind* a tool's cutting edge.
- wear sensible, protective clothing.
- use heavy-duty gloves when handling caustic solutions, stains, glass and fibreglass insulation.
- wear goggles to protect the eyes when sanding, chipping out or doing any other messy work.
- wear a mask for dusty work and consider ear plugs or muffs if using a very noisy machine.

*Do not*

- race to accomplish one particular task in a single heavy session; you will only make mistakes.
- inhale chemical fumes when using chemical strippers, adhesives and other solvents, and do make sure the room is adequately ventilated.
- use blowlamps (propane torches) near curtains or in any confined spaces. Hot-air strippers are safer for the beginner to use.
- decant any chemical products into drink bottles or food containers, or leave them unlabelled where they could be used mistakenly.
- ever work with asbestos. If you discover any (a blue or grey fibrous material with a powdery surface), seek expert help.
- tackle any job which is beyond you or which you feel is unsafe. Call in a professional to help you.

# Stripping Surfaces

Most decorating jobs require you to do a fair amount of work stripping off old coverings or layers of paint first. It can be hard work that is made much easier with the modern tools readily available, such as hot-air strippers for woodwork.

### Stripping wallpaper

Normal wallpaper can be removed by soaking with warm water and a little household detergent. Apply with a sponge, brush or a hand-held spray, leave to soak and apply more water if necessary. A wallpaper scraper can then be used to strip away the old paper. Work from the bottom of the wall upwards, taking care not to dig into the plaster. Try and clear up the mess as you go along. Take care when working round light fixtures and switches. A proprietary stripping compound can also be used which speeds up stripping.

If it is a washable paper you will need to score the surface first to enable the water to penetrate. Use a wire brush, handyman's knife, serrated-edged scraper or a coarse abrasive paper to break up the surface, then soak as above.

The top layer of vinyl or polyethylene wallcoverings are usually easy to peel off. Lift a corner and pull upwards. A backing layer will be left behind, which can be used as a lining paper if it is well stuck and not damaged. If you need to remove it, soak and strip in the usual way.

Dry strippable wallcoverings can be removed easily, starting from a bottom corner of each sheet and pulling it gently. They leave the wall ready for redecorating.

Heavy relief wallpapers which have been painted over and some washable papers are much easier to remove using a steam wallpaper stripper. These can be hired or rented and are normally electric. They force the steam through a large

## STRIPPING WALLPAPER

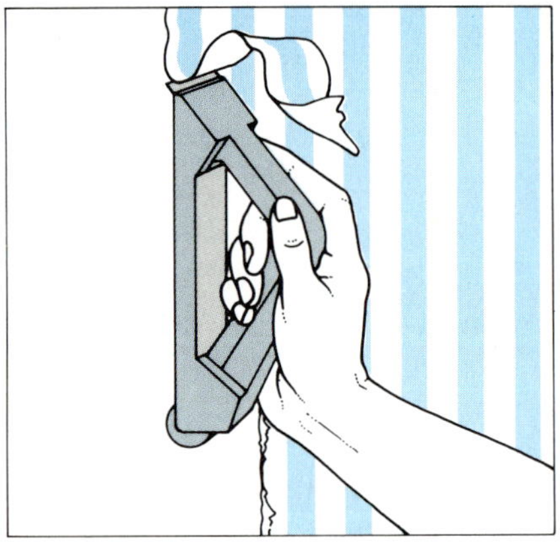

**1** Look for a wallpaper stripper with a roller at the back that will keep the blade at the correct angle.

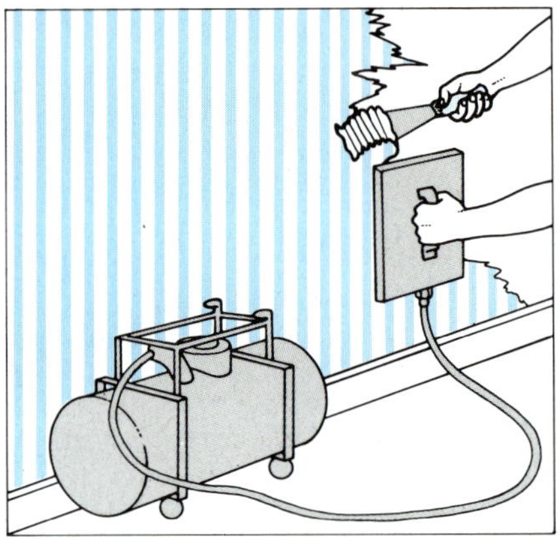

**2** For stubborn paper, hold the plate of a steam stripper against the wall to soften the adhesive.

**3** Score the surface of washable papers with a serrated scraper to allow water to penetrate.

## STRIPPING PAINT

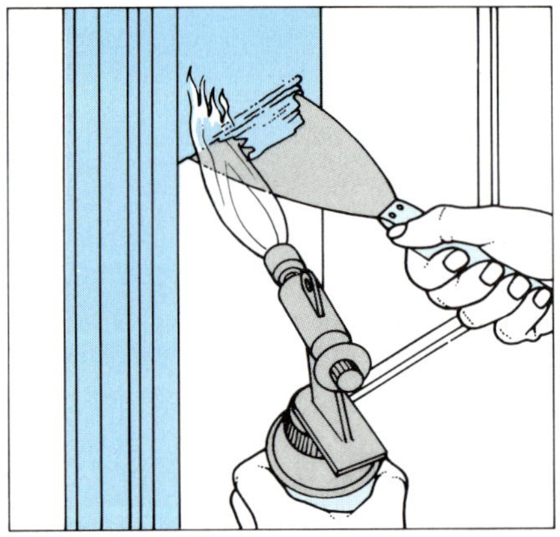

**1** Keep a blowlamp (propane torch) flame moving to prevent scorching; scrape paint into a metal tray.

**2** Use a shavehook for mouldings, and a hot air stripper to reduce the risk of scorching.

**3** Rub down mouldings with a flexible abrasive block which will take the shape of the moulding.

plate which penetrates the top surface of the wallpaper and gets to the paste beneath. You will still need to use a scraper but it is a much quicker process. Wear a protective waterproof glove on the hand using the steamer to prevent any scalding.

Once stripped, let the walls dry before filling and re-decorating.

## Stripping paint

You may not need to strip off all the old paint unless it has perished or unless you want to get back to the bare surface to prime or use a new treatment. Paint in good condition on ceiling, walls, wood and metal can be washed down, 'keyed', any cracks or chips filled, and then repainted. Stain is a different matter, and cannot be removed. Here one option is to sand down and paint over it in a darker colour – a lighter one will allow patches of stain to show through. Alternatively, sand the stained wood and paint over it with aluminium wood primer; apply two coats with 24 hours between each. Paint over this with oil-based paint.

If the surface paint has blistered or perished, or if on metal rust is breaking through, you will need to strip off all the old paint. Once that is done, use a coat of primer and then undercoat and topcoat.

You can use a hot air stripper to soften old paint, scraping this off with scrapers and shavehooks. Work on a small area at a time, and clear up as you go along. You can also use a blow lamp (propane torch) but only use one if you feel confident, as you can easily scorch the wood. There are also various chemical strippers available. A liquid type can be painted on with an old paintbrush, which causes the old paint to bubble up and become easy to scrape off. As the liquid is caustic, wear rubber gloves to apply it. Easier to use is a thick paste stripper that can be spread on with a trowel. When the paste is later scraped off, the paint comes off with it in sheets. With either type, rub over the surface afterwards with steel wool, then wipe thoroughly with white spirit (mineral spirits). The chemical strippers are particularly good for moulded, carved and other intricate surfaces: use a shavehook to remove the paint.

If you are stripping doors or shutters it is much easier to take them off their hinges, lay them flat on a trestle or table and strip them in a well-ventilated area, or outdoors; or have them stripped professionally.

*In this simple alcove the natural texture and colour of the wood itself is allowed to make a powerful decorative statement.*

## Stripping varnish

Varnished surfaces are similar to painted ones and can be washed, rubbed down and re-treated. Use a scraper or shavehook to remove any flaking chips of varnish, then use a chemical stripper to remove it. Alternatively, sand down using sanding discs and a power tool, or for smaller areas use abrasive paper wrapped round a sanding block.

# Filling Holes

Small holes and cracks in plastered walls or punctures in plasterboard (gypsum board) are not difficult to repair; larger areas of loose or crumbling 'live' plaster may be harder to fill. Plastering is not an easy skill to acquire and it might be wise to call in some professional help.

In some cases you can cheat, and just cover a poor surface with wood or a laminate. If you want to hang a wallcovering or ceramic tiles, use new plasterboard (gypsum board) to cover the offending wall, nailed to a framework of battens (furring strips) as for wood cladding. Tape the joints flush. Textured paint can be used as a cover-up but needs to go on to a fairly smooth surface.

### Walls and ceilings

Tackle small cracks in plaster by first raking out any loose material, then undercutting the crack with the edge of a filling knife. Moisten the surface well to ensure good adhesion and press filler into the crack with a filling knife (right).

For larger cracks and holes, you may have to use plaster rather than filler, and do a thorough patching job. Modern 'one-coat' plaster saves a lot of the work necessary with the traditional undercoat and finishing plasters. Most dry to a white finish. First, remove all the loose plaster and get right back to the original sub-structure. Wet the area thoroughly as plaster absorbs a lot of water and paint on a PVA bonding agent. Mix the plaster with clean water to a thick creamy consistency and apply it with a plasterer's trowel in layers, letting each dry in between, to just above the original plaster surface. Level it off by drawing a straightedge upwards over the repair, flush with the plaster each side. When nearly dry, smooth and harden off with a plasterer's float, wetted with water.

**FILLING: PLASTER CRACKS**

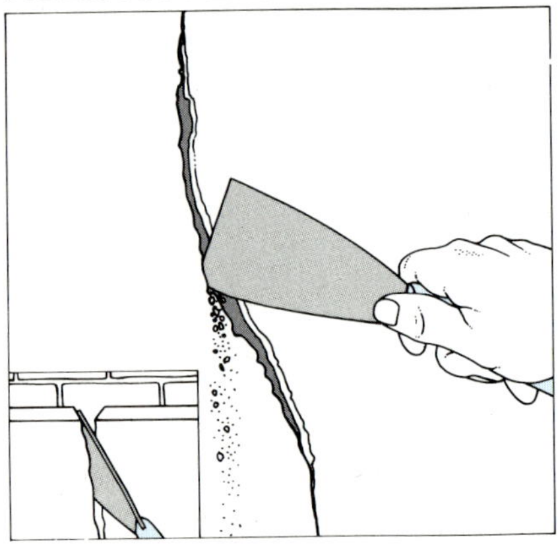

**1** Rake out the crack to a V-shape (inset) with a filling knife, to keep the filler from falling out.

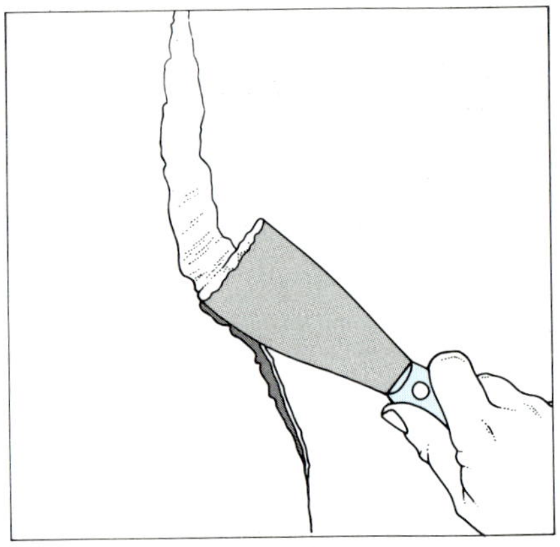

**2** Dust out and wet the crack, push in filler firmly, and level off slightly proud of the surface.

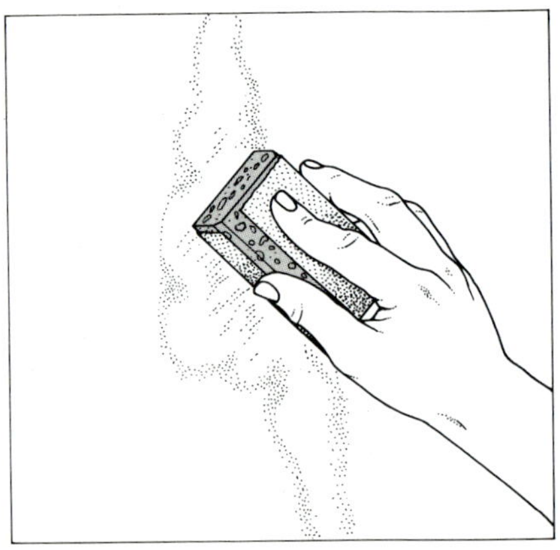

**3** Allow the filler to dry, then rub down flush with the surface with some abrasive paper.

**PLASTERBOARD HOLES**

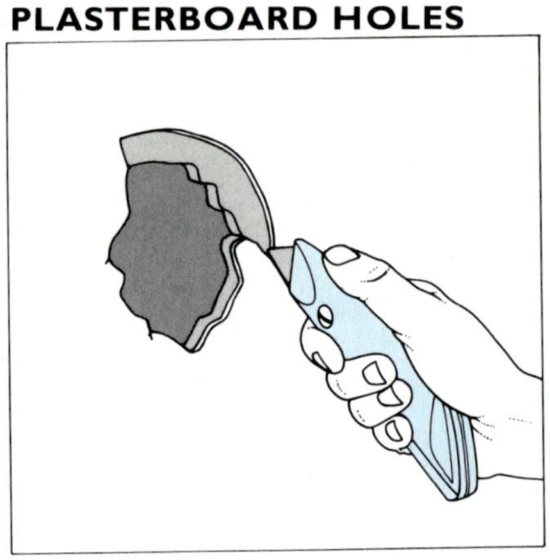

**1** Cut through the finishing layer of plaster to leave a ledge about 10mm ($\frac{1}{2}$in) wide round the hole.

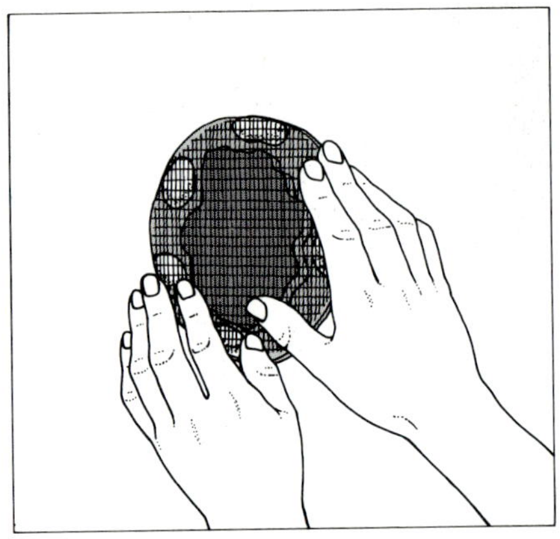

**2** Cut a piece of scrim tape the size of the hole and fix it to the ledge with blobs of plaster.

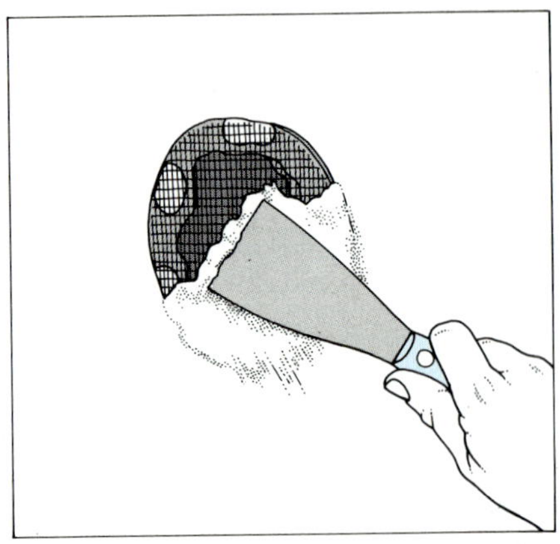

**3** Carefully but firmly apply a layer of finishing plaster over the scrim tape and level off flush.

*The interesting architectural shapes in this room catch the attention, so it's important that there should be no irregularities in the surface of the plaster. The careful filling and smoothing of any holes is essential at the preparation stage.*

For more complicated repairs it is often advisable to fill the hole with traditional undercoating plaster and to complete the repair with a layer of finishing plaster.

An easy way to fill medium-sized holes in walls and ceilings is to crumple up some wet newspaper and use it to fill the hole partially before adding the new plaster or filler.

## Dealing with damaged corners

External corners do get chipped, and they need careful repairing. First, hack off any loose plaster and brush away the dust. Dampen the area, pin a wooden strip lightly to the edge of the wall with masonry pins and apply plaster to the wall now at right angles to the strip. When the plaster has hardened remove the wooden strip and attach it to the other side of the corner, then replaster the part of the hole now uncovered. When almost set, round off the external angle with a moistened finger or a small sheet of polyethylene. Sand flush with the wall when the new material is completely dry.

## Plasterboard (gypsum board)

Small holes can be repaired with a special scrim tape. Trim round the hole to make a neat edge, then fix the tape, cut to size, with some plaster to the hole. Spread plaster over the tape, leave it to dry and sand flush.

If the hole is larger, you will need to cut the damaged board back to the studs or joists. Cut a piece of plasterboard (gypsum board) to size, and patch the hole by nailing it in. Put jointing or scrim tape over the edge, then lightly plaster over the patch.

### FILLING CHIPS IN WOOD

Any woodwork with chips or holes can be filled with wood filler and painted. If the holes or chips are bad, strip the item first. For chips on mouldings or external corners, use a wooden strip held flush to one surface and fill the hole created; when dry, move the strip to the other surface, fill the hole then sand when dry and repaint. Use the technique below to conceal the nails or screwheads in picture, dado or chair rails, or skirting boards (baseboards).

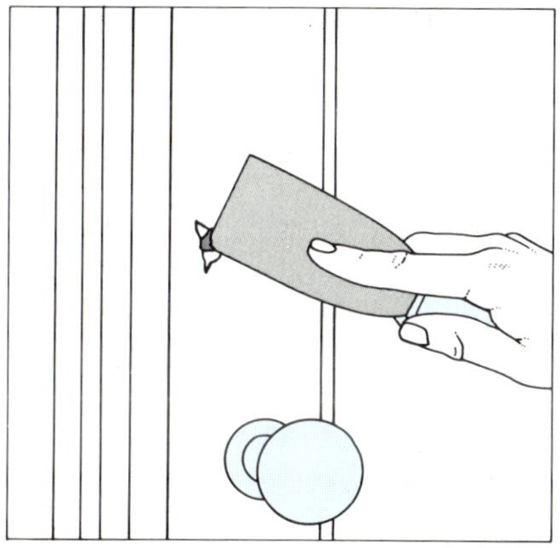

**1** Remove any flaking paint round the chip and fill it slightly proud with fine-surface filler.

**2** When dry, sand flush with abrasive paper, prime and repaint.

# Renovating Floors

Your choice of flooring will in the end depend very much on the state of the existing floor and how much repair work you are prepared to do. If you want to lay tiles or a new flooring you will need to make sure the existing floor (subfloor) is as level and as smooth as possible, and also that it is not damp: test by leaving a square of polyethylene under an inverted saucer overnight. If there is any moisture on the underside of the polyethylene in the morning you have a damp floor which will need to be treated professionally before any new flooring is laid. Uneven floorboards or bumps in the subfloors will need to be repaired as they could pierce new floorcoverings, or cause tiles to push up.

If you have uneven concrete floors, cover them with a floor levelling compound. Mix it up with water following the instructions and pour on to a depth of 3mm ($\frac{3}{8}$in). Lightly trowel the floor and leave to find its own level. Ceramic tiles can be laid on top of this compound, when dry, with adhesive.

## Wooden floors

Floorboards, if they are in good condition, can be stripped, sanded smooth and sealed, or stained and varnished. They can also be painted, perhaps stencilled or given various

*The owners of this house have made the most of their damaged and old floorboards, without attempting to make them look as good as new. Gaps between the boards and splintered holes have been filled with corks from wine bottles, then the whole has been varnished. The result is charmingly eccentric.*

**REPLACING FLOORBOARDS**

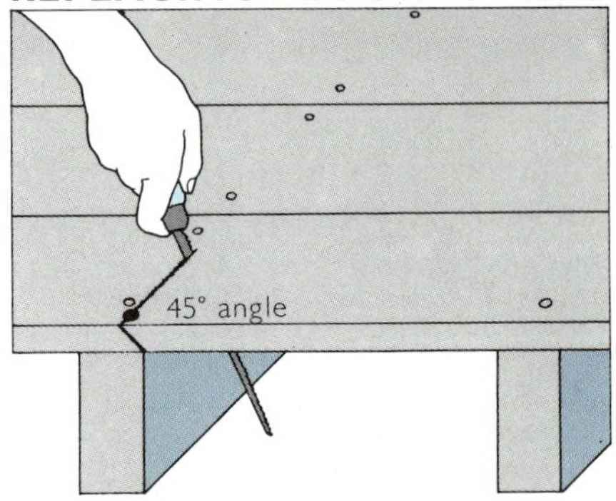


**1** If it is difficult to lift the whole board, drill a starting hole and cut carefully at 45° to the surface with a pad saw (keyhole saw) or power jigsaw (saber saw) along a joist.

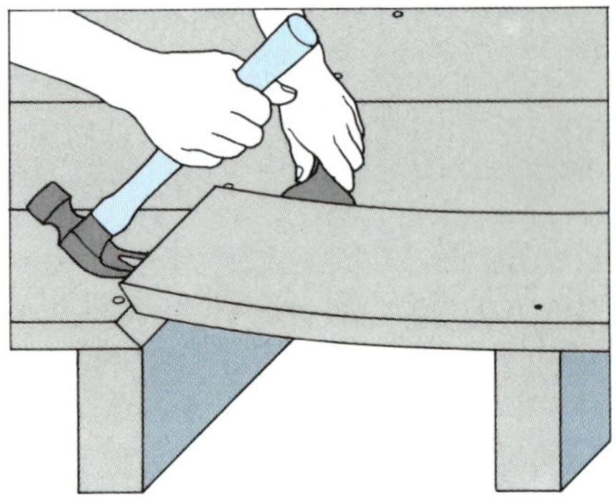

**2** Hammer a bolster (wide) chisel into the cut, lever up the end of the board, and insert a claw hammer under the lifted end. Work along the board with the chisel to lift it.

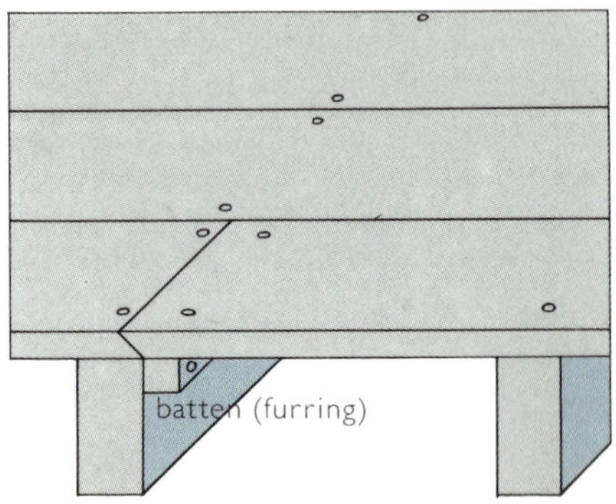


**3** Screw a wooden strip along the joist, flush with the underside of the board, cut the replacement board to 45°, and nail it to the wooden strip, 25mm (1in) from the edges.

| | |
|---|---|
| USING AN OVERLAY | 86 |
| PAINTING FLOORBOARDS | 106 |
| STAINING FLOORBOARDS | 108 |




other decorative treatments. If the floorboards are poor and you want to lay a new flooring, an overlay may be the only option.

Gaps between the floorboards are unsightly, let in draughts and trap dust and dirt. They can be filled with narrow strips of wood or with wood filler, although both these processes are time-consuming. It may be better to lift the boards using a claw hammer and bolster, or wide chisel, and re-lay them. Shunt all the boards along so that they lie tightly against each other – which will leave you with a gap. Fill with new boards, cut to size by your supplier.

When lifting and replacing damaged or rotten floorboards remember that electric wires and pipes pass underneath the floor. Switch off the electricity supply, and take care not to puncture pipes when re-laying boards – they can sometimes be very near the surface. Make a diagram of the wiring and water systems while the boards are up.

A wooden floor can only be stripped and sanded once the boards are repaired and made good. First replace any floorboards or sections as necessary. Ensure all the boards are firmly fixed down, punch down nailheads or countersink any screws below the surface, and pull out any old tacks or pins used to secure any previous floorcovering, as these will tear the abrasive paper in the sanding machine.

Next, hire or rent a floor-sanding machine, which strips off the top surface of the boards with abrasive paper, smoothing, cleaning and lightening the floor at the same time. It also vacuums up the dust as it works, but sanding is still a very dusty and noisy job. Use protective clothing, wear goggles and a face mask. Try and work with the windows open, and tape up the inside of the door to keep the dust in.

## SANDING FLOORBOARDS

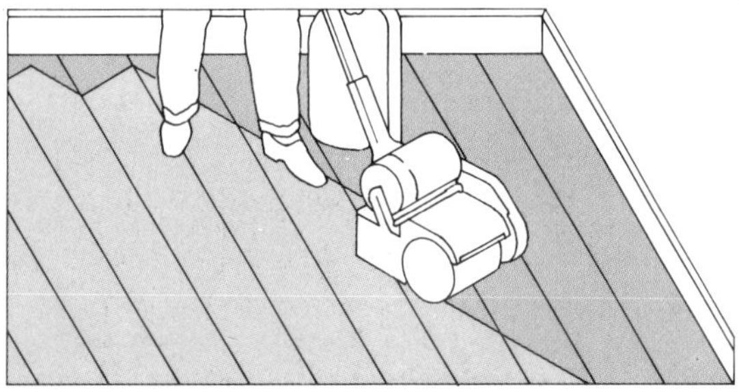

**1** Punch nailheads below the surface, pull out any tacks, and screw down any screws. Fit a coarse-grade abrasive to a drum sander and, starting in one corner, sand the floor in diagonal strips.

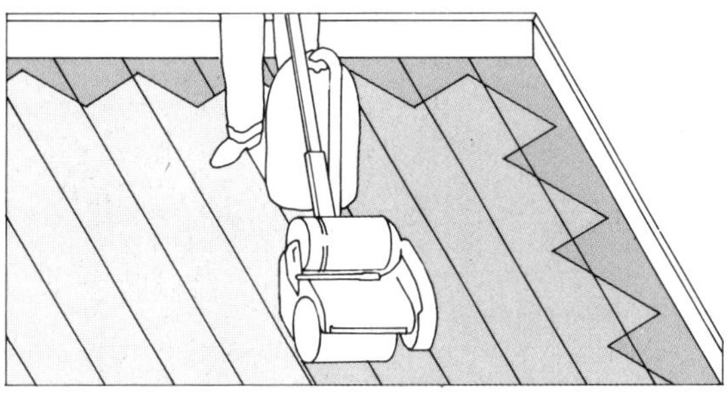

**2** Change to a medium-grade abrasive and sand the floor at right angles to the first direction. Then, with a fine-grade abrasive fitted, sand the floor parallel to the boards (with the grain) to achieve a smooth finish.

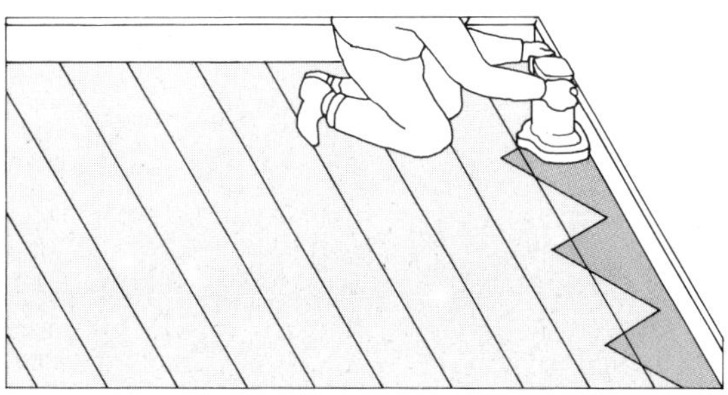

**3** At the edges where a drum sander will not reach, finish with a disc, belt or orbital sander, again using decreasing grades of abrasive. Leave overnight for all dust to settle, then vacuum clean and wipe with white spirit (mineral spirits).

Begin by moving the sander across the floorboards diagonally starting in the corner furthest away from the door. Sand again on the other diagonal, then again along the boards. Use abrasive papers of decreasing grades, switching to a fine grade when sanding with the grain of the wood. To sand the corners of the room you will need an edge sander.

Leave overnight, then sweep up and vacuum the floor, sanding any stubborn or rough spots that still remain by hand. Finally, wipe the floor clean with white spirit (mineral spirits), and then apply your finish – varnish, polish, stain or paint. To make a painted or stained floor hard-wearing, you will need perhaps three or even four coats of polyurethane varnish over the top.

## Using an overlay

An overlay of hardboard, plywood or flooring-grade chipboard (particle board) sheets may be necessary to eliminate draughts and provide a flush surface for a flooring. If you want to lay ceramic or quarry tiles on a timber floor use plywood sheets of 6mm ($\frac{1}{4}$in) thickness and screw them down. Leave 100mm (4in) between each. A very uneven floor may, in exceptional cases, need the application of a 10mm ($\frac{3}{8}$in)-thick layer of a latex-based screed or

*Left: The warm and burnished floorboards in this passage and bedroom overcome any suggestion of austerity in the furnishings. The natural colours in the wood combine with natural light and the textures in the door surround to produce an effect that is powerfully simple.*

*Opposite: Even after carpeting some floorboards may let through draughts. A covering of hardboard sheets will eliminate these and make the entire house cosier.*

| | |
|---|---|
| PREPARING FLOORS | 140, 150 |
| TILING FLOORS | 150 |
| CARPETING | 170 |



compound over the plywood (prime first), but it is rarely necessary to go to these lengths: the tile adhesive or cement will absorb any bumps. If there are uneven joins, sand these down before continuing.

If you decide you need to cover up old floorboards with hardboard, this will first need to be conditioned to prevent buckling. Brush the rough side of each sheet with water, and lay out in the room with the rough sides up for 24 hours. Other coverings need no special preparation.

Nail or staple down the sheets and stagger the joins. Lay hardboard shiny side down so that the rough surface gives adhesion for the new flooring, and secure the sheets with nails (for hardboard) or screws (for plywood and chipboard).

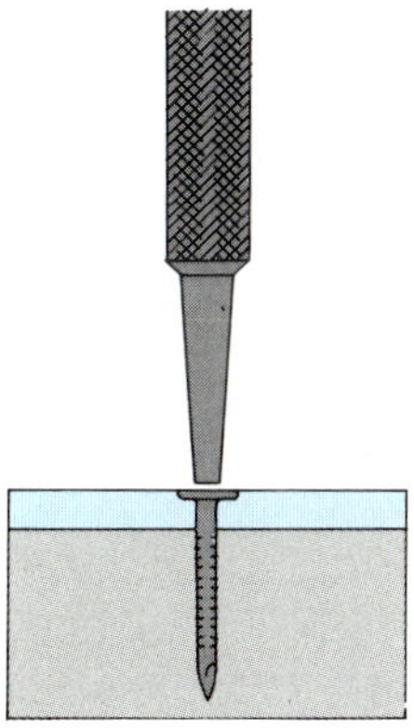

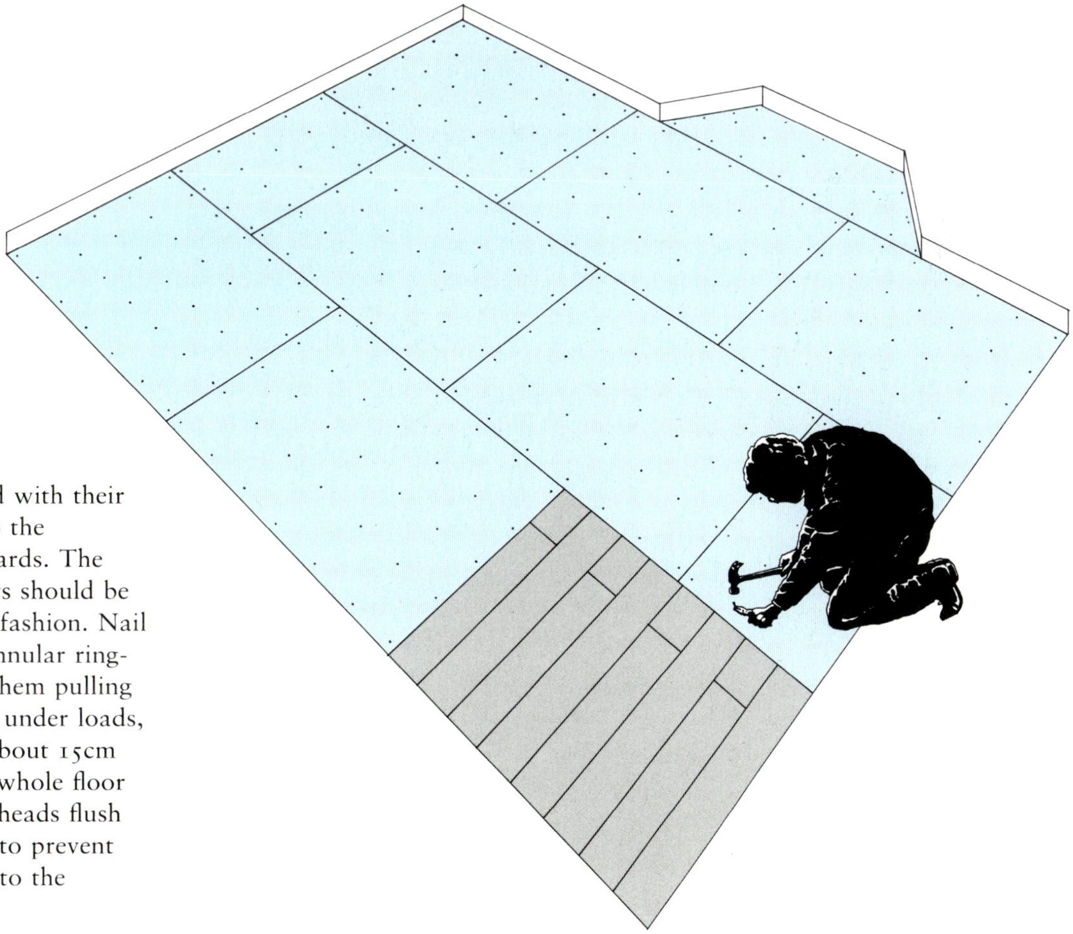

Lay sheets of hardboard with their length at right angles to the direction of the floorboards. The joints between the sheets should be staggered in brickwork fashion. Nail down the sheets with annular ring-shank nails to prevent them pulling loose as the floor flexes under loads, and space the nails at about 15cm (6in) intervals over the whole floor surface. Punch the nail-heads flush with the surface (inset) to prevent any damage happening to the floorcovering.

# Renovating Doors

A door should be a pleasant architectural feature in a room and in keeping with the style of the house, but all too often they are neglected as decorative vehicles. Old doors will often benefit from loving restoration, but modern ones can also be revitalized by repainting and adding new accessories. In dark areas, for example, it might be worth thinking about replacing wood panels in a door with decorative glass to give more light.

It is much easier to work on doors if you take them off their hinges and place them on trestles. Start by removing all the door hardware – knobs, handles, finger plates, knockers and letter boxes – and carefully lift the door off its hinges. This can be very heavy, so balance the bottom on a wedge of wood. If the hinges are old or weak, it may be better to replace them with rising butt hinges that will make the door easier to lift off in the future. If taking the door off its hinges is not possible, take care with stripping and finishing.

When stripping a door back to the wood using a caustic solution it is sensible to work in a well-ventilated area like a garage, or outside. Balance the door on trestles, a workbench or a strong table. If you have several doors to strip, have them dipped professionally to save time.

## Restoration work

Often panelled doors with attractive mouldings were covered up with plywood or hardboard to suit the style of the day and make them easier

*Above: Exploit the qualities of gloss paint on your doors and woodwork. Flush doors with no panels can be dressed up with moulding, glued or nailed to one or both faces.*

*Right: Gleaming gloss paint need not be your objective: these doors look charmingly dilapidated.*

**DOOR HARDWARE**

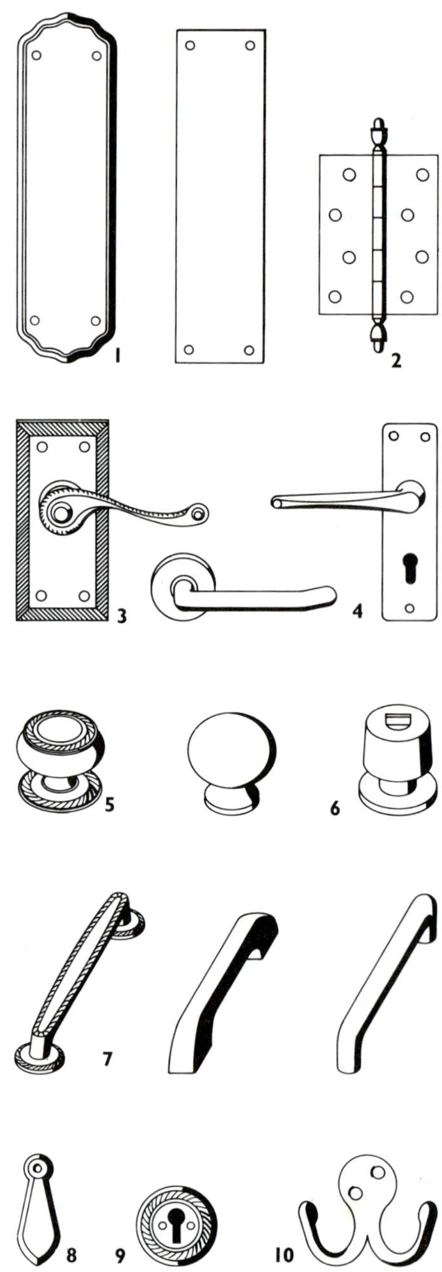


**1** Finger plates; **2** Butt hinge with removable pin; **3** Lever latches; **4** Lever lock; **5** Knobs; **6** Locking knob; **7** Pull handles; **8** Covered escutcheon; **9** Plate escutcheon; **10** Coat hooks.

WOODWORKING TOOLS 76, 160
FILLING HOLES 82
PAINTING DOORS 103



to paint. Beautiful stained, or etched, glass panels may have been removed because of damage or breakage, and just replaced with frosted panes. You can restore these doors to some of their former elegance by removing coverings, or replacing ugly glass, as well as renovating and adding door accessories.

If yours is an old property check to see if flush doors are panelled underneath. Open the door fully, and you should then be able to tell from the hinge edge whether they have been covered with hardboard or not. If you can't, strip off a little paint for closer inspection. Carefully remove the covering by inserting a fine chisel blade between the two layers and levering outwards to pull off the cover. When the original door is exposed remove any nails and carefully fill all the holes. With this covering removed the door might rattle – if so adjust the door stop.

## Doors that stick

You will often find that doors may not fit very well in their frames and can stick when you try to open or shut them. Try and find out what is causing the problem. Bathroom or kitchen doors can swell because of condensation, or doors which are used a lot, such as living room doors, can develop loose hinges. These problems are easy to fix.

If the hinges are loose, tighten the screws or replace with longer ones.

If the hinges are in good order but the door still sticks it has probably swollen slightly. Find out where the trouble is by sliding a piece of thin card between the door and the frame and mark where it sticks. If the sticking is not too bad, try rubbing the tight areas with some wax.

If the door is sticking badly, support it firmly and plane the wood off the side of the door. Plane slowly until the door closes.

## REMOVING DOOR PANELS

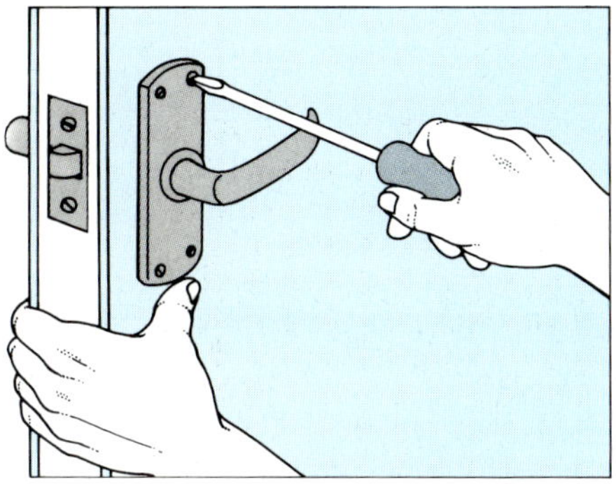

**1** To restore a panelled door that has been made flush with sheets of hardboard (usually detectable on the hinge edge), first unscrew and remove all the door hardware.

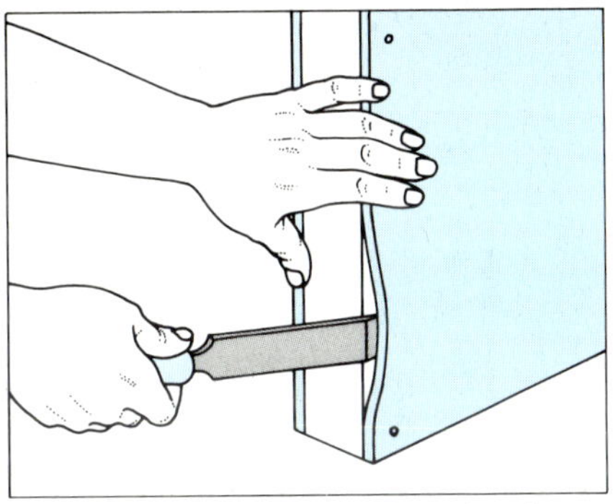

**2** Tap a wedge of wood under the open door to steady it and scrape a little paint off the opening edge to show the hardboard. Carefully lever it away with a chisel.

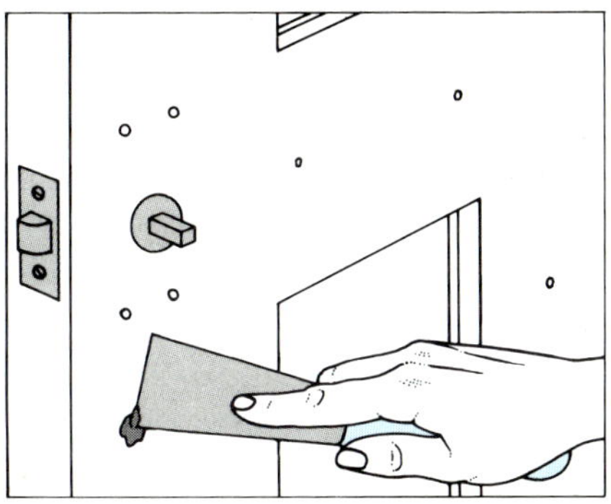

**3** Remove all the hardboard pins with a pair of pincers and fill the nail holes with fine-surface filler. When dry, rub smooth with abrasive paper and repaint.

## ADJUSTING DOOR STOPS

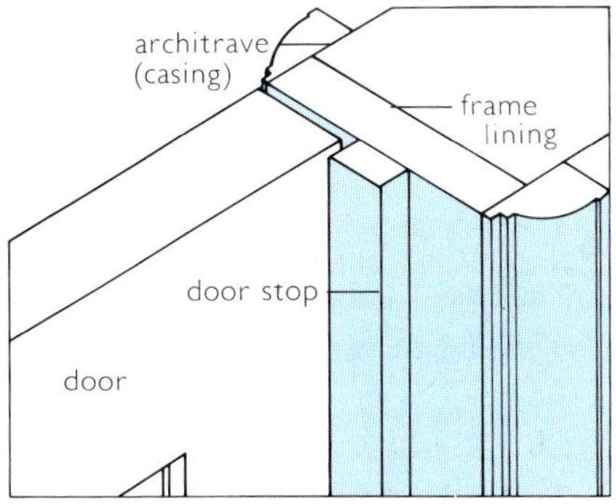


**1** The doorstop is nailed to the frame lining down both sides and across the top of a door frame. It will have to be moved closer to the door after removing a flush panel.

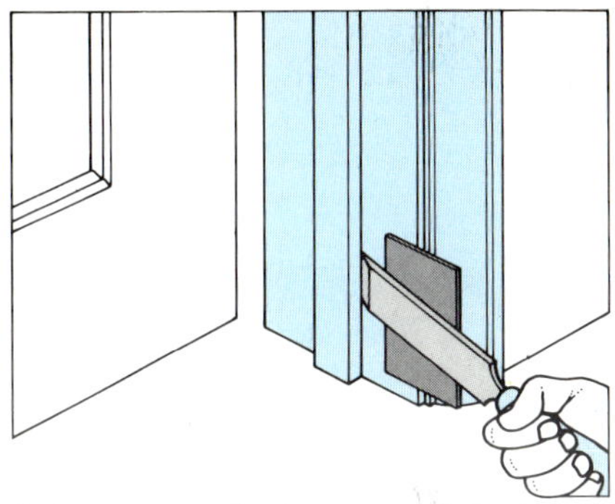

**2** Starting at the bottom of the latch side of the frame, lever away all the doorstop with a chisel, using a scrap of hardboard to prevent any damage to the lining.

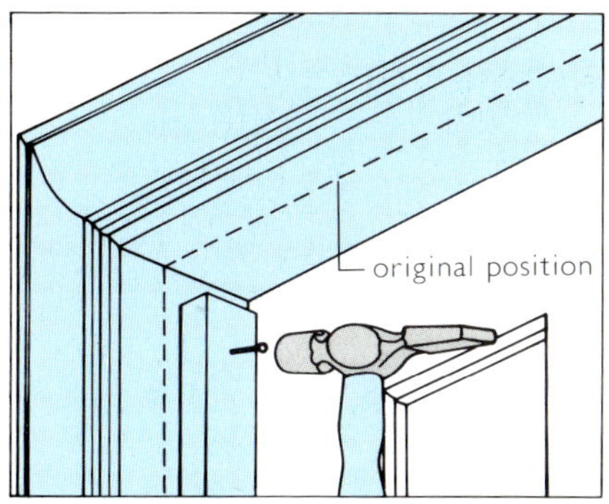


**3** Close and latch the door, hold the door stop firmly against the door on the latch side, and then nail it to the lining through different holes. Repeat this for the other pieces.

# Renovating Windows

Window frames are today made from wood, metal or PVC. Modern metal window frames are made from aluminium, or in some cases a specially-treated steel, and need little upkeep. Rot may affect wooden window frames, starting at the joints where the vulnerable end grain is exposed – this is why frames need to be primed and then painted, although nowadays wooden frames may be finished with microporous paint or preserving stains.

If a wooden frame is starting to go weak at the joints, you can stop the rot in its early stages with a special treatment. Remove all the rotten wood with a sharp knife or chisel, brush down and apply a wood preservative followed by a hardening chemical. Patch any holes with two-part wood filler, sand when dry, prime the area if necessary and repaint. If the rot is severe, you may have to cut out the rotten piece and replace it. The method will depend on the extent of the damage and the type of window.

The development of microporous paint means any moisture in the wood can escape, without breaking up the surface paint film or seeping back into the wood and starting the rot in the first place. (Special preservative plugs may also be inserted in the vulnerable joints by drilling a small hole first.) Metal frames painted with microporous paint are also less likely to rust.

If your windows are in very bad condition or you are installing double-glazing, then you may well decide to put in new windows. This is best done by a professional. Ask for the sealed unit type, with double-glazed panes already fitted into the frame. Secondary double-glazing (storm windows) works by fixing a second window inside the frames but this is less efficient and can be prone to condensation between the panes.

**REPLACING A WINDOW PANE**

**1** Stick masking tape over the broken pane and ease out the pieces, wearing thick gloves.

**2** Pull out and save the glazing sprigs (points) or clips, and remove all putty with an old chisel.

**3** With a ball of soft putty in one hand, feed a bead of putty all round the rebate (rabbet) and press in.

**4** Lay the bottom edge of the new pane in position and press it into the putty round the edges.

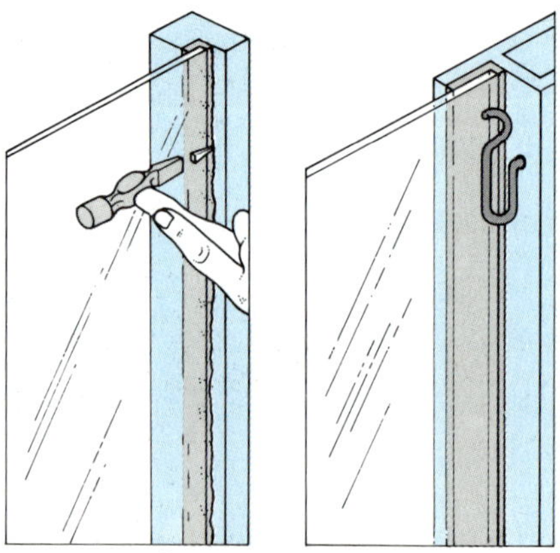

**5** Tap in glazing sprigs (points), sliding the hammer across the glass, or insert clips in metal frames.

**6** Apply a covering bead of putty and smooth it to a 45° angle with a putty knife, mitring the corners.

## Replacing glazing

Over the years window panes may get broken. If you cannot get replacement glass immediately, tack or tape a sheet of thick polyethylene to the frame as an emergency repair. Leave the pane intact if you can and remove it with great care wearing gloves; if the glass is broken, there will be jagged edges that can cut as well as little chips and slivers that can lurk in carpets. When you have removed all the glass, putty and glazing sprigs or chips, rub the surface smooth with abrasive paper, dust down and prime. Measure up the window, or make a template from stiff card or paper if you know your frame is not square or if it is an awkward shape. Order the glass 3mm ($\frac{1}{8}$in) smaller on both height and width than the inside of the frame or template – this allows for expansion and contraction due to temperature changes. Be guided by the merchant when selecting a thickness. Check the glass fits, then use bedding putty

*Draw the eye away from an aluminium window frame with an extravagantly draped curtain arranged to cover the window at all times. Use a lightweight fabric that hangs well and lets the sunlight in.*

### PATCHING A SILL

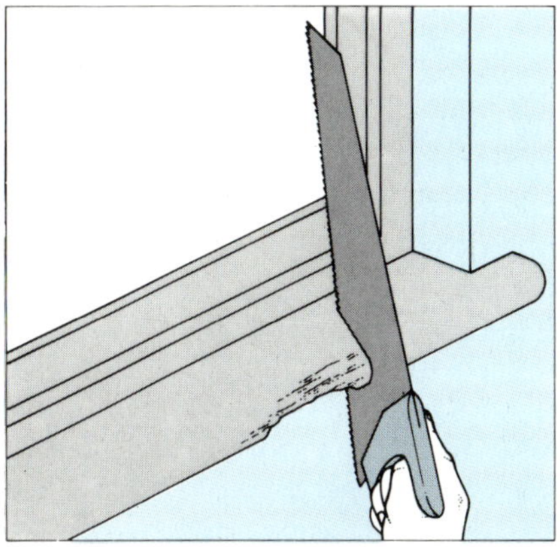

**1** Make an angled cut each side of the damaged area with a saw and chisel along to remove it.

**2** Cut a patch of wood the same thickness as the sill, using the opening as a template for a tight fit.

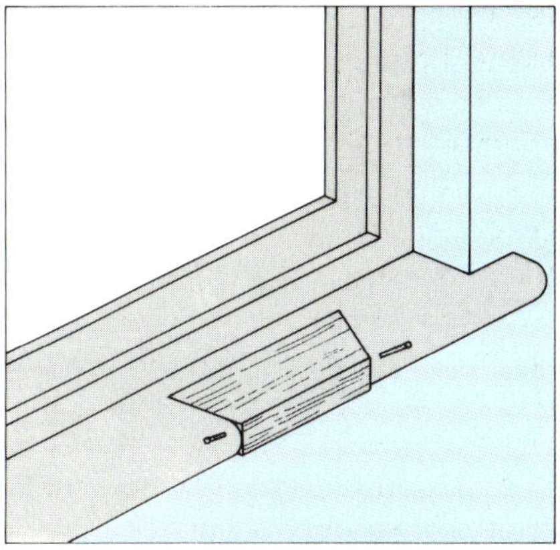

**3** Glue and nail in position with waterproof adhesive, plane flush with a block plane, and fill joints.

to fix into place. Remember always to put any pressure on the edge of the glass, *never* the middle.

If your frames are metal, remove any rust and apply a rust inhibitor, then use a putty suitable for metal windows. Fit new glazing sprigs in the positions of the original ones, marking these on the frame in pencil when removing the sprigs and glass.

## Replacing a sash cord

Sash cords wear with age and if they break can cause accidents. Never lean out of a sash window without wedging it first. Replace all old cords at the same time, even if only one is broken, using modern, strong nylon cord. Lever the staff bead (stop moulding) out very carefully on both sides of the window, as this has to be replaced once the new cords are in position (see right).

## Simple window repairs

Window rattle in the home is easy to resolve. Casement windows rattle if the catch is not holding them tightly enough. Fit draught excluder (weather stripping) all round the frame – the self-adhesive foam type is the easiest to use. If sash windows are rattling, this is normally caused by age and too much space around each sash. Fit a nylon-pile draught excluder (weather stripping) so that the sash can slide along it.

There is nothing more frustrating than windows that stick when you are trying to open them. Often they only need some basic repair work to get them moving freely again. The problems are normally caused by a build-up of paint, swelling because of dampness, or just loose joints.

To solve the paint problem all you need to do is to strip the window back to the wood where the problem occurs. Use a hot-air or chemical paint stripper for ease and speed and check there is enough clearance

### SASH WINDOWS

This illustration shows the parts of a vertically sliding sash window. The weight of each sash is counterbalanced by two weights attached to it by cords passing over pulleys.

To replace sash cords, you will need a helper. Lever off both staff beads (stop mouldings), starting at the middle. Cut the sash cords close to the inner sash, lower each weight slowly and lift out sash. Lever off parting beads (strips) and remove outer sash in the same way. Remove pockets, and remove and mark the inner and outer weights. Remove the old cord from the sides of the sashes and mark the positions of the top tacks – do not re-nail above these or the windows will not close.

Cut new nylon cords the same length as the old ones and tie them to the weights. Pull the outer sash cords up and over the pulleys by feeding down a weighted length of

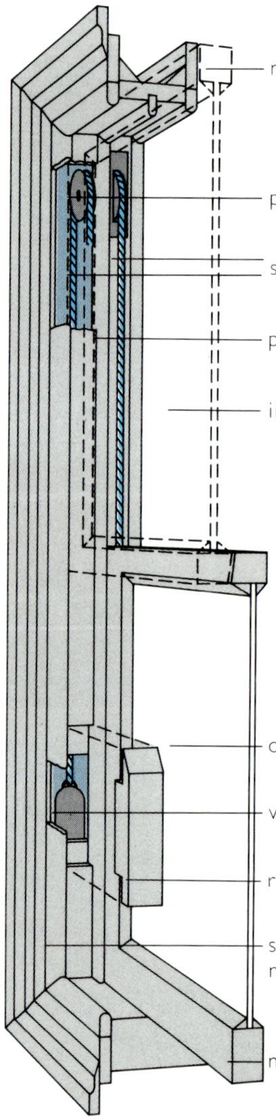


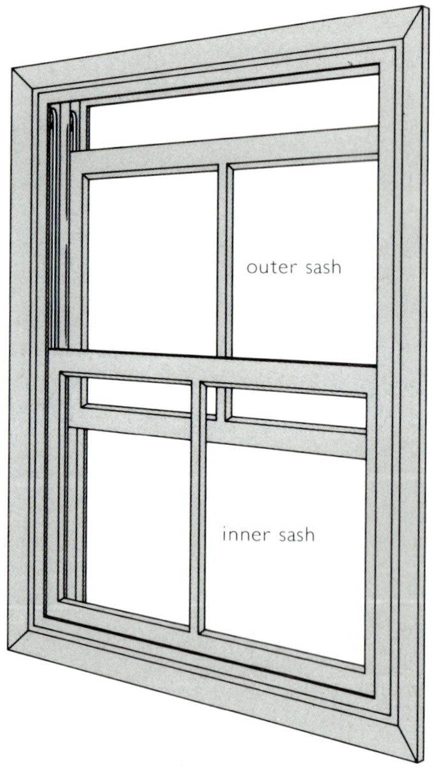


string and attaching the cord to it. Tack the free end of each cord to the same depth as the original cord in the grooves on the sides of the sash. Hang the sash and check for free movement. Replace the parting bead (strip), hang the inner sash in the same way, replace the staff beads (stop mouldings) and oil axles.

between the window and the frame. Plane gently if necessary. Prime the wood and then repaint.

If your window frame has swelled because of dampness, again strip the relevant paint back to the wood. If the wood still feels damp, dry it with a hair dryer or fan heater. Rub down the area that sticks with coarse abrasive paper or, if necessary, plane a bit of the wood off. Once the fit is right you can again prime and repaint the wood, as normal.

If your window problem is caused by loose joints, strengthen them with flat steel L- or T-brackets. Close the window and drive some thin wooden wedges into the area between the window and the frame to close the gaps in the joints. Secure the brackets to the outside of the window so that they are not visible from inside the room. Place the brackets in position, mark holes, drill, screw in position and paint.

To make a neater repair you can hide the brackets. Mark the outline on the frame and make a recess using a chisel and mallet, then drill and screw the brackets in place. Cover the bracket with wood filler and sand flush when dry. Prime and paint the repair so that it blends in with the rest of the window.

Loose hinges can make casement windows stick. Try just tightening up the screws. If this does not cure the problem, remove the screws and drill out the holes. Glue small pieces of wooden dowel into the holes and, when dry, drill holes to accommodate pilot screws, which should cure the problem.

*It is often important to keep sash windows, despite the intricacy of their construction, for the sake of architectural and also decorative consistency: here they provide just the element of character and charm that the room needs.*

Part 5

# THE APPLICATION

So now you've planned your decoration and prepared your surfaces; you've stripped off all the old wallpaper and paint in sight and are gazing round at the scene of desecration you have created. Now is the moment when it all seems too much, living in this mess is just too difficult. Without losing heart, think how beautiful your rooms are going to be by the time you reach page 183. Now you can at last start to be positive, you can put your overalls on and set about the real business of decorating your rooms.

The common decorating media require varying degrees of skill, time and common-sense – but everything that follows is well within the reach of even the most amateur of amateurs. The secret is to be as brave and as adventurous as your pocket will allow; but do choose effects that you can reasonably accomplish within the hours of daylight at your disposal. All decorating jobs will seem less problematic if you do them in natural light, while fitting such tasks as wallpapering and tiling in during snatched evenings will only put off the day when you can sit back and admire your handiwork.

Look to use the media with panache and originality. As you look at the pictures in this book and in magazines, remember that there is one thing they cannot convey: texture. Exploit its potentiality as you tackle each medium, for it is one quality that can be used to make a subtle decorative point for you.

*Clouds painted on the ceiling can produce a powerful illusion of airy space. Here paint, tiles, lighting and neutral colours all combine to reinforce that illusion: one could happily dream of heaven here. Notice how the wall-lights throw the light, and therefore the attention too, upwards, while an emphatic rug firmly anchors the total effect.*

# WORKING WITH PAINT

Paint is the most versatile of all decorating materials. It can be used anywhere in the home and can bring a dull room to life again. It is a very flexible decorating medium, which can be applied with a brush, roller, spray or pad, and manipulated to create many different textures, finishes and patterns.

## Types of paint

There are various different types of paint available but they fall into two main categories: oil- or alkyd-based paints come in the form of primers, undercoats and top coats (and will be described as oil-based from now on); water-based paints include acrylic primers/undercoats, top coats and emulsions (latex paints). As a general rule the two types of paint should not be mixed: oil-based top coats should go over oil-based undercoats. and emulsion (latex) should go over a watered-down coat of the same paint – especially on new plaster. On walls, however, it is acceptable to use emulsion (latex) as an undercoat for eggshell/lustre (oil-based) paint.

**Oil-based paints** can give either a gloss, lustre (eggshell or semi-gloss) or matt finish that is hard-wearing and easy to clean. They are particularly suitable for areas such as doors, windows and wooden floors, where maximum protection and durability are needed. The gloss varieties are commonly used on metal and woodwork, but oil-based paint can also be used on walls and ceilings where a tough, washable surface would be most suitable. (Do not use over wallpaper as the latter becomes very difficult to remove.) The normal thinner for oil-based paint is white spirit (mineral spirits), which must also be used to clean brushes in most cases; however, some paints have a brush-wash additive that enables them to be washed in hot water and liquid detergent.

# WORKING WITH PAINT

*Four rooms demonstrate the potential of paint. Lloyd Loom chairs were spray-painted to give them a new lease of life (above, left), and to incorporate them into this prettily decorated room.*

*Flat colour can be manipulated to break up surfaces – perhaps with a broad stripe in a bolder colour – or to enhance interesting architectural shapes (above and far left).*

*Brown dots (left) were painted randomly over a white background, creating a lively and rhythmic surface that is enhanced by the stripped but un-renovated woodwork, and wavy lines painted below the dado or chair rail.*

# Types and Quantities

## PAINTS, STAINS AND DYES

Picking your way through the vast array of paints, stains and varnishes available today is not easy. The following list is intended to serve as a guide to the more commonly available types. When selecting a finish, particular attention should be paid to its compatibility with undercoats and primers: to avoid mistakes read the instructions on the can before you buy.

Extensive colour charts are available from all the manufacturers, including paints which are specially colour-mixed.

### Preparation paints

**Primers** All raw wood and metal needs priming to cut down absorption and provide a key for subsequent coats of paint. Apply all types with a brush.

Oil-based primers are used in wet or steamy conditions to give wood durability and seal the wood against moisture.

Aluminium primers are suitable for resinous timbers and hardwoods; no knotting is needed.

Alkyd-based primers are more manageable and are available in rapid drying form, suitable for interior or exterior use.

Acrylic-based primers are quick drying and are suitable only for interior use; may also be used as an undercoat.

**Undercoats** An undercoat is essential for traditional finishes, its chief function being to even out the grain on wood and prevent previous colours from showing through. Emulsion (latex) paint is a quick-drying, cheap undercoat for oil-based paint on bare plastered walls or relief wallcoverings and lining paper, although the more usual undercoat is alkyd- or oil-based. It is not suitable for woodwork. Select the correct colour for the top coat. Apply with brush, pad, or thinned with spray. Always use primer and top coat from the same manufacturer.

### Top coats

**For primed and prepared surfaces**
Oil-, alkyd-based or co-polymer paints are the most common types. Liquid gloss paint needs an undercoat and needs more skill to apply. Available in semi-gloss and full gloss finishes. Top coats are also available as non drip, or thixotropic, paints. These are easier since they are to a great extent self-smoothing, but care must be taken not to brush them out too much. Eggshell/lustre types are available for woodwork and can also be used for walls: use over an undercoat or emulsion base. They give a more reflective surface than emulsion (latex). Some top coats for wood or metal have added poly-urethane to withstand knocks and scrapes. For extra protection a clear polyurethane varnish may be applied over the final coat of colour. Apply top coats with brush, pad or spray.

**Microporous paints for wood** These paints are specially formulated to allow wood to breathe: this has the advantage of allowing moisture to evaporate through the skin whilst still maintaining resistance to weather. Microporous paints give a sheen finish, but are usually for outdoor use; may need to be applied over a primer but need no undercoat. Apply with brush. Previously painted wood must be stripped and re-primed if necessary.

**Emulsion (latex) paints** Water-based (latex) paints are easy to apply to walls and ceilings by brush, roller, pad or spray, and do not generally need to be applied over an undercoat or primer. A variety of finishes are available from matt through to silk which dries with a light reflective sheen. Emulsion (latex) is now also available in non-drip, or thixotropic, form. Higher durability and resistance to moisture is achieved through the addition of vinyl or PVA at the manufacturing stage. The first coat may be thinned by up to 10% with water. Apply with brush, roller or pad; can also be sprayed.

**Textured paint** Emulsion (latex) paints used for covering rough plaster or sand and cement surfaces. Often very difficult to remove. A variety of patterns may be achieved through the use of various tools, such as rollers or sponges.

### Stains, and transparent coatings for wood

If you wish to retain the natural look of wood there are a number of methods used to seal and protect the surface.

**Stains** The colour may be changed dramatically or subtly by applying stains. Water- or spirit-based stains or dyes can be bought pre-mixed. These soak into the grain making it impossible to change the colour without painting over it, so you need to be sure that you have the right colour before you start. These stains require rubbing down afterwards and sealing with shellac or polyurethane varnish. Apply with brush or rag.

Stains mixed with polyurethane sealers are another method of colouring wood. These can be removed with chemicals if you decide to change the colour in the future. No further treatment is necessary after the application of these stains. Apply with brush or rag.

**Waxes** Should be applied on top of polyurethane sealer for good protection. Most waxes now contain silicone. A limited range of coloured waxes are available. Apply with rag.

**Linseed oil** A traditional finish built up in coats to give a natural look to all kinds of hardwoods. Best used on darker timbers such as mahogany. Mix 50:50 with genuine turpentine spirit. Apply with rag.

**Teak oil** Quick-drying finish that darkens the wood, resists marks and gives greater durability than linseed oil. Apply with rag.

**Polyurethane (one pack)** A tough water-resistant finish that gives a long-lasting, transparent, washable surface. Available in matt, silk or gloss finishes. Apply with a clean unused brush; lightly sand down between coats.

Thixotropic or jelly paint is usually oil-based and non-drip: it is particularly useful for the beginner as runs and sags can be avoided. It should not be stirred or thinned. Also oil-based are many of the specialist paints commonly used in decorative paint finishes, such as glazes and lacquers.

**Water-based paints** are often easier to handle as the brushes are washable in water. Emulsion (latex) is the most popular and versatile type: it is widely used for walls and ceilings, and on these surfaces can be painted over with any other type of paint. Emulsions (latex paints) can produce matt, silk or sheen, or glossy finishes, but without the hard-wearing qualities of oil-based gloss. They are extremely easy to use, and are thinned with water. Some emulsions (latex paints) now come as a solid block packed in a shallow tray, ready for application by roller: the paint does not drip or run and is therefore ideal for painting ceilings.

## Materials and preparation

First you must decide on your colour scheme, remembering that paint cards and colour chips do not really give a true idea of the intensity of a colour. Bright or dark colours will look much stronger on walls, ceiling or woodwork whilst the pale ones will tend to fade into insignificance.

Always test your chosen paint on a small area before buying the full amount. Some colours which seem fine on small swatches will be just too strong over a large expanse of wall or ceiling. When you are sure,

*'Tame' a brick wall and exploit its texture by painting it with a sophisticated sheen or silk type emulsion (latex). As brick has a porous surface it will need several coats, so calculate the amount of paint required carefully.*

## ESTIMATING QUANTITIES OF PAINT

The covering power of paint and the number of coats required will depend on the type of paint used. It will also depend on how porous and smooth the surface is, and the thickness of the coat applied. Top coat covering power will also depend on the number of undercoats you have applied.

| **Paint Type** | **Nominal Covering Area** *$M^2$ PER LITRE ($YD^2$ PER $\frac{1}{4}$ GAL)* |
|---|---|
| Universal primer | 7–8 (wood) 9–11 (metal) 5–9 (plaster) |
| Aluminium primer/sealer | 11–13 |
| Acrylic primer/undercoat | 15–16 |
| Alkali-resistant primer | 9–11 |
| Primer/sealer | 10 |
| Stabilizing primer | 6–12 |
| Metal primer | 9–11 |
| Undercoat | 15 |
| Microporous paint | 15 |
| Gloss (liquid) | 17 |
| Gloss (non-drip) | 12 |
| Silk finish (oil-based) | 12 |
| Eggshell finish (oil-based) | 15 |
| Emulsion (latex), matt | 14 |
| Emulsion (latex), vinyl silk | 15 |

buy enough paint to complete the job as there can be problems with colour-matching at a later date. Always buy the correct undercoat and primer (if needed).

Next, decide whether you want to use a brush, roller or paint pad, and sort out all the tools and equipment you need for preparation and painting. It is usual to paint woodwork with a brush, although some people prefer small paint pads. Walls and ceilings can be painted by brush, pad or roller, depending on the surface. Select a range of different-sized paint brushes from 19mm ($\frac{3}{4}$in) to 125mm (5in) to suit all purposes. All tools are an investment, so take care of them. Wash brushes, rollers and pads thoroughly in the appropriate solvent, and store carefully. During short painting breaks just wrap brushes in kitchen film or foil. For longer storage wash thoroughly then wrap in foil and secure with an elastic band.

Stored, opened paint containers will develop a 'skin' on the surface. Cut around the edge with a sharp knife and try to remove it without breaking it. Store containers upside down if possible.

Areas which prove difficult to paint such as radiator panels and

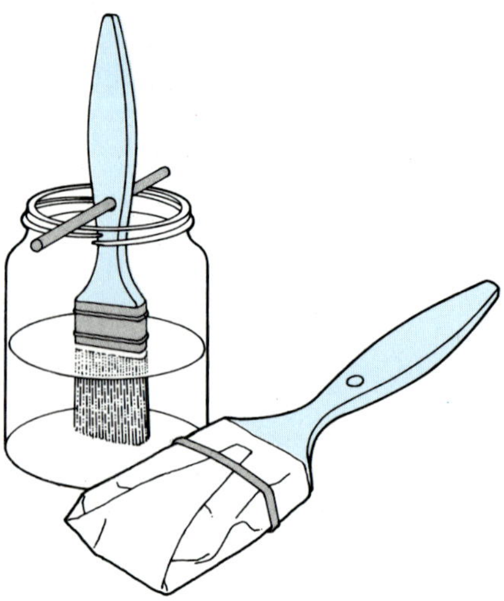

**PAINT EQUIPMENT**

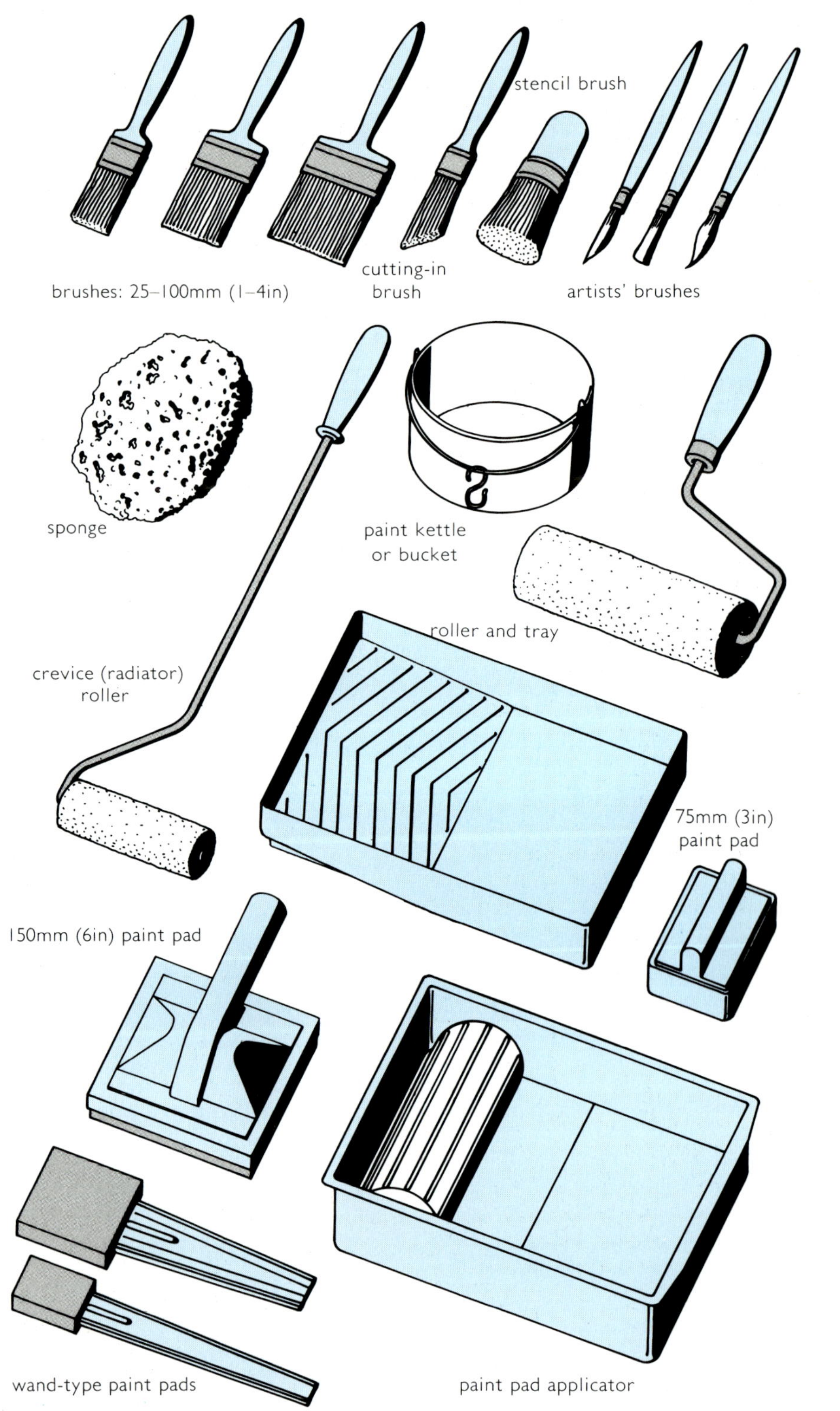

grilles can be painted successfully with a sprayer or aerosol paints.

Always paint in a good light, and try to avoid starting in natural daylight but having to complete under artificial light, as this could confuse you. If you are using emulsion (latex) paint, shut the windows before you start to prevent the paint from drying too quickly, and open them as soon as you have finished the job to accelerate the drying process. When you are painting a large surface, like a wall and/or a ceiling, try to complete it in one session. If you stop halfway, a hard, dried line will form which will always be apparent.

The first step in painting any large surface, such as a wall or a ceiling, is to cut in around the edges with your chosen paint. This means painting a strip roughly 5cm (2in) wide all around the perimeter of the surface, which will hide the feathered edges of brush strokes and prevent you scraping or touching the surface at right angles with your large, clumsier brush or roller. Use a small brush for this job, preferably one with its bristles cut at an angle. Cutting in will particularly help a beginner in awkward places such as internal corners, when paint could be accidentally daubed on an already painted wall or ceiling.

If you have a decorative moulding between your walls and ceiling, paint this before the ceiling. If you are putting one up, paint it first.

Begin painting walls in the corner nearest a window, working away from the light. You will need to apply two or even three coats.

If you are dealing with an area like the stairs, landing, hall and stairwell, start with the ceilings, then continue with the walls of the landing and stairwell, starting at the top. Next, paint the woodwork, leaving the stair treads, banisters, handrail and newel posts until last.

**ORDER OF WORK**

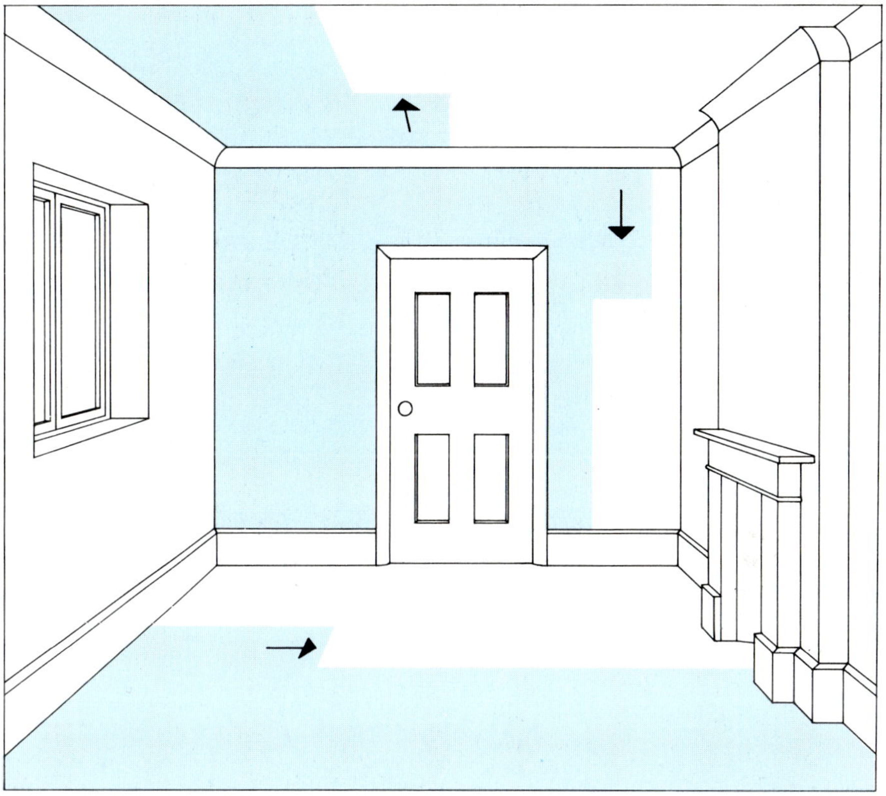

*Above: Paint a ceiling in strips parallel to the window wall, working away from the light. Start painting walls in sections in a corner adjacent to the window wall, again working away from the light. To enable you to leave the room when you have finished painting a floor, start painting against the wall opposite the door and then work backwards.*

*Left: When painting any large flat surface, first cut in around the edges between it and adjacent walls, the ceiling and window and door frames with a small angled cutting-in brush.*

# Basic Techniques

Painting techniques vary, depending on the type of paint you are using and the tools. You can often cover areas much more quickly with emulsion (latex) paint, for example, than a non-drip gloss paint, which requires careful application on doors, wooden mouldings, window frames and radiators. The technique you use will also vary with the surface you are painting. A smooth, plastered wall can be easily painted with a roller, while a heavily embossed wallcovering will need to be painted with a brush to work the paint into the indentations. A flush door is easier to paint than a panelled one.

Emulsion (latex) paint will brush on straight from the can, but you can pour it into a paint kettle or pot to enable you to use a wider brush. Thin the paint with some water if it is too thick or if you want a thinner first coat, as an undercoat.

For large areas use a 100 or 125mm (4 or 5in) brush and coat with a generous layer of paint. Start at the top corner of the wall nearest to the window, and work away from the light in rough squares, going from top to bottom. Work methodically in small sections. If using emulsion (latex), cover the area fairly quickly, as this type of paint dries fast – silk and satin finishes dry faster than matt. (Oil-based paint dries more slowly in any case.)

Load the brush with paint, covering about one third of the length of the bristles, and apply it to the wall starting in the middle of each square section and brushing out towards those already done: the aim is to avoid a hard edge, created by covering the joins with more than one coat. Without reloading the brush, work the paint over the surface until evenly applied, then finally 'lay off'; this means brushing lightly from the leading edge back into the painted area. Lay off matt emulsion (latex)

with criss-cross strokes.

A roller is quicker and easier to use than a brush on a big area. Pour some paint into a paint tray, dip the edge of the roller in this and run it up and down the tray until there is an even layer of paint on the roller sleeve. Take care not to overload it, or you will get paint spattering all over the surrounding area. Run the roller over the surface, starting at the corner and working in rough squares as before. Use a criss-cross pattern, and take care to fill any gaps.

A paint pad requires a similar technique. Load using the special tray with its roller, or use a paint kettle, and apply in random directions in rough squares as before.

### Painting woodwork

The major items of woodwork you will be painting are doors and windows; items such as skirting (baseboards) should be painted along their grain and, like all wood, need priming and undercoating first. Paint each item in one session: if you stop halfway you will get an ugly hard edge that will be impossible to eradicate later.

If you are using an oil-based paint, and particularly a gloss, the secret of success is not to overload the brush. Stir the paint well, unless using a thixotropic or non-drip type which should not be stirred at all, and pour some paint into a paint kettle if preferred. Flick the bristles of the brush to loosen them and remove any loose hairs, and dip the ends into the paint. Wipe off any excess paint on the side of the can or kettle.

*Low ceilings and awkwardly-shaped rooms will benefit from being painted in a single colour. White throws interesting shadows in shades of grey in any room, but will make the most of beams and shallow-angled corners such as here.*

## PAINTING WALLS

**1** Brush emulsion (latex) paint in vertical strips of squares (or horizontal strips if you are working on a platform or table).

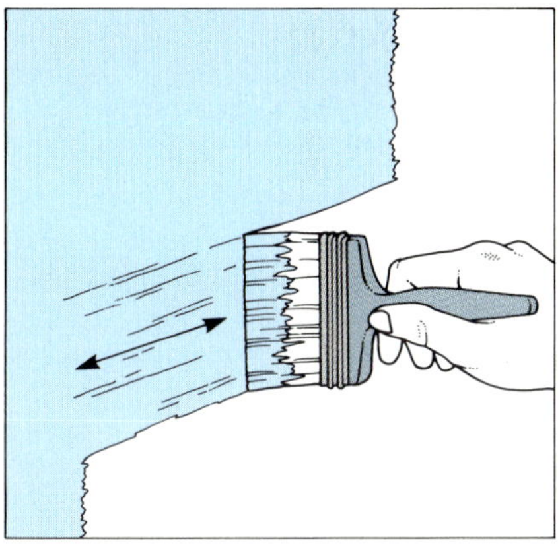

**2** To paint each square, first lay on the paint horizontally with a well-loaded paintbrush.

**3** Then lay off with light upward strokes of a lightly loaded brush (downwards near the ceiling).

**4** Apply emulsion (latex) paint with a roller in vertical strips of overlapping criss-cross strokes.

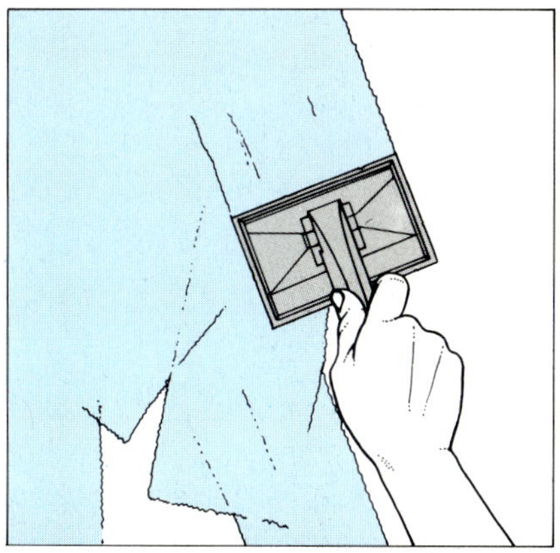

**5** Use a paint pad in the same way as a roller, keeping the surface of the pad flat on the wall.

Avoid 'sags' or runs of paint; any that appear should be rubbed down when dry and hard, and the area repainted.

Always remember to remove all door and window hardware – handles, knobs and catches – before starting work.

Flush doors are not too difficult to paint because they have a flat surface. Start at the top corner on the hinge side: you are going to paint in wide bands across the door, divided in half. Start with two or three light strokes covering one half of the top 'band' and following the direction of the wood grain. Change direction and cross-brush, working the paint over the surface evenly. Finally lay off in the direction of the grain. Repeat on the other half and work down the door in this way. Take care not to get a hard edge at the joins – brush from the centre of each section towards the edges and gently skim over the surface with the tips of the bristles to prevent this.

Leave to dry for 12–24 hours. If another top coat is needed, lightly key the first coat with abrasive paper before applying.

Panelled doors should always be painted following the diagram, which is designed to avoid any ugly ridges or unsightly paint runs. Take care to prevent accumulations of paint on mouldings.

It is not essential to paint the tops of doors, unless they will be seen from above – from a staircase for example – or are prone to moisture. When a door is to be a different colour on each side, paint the hinge edge the same colour as the outer face, and the outside, or latch, edge the same colour as the inside.

## Painting windows

These can suffer from condensation problems so take care always to prepare them properly.

One of the difficulties with windows is keeping the paint off the glass, although you should let it overlap slightly to protect the frame

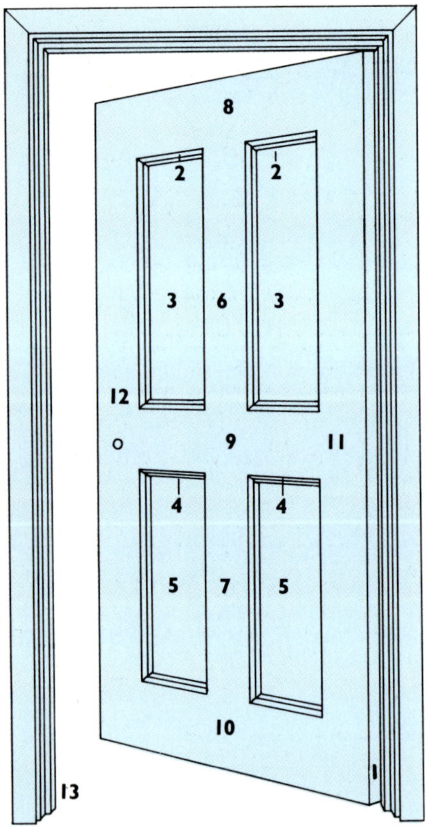


Paint a panelled door in the order shown, starting with a 25mm (1in) brush for the edges and mouldings, and changing to a 50mm (2in) brush for the panels and other sections.

**PAINTING FLUSH DOORS**

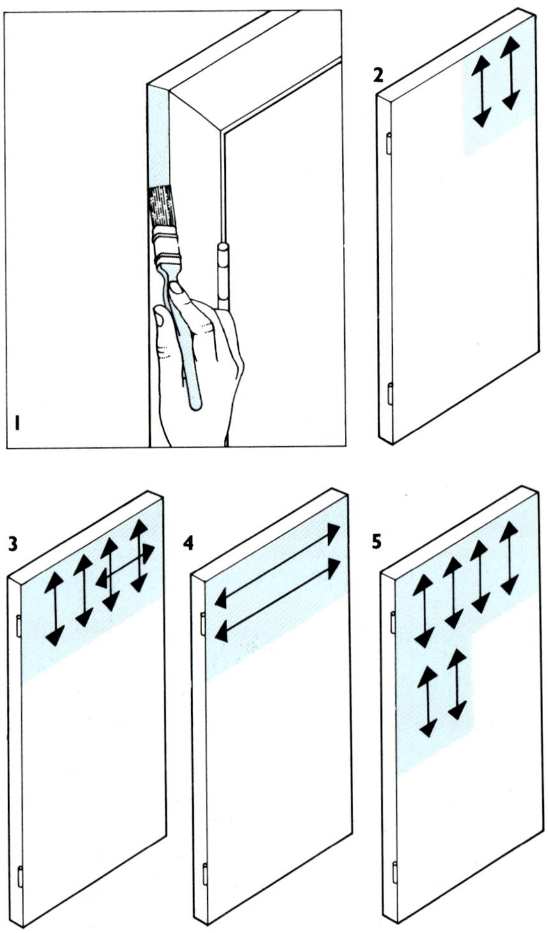


**1** Paint the frame and the opening edge of the door with a 25mm (1in) brush.

**2** Paint the face of the door in squares half the width of the door, using vertical strokes with a 75mm (3in) brush.

**3** Lay off the first square with light strokes horizontally and lay on a second square next to it.

**4** Lay off the second square and lightly brush horizontally over the whole strip to merge the join between the squares.

**5** Paint a square below the first strip and continue in this way down to the bottom of the door laying on, laying off and merging. Always brush towards the door edges to prevent paint build-up.

RENOVATING DOORS, ETC. 88
PAINT TYPES 98

Paint casement windows early in the morning so that they will be dry enough to be closed again at night. Use a cutting-in brush for the glazing bars and a 25mm (1in) brush for the remainder of the work. Paint in the order shown and then take about 3mm ($\frac{1}{8}$in) onto the glass to create a good seal.

and putty joint. Mask the glass with masking tape round the edge. Peel this off once the paint is touch-dry, but before it hardens fully or you may lift off flakes of paint with it. You can prevent smudging on the glass by using a paint shield. Scrape off any paint splashes when dry with a special window scraper.

Window frames should be painted in a carefully planned sequence. With casement windows and any type with glazing bars, the principle is to start nearest the glass with the rebates (rabbets), then proceed to the glazing bars themselves, then on to the frames. Many windows have fairly narrow glazing bars, so work with a 25mm (1in) brush, and try to obtain a cutting-in brush with its bristles cut at an angle to help with the corners.

*The special texture of a high-gloss paint is exploited to its full on these flush doors. The highly reflective surface makes an interesting counterpoint to the decoratively stencilled floor, and also helps to suggest modernity and drama amongst the rather traditional, country-style furniture.*

## PAINTING SASH WINDOWS

Paint sash windows in two stages. First lower the outer sash as far as it will go and raise the inner sash to about 150mm (6in) from the pulley head. In this position paint as much as possible of the outer sash, the bottom edge of the inner sash, and the tops of the pulley stiles. Let all this completely dry, then reverse the positions to paint the rest of the window.

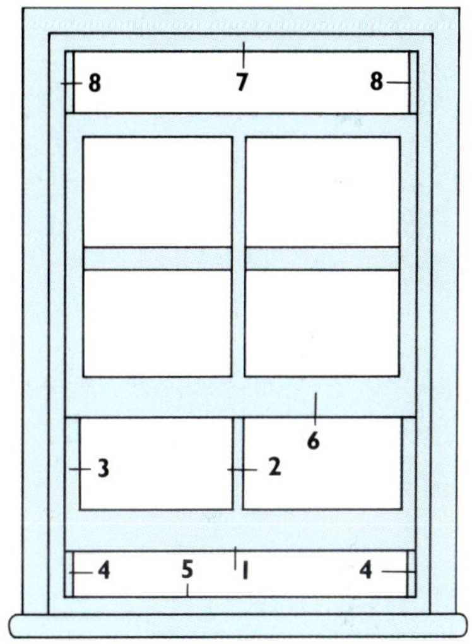


Outer sash down, inner sash up.

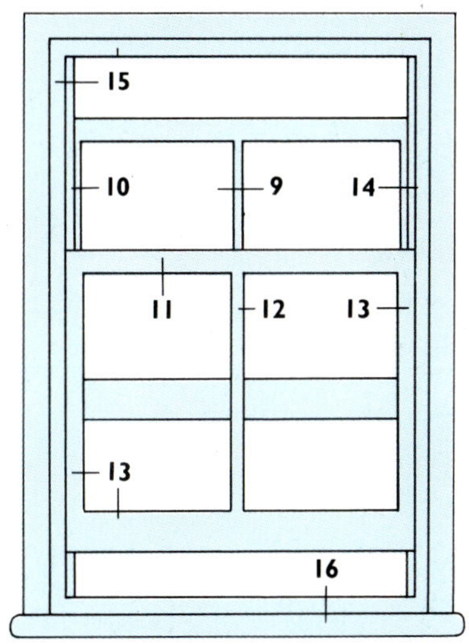


Outer sash up, inner sash down.

# Painting Floors

Floors can be painted or stained to rejuvenate them and add some colour, or they can be made into the single, dominant, decorative feature, with bright tessellations, stencils or even a special paint finish. The process of marbling, for example, works particularly well on floors, especially if you use different colours to create border or inlaid effects, perhaps to simulate the classically decorative marble floors found in Italy. *Trompe l'oeil*, though requiring artistic skills, does create beautiful illusory effects and can make bare boards look as though they are carpeted. For all these treatments, you will find paint a more flexible – and reversible – medium than stain.

Before you begin you need a smooth, keyed surface to work on. Deal with any loose or damaged floorboards first, then strip the boards of any old varnish or polish.

Oil-based paints, either gloss or matt, plus the necessary primers and undercoats, should be used for painting floors to create a hard and durable finish – but avoid areas of heavy traffic. They are suitable for concrete, stone, brick and wood. Emulsions (latex paints) could also be used but must then be covered with a protective polyurethane varnish.

*A painted floor can be the single decorated element in a room, without any sacrifice of dramatic effect. Geometric patterns in a limited number of colours are simple to do and very effective.*

Always remember, whether you are sanding, sealing, staining, painting or decorating a floor, to start in the corner furthest away from the door and work towards it, so that you do not find yourself trapped in a corner of the room.

| | |
|---|---|
| SURFACE PREPARATION | 74 |
| RENOVATING FLOORBOARDS | 84 |
| PAINT TYPES | 98 |
| PAINT FINISHES | 110 |



## PAINTING PATTERNS ON FLOORS

Establish a regular shape such as a rectangle on the floor, and lay it out with string lines tied to nails knocked lightly into the floorboards, with one of the longer edges lying parallel to a long wall of the room. Check that the corners are square by measuring the diagonals – these should be the same length. Adjust the corners if necessary, chalk string lines and snap onto floor (insets).

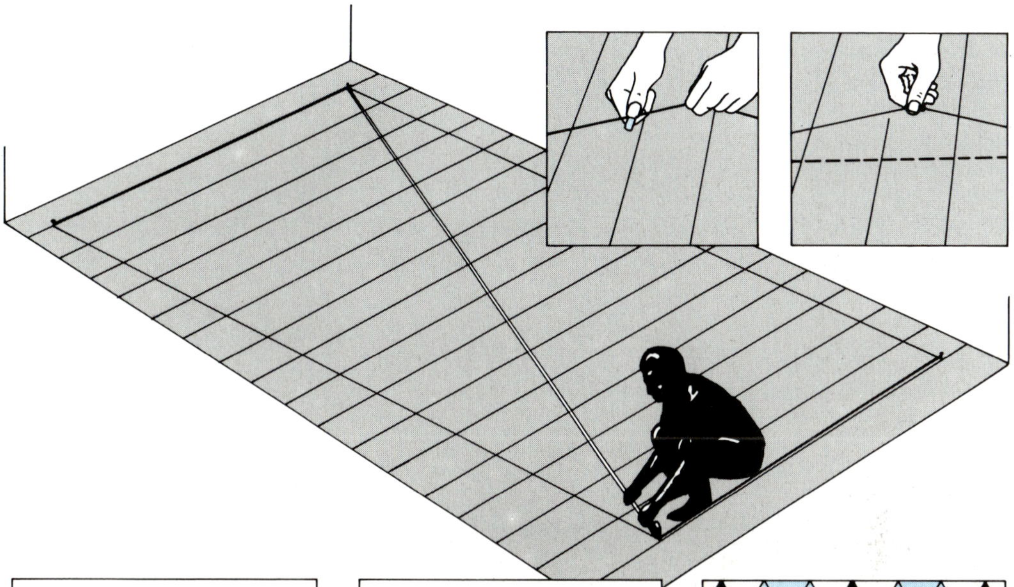

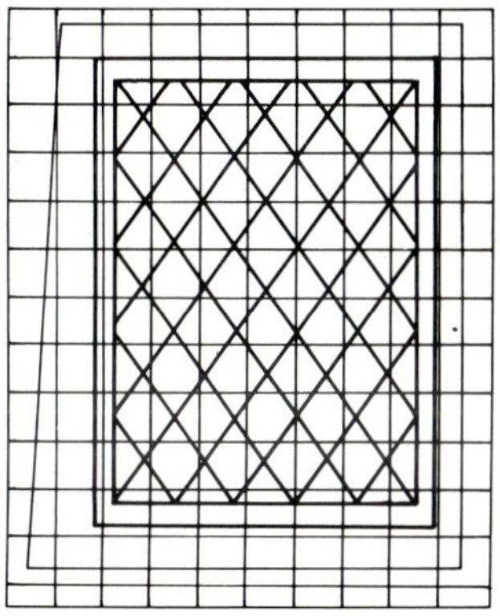

For all but the simplest patterns, a scale plan of the floor is essential so that the pattern can be drawn out on paper before marking onto the floor. Most rooms are not regular, so align the border line of the pattern with the wall against which it will be most obvious. Construct the pattern within this border, using compasses for circles and set squares for 30°, 45°, 60° and 90° angles.

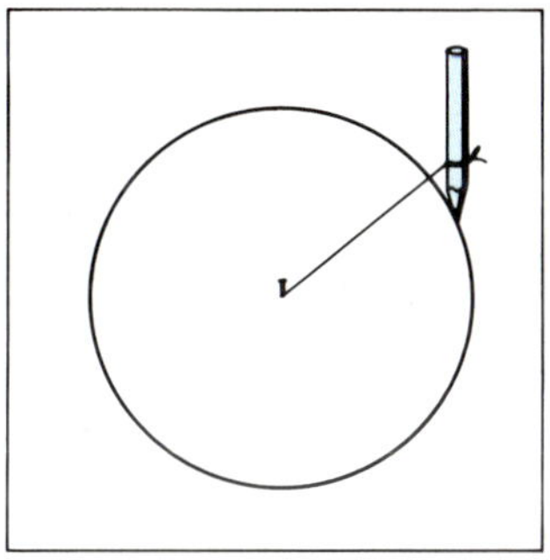

**1 Circle** Tie one end of a length of string loosely round a nail at the centre and the other to a pencil. Keep the string taut.

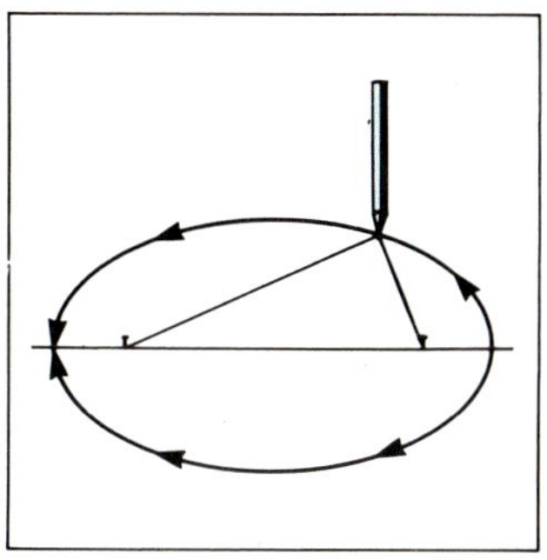

**2 Ellipse** Use two nails and a loop of string with a pencil attached. Draw one half, then the other.

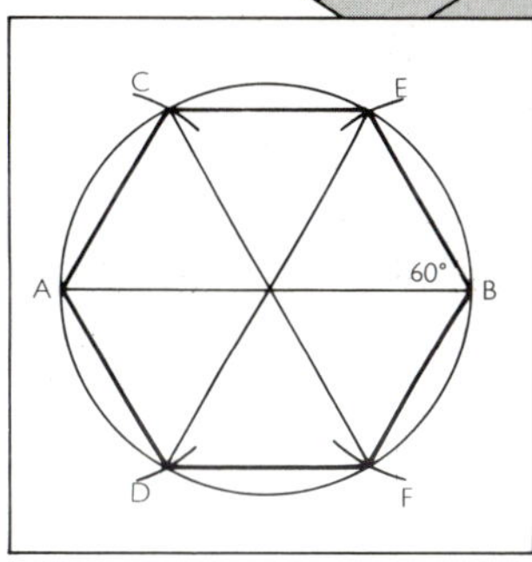


**3 Hexagon** Draw a circle and line AB. Keeping the string the same length, draw arcs from A and B to cut at C, D, E and F.

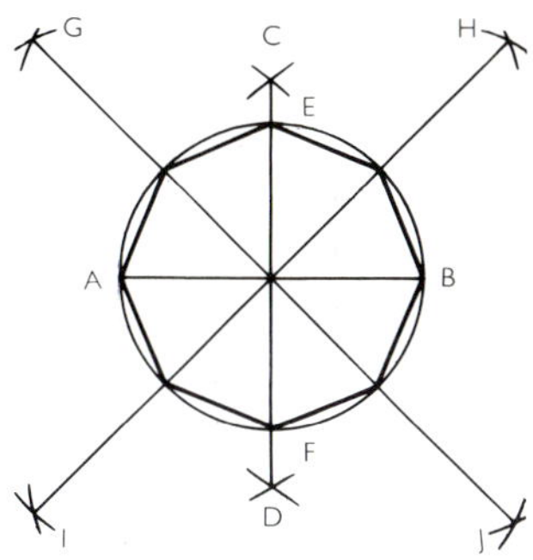


**4 Octagon** Draw a circle and AB. Draw arcs C and D from A and B. From E and F draw G, H, I and J.

**5** A simple tessellated pattern. The design is made up of 60° triangles (as in the hexagon) and diamond shapes.

**6** A lattice pattern with squares and rectangles. Check right-angle corners by measuring diagonals.

# Staining Floors

Timber should not be left in its raw state; it does have to be sealed in some way to protect it from knocks, scratches and general wear and tear, and to make cleaning and upkeep easier. Apart from paint, your options are varnish, stain, or, for hardwoods, spirit-based sealant which can then be polished. Whatever you choose, your floors will need to be in good condition if you are going to leave them uncovered. They can be left with the natural beauty and warmth of the grain showing through: seal them with polyurethane varnish or apply a neutral, combined stain/seal for protection. Coloured stains are also available, and give a very attractive effect that still leaves the grain of the wood visible. If you ever change your mind and want to paint over it, stained wood should be sanded, primed and undercoated first.

Two or three coats of polyurethane varnish are necessary for raw timber or floors painted with emulsion (latex) paint. Polyurethane-based ones cover the wood with a clear gloss, matt or semi-matt finish to suit your taste. There is another type of oleo-resinous seal, which soaks into the wood giving a scratch-resistant and lustrous surface. These are all sold under various brand and trade names; make sure you buy the right type for use on floors. Apply with a brush or as instructed by the manufacturer.

Stains come in two main types. Some need to be varnished to seal them, while some combined types both stain and varnish the wood all in one go. Stains are usually applied with a clean, lint-free cloth.

All sealants make wood look darker and most stains can seem much stronger when actually used on the wood than they did on the shade card. Before starting work always test stain on a small, spare

piece of wood (or a hidden corner) before you do an entire surface.

Creating patterns with stain needs careful planning, as you will almost certainly encounter 'bleeding', caused by the grain absorbing the stain itself. One easy way round this is to use the gaps between the boards themselves as the boundaries of each colour: you could use just two colours alternately, or many more. When staining across the grain of the boards, score a shallow line with a handyman's knife to the grain's depth to make a grooved boundary. (For this reason, geometric patterns are the easiest.)

*Work with, not against, the floorboards themselves when using stain. Easiest of all is to stain ordinary boards in alternate colours, as below: the result is subdued and elegant. More colours used in the same way expands the possibilities. Bolder and much more dramatic is the pattern opposite. The design is still sympathetic to that of the wooden flooring, but the large squares could have been broken up by simply scoring and staining across the grain. The bold geometric theme is picked up throughout in the soft furnishings as well as in the border running around the walls.*

## STAINING A FLOOR

Wood does not need priming or undercoating before you apply stain to it, but it does need to be in good condition. Thorough sanding is essential to ensure even absorption; bear in mind, too, that end grain will absorb more stain than cross grain, so will look darker. Some types of stain will need to be sanded again, then sealed with two or three coats of polyurethane varnish for protection against knocks and spills; other types have a sealant incorporated into them.

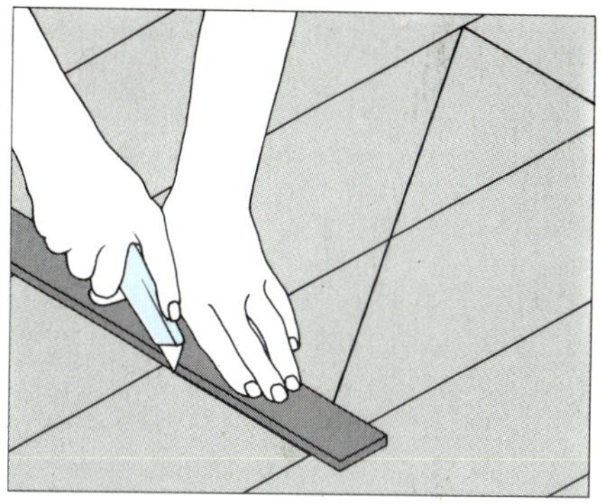

**1** Prevent stain from running along the grain by scoring pattern lines to the grain depth with a handyman's knife against a straightedge.

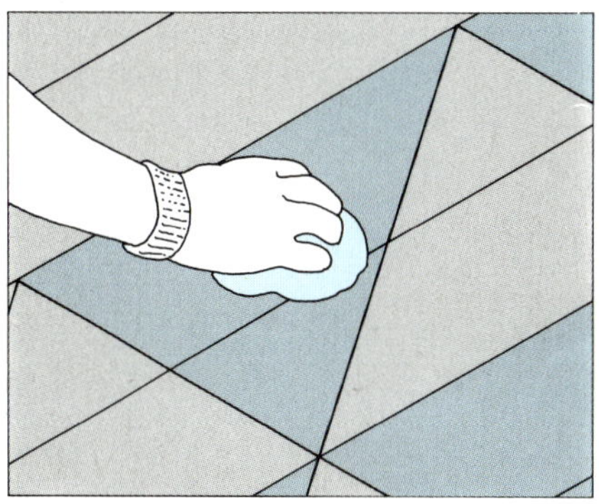

**2** Apply wood stain with a folded pad of cloth, working along the grain; use a small brush at the edges of patterns and in angles. Further coats will darken the colour.

# Paint Finishes

A new London shop devoted to special paint finishes has no less than 75 different examples on the walls for clients to choose from. With such a choice, where, unnerved beginners ask themselves, do you start?

The easiest finishes use paint straight from the can and sponge, flick, or rub it on to the walls or other surfaces. The colour or colours are pre-mixed, you can go at your own pace instead of rushing to distress a drying glaze, and you can appraise the effect immediately. Using the same simple technique but more than one colour of paint gives a richer, more subtle effect.

A safe rule when you are worried about colours 'going' together, is to choose different shades of the same colour as shown on a paint chart – it is best to go more cautiously at first, and end up feeling happy with the result. A very safe colour scheme can be livened up with stencils in a contrasting colour later, or with a further layer of distressed colour or tinted varnish.

### Sponging

This is one of the easiest techniques to do and the effects range from the naïve to the sophisticated. It can be done on sub-standard walls, and is an excellent way to disguise uneven surfaces or imperfect plaster. It is also the ideal technique for camouflaging awkward shapes and features, such as ugly pipes or sloping ceilings: sponging over anything produces an even, coherent effect.

One colour sponged on white will give you a range of tones of that colour. Sponging a Delft blue on a white ground, for instance, with a sponge wrung out in water will give pale and deep blue prints, depending on how often your prints overlap each other and how much white base is exposed. More than one colour can be applied over a base, but let one

*Above: Sponging, in this case in shades of green plus a little black, can dramatically change the appearance of fixtures.*

*Left: A kitchen wall was stripped, then repainted with various techniques to look like flawed plaster.*

*Opposite: This luminous wall was achieved by painting a coat of varnish diluted with turpentine over a white base coat, then squeezing tubes of artist's colours down the walls. While still wet, another coat of diluted varnish was applied.*

# WORKING WITH PAINT

coat dry before you apply the next. Try pink and beige, or cream and brown, for a soft, mottled effect.

For both this and ragging, an emulsion (latex) base will need one or two coats, then sponge over with a water-based paint. An oil-based ground will need two coats and should be undercoated as normal, then sponged over with oil-based paint or glaze.

*Method* Always test the print made by the sponge on newspaper before applying it to walls or furniture. Use a natural sea sponge for the best print. Rinse the sponge in water before using and wring it out very thoroughly so it is just damp. Pour some paint on to a plate or saucer, then you are ready to experiment.

Start sponging a window wall to show fewest mistakes, and leave some base colour showing. When you reach a corner, stop and review the effect. If it looks too 'jumpy', soften the effect with a sponge wrung out in diluted colour; do the same with a patterning that looks too oppressively rhythmic, or uneven. If too much colour has been built up, sponge over when dry with the base colour to even it up.

*Sponging off* (see diagrams) is a slightly different process which needs two people. It is best done with a tinted oil-based glaze, which one person applies with a brush over the ground colour in vertical strips about 60cm (2ft) wide, whilst the second follows with a sponge, dabbing it on to remove some colour and reveal the base coat.

## Ragging

*Ragging on*, as the name implies, is a decorative finish achieved by pressing crumpled up, dry rags into paint, then making a print on the wall. It gives a rather more decided patterning than sponging, although the technique is the same, and it can look

### SPONGING ON

**1** Thoroughly prepare the walls, and apply two coats of the chosen base colour. Allow to dry overnight.

**2** Wet and squeeze out a natural sponge, and apply the glaze or wash quickly and evenly across the wall.

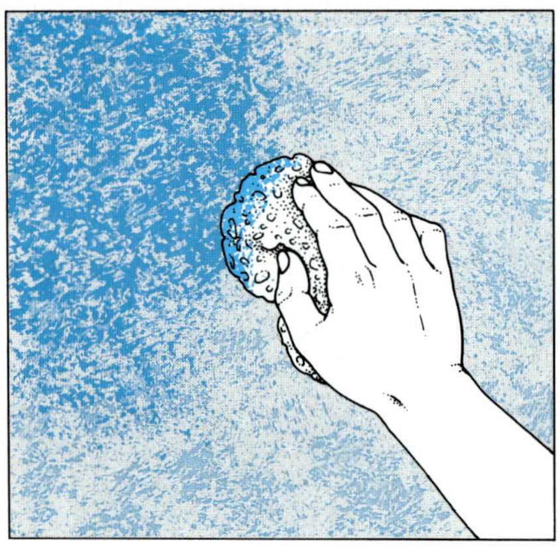

**3** If using two colours, apply the first quite thinly, let it dry, and use a new sponge for the second.

### SPONGING OFF

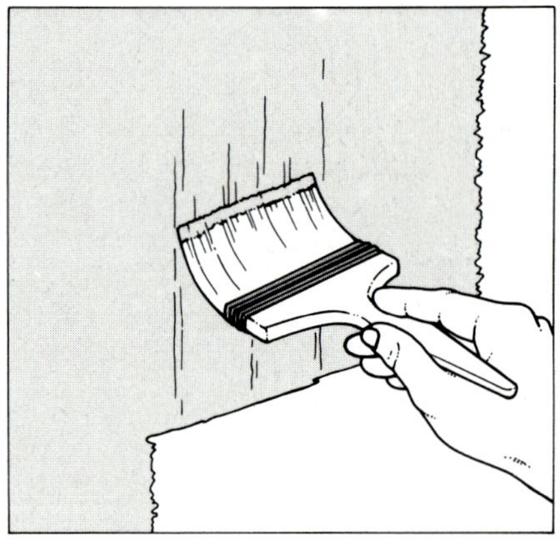

**1** Prepare the walls, and cover with two coats of base colour. You will now need a second person.

**2** One person applies a continuous film of glaze or wash, working in strips about 60cm (2ft) wide.

**3** The second person follows, dabbing the wet film with a dry sponge to reveal the base coat.

striking, even damask-like. Ragging on can be done over a silk emulsion (latex) or oil-based ground, like sponging, and is also an easy technique for one person working alone.

Any soft clean rags can be used, from fine cotton to chamois leather, but have a plentiful supply on hand, as the rags quickly become loaded with paint. Your print will vary with the texture of the rag, so experiment on paper first. Re-fold your rag from time to time.

Thin your paint with white spirit (mineral spirits) or water, depending on the type of paint being used, and use a little at a time. When the wall is dry, try ragging on another coat in a tone of the same colour to blur the contrasts, or rag over with a transparent glaze.

*Ragging off* is a similar process to sponging off, and again two people are needed for a wall area as it will need to be done in one go. The best method is for one person to brush a thinned, tinted transparent oil glaze over an oil-based ground colour, one 60cm- (2ft)-wide vertical strip of wall at a time (see diagram). The other person follows behind quite quickly, pressing the rags into the wet glaze evenly but rapidly, lifting off the top colour to reveal the base coat. Rebunch the rags from time to time.

## Rag-rolling

This process is similar to ragging off, the difference being that the rag is rolled into a sausage-shape and moved up and down over the wet glaze to create a broad, blurry stripe. The total effect is not unlike watered silk (see diagram). Re-roll and renew the rags from time to time.

*Rag-rolling can be an illusionistic technique too, re-creating the look of silk or damask. Dark, rich colours will add to the suggestion of sophistication and luxury.*

### RAGGING OFF

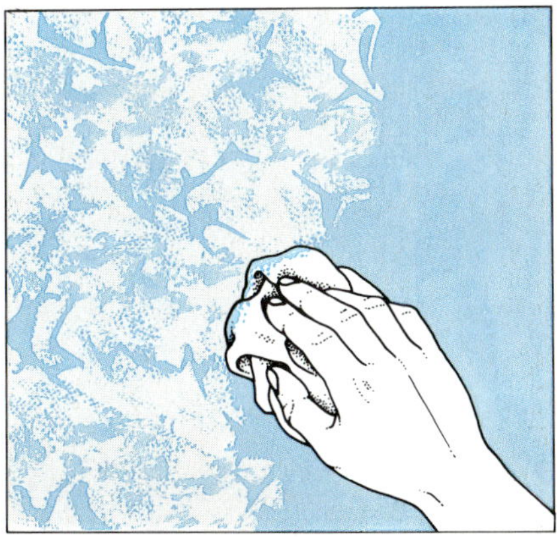

To create a different effect to sponging off, dab off the wet film with a crumpled rag.

### RAG-ROLLING

Alternatively, roll up a rag and then roll it over the wet paint surface, avoiding any slipping.

*Illusionistic paint effects always look better as free interpretations rather than slavish copies of the natural material. The wood graining (above) is one such example: the combing technique explained in figs. 3 and 4 on page 117 has been exploited and freely handled to bring rhythm and texture to the woodwork. Marble is another material commonly re-created in paint. In this bathroom (right), the walls are painted with long, flowing streaks, over a dappled background.*

## Marbling

Marbling ranges from a complex, skilfully built-up effect to a simple streaking of rubbed or feathered colour. Take a long, close look at real marble and have it by you, if possible; but do not overdo the realism. A simplified, impressionistic effect will look better than a laboured and tight effort. Small areas, such as table tops, can be marbled in one sweep but walls need to be tackled in alternate squares, returning to fill in when the first set are dry. Vein effects are then added to complete the effect.

*Method* Pale cloudy marbles with occasional patches of veining are the easiest to begin with. These should be done over a well-keyed base coat which, for best results, will have been painted with two coats of eggshell or semi-gloss oil-based paint. Use the lightest colour visible in the piece of marble you are copying, or white. The smoother the surfaces, the better the finished effect.

Brush or sponge an oil-based glaze, tinted cream or grey with

white undercoat and a little ochre or black artist's colour, over the base coat. Brush out smoothly and evenly.

The first coat of loose, paler veining can be added in grey or shades of raw umber. Apply with a sable brush, or a large goose quill if you can find one, 'fidgeting' the paint across the surface to make zig-zags, 'branch lines' and the odd pebble shape. Use a dry brush – or a painter's dusting brush – to tease these markings out gently, to soften and blur them a little. Apply the darker-coloured veins on top of the first but paint them at different angles, intersecting with the first set. Fidget and soften them as before.

Soften the whole surface further by dabbing with some soft paper towel. If you want to blur it a little more, lift off patches of glaze with a brush or rag dipped in white spirit (mineral spirits). When completely dry, the whole surface needs to be protected with clear, semi-gloss varnish: apply two coats in areas of heavy traffic, such as hallways.

## Transparent glaze formula

The easiest glaze for beginners is made up of equal parts of transparent oil glaze – a proprietary product sold under various brand names – and white spirit (mineral spirits). This mixture is colourless. To tint it, add tubes of artist's colours dissolved in a little white spirit (mineral spirits). Stir the colour in gradually but thoroughly. (Some decorators use small model-painting tins or cans of coloured enamel instead, for speed, allowing about one tin to a litre of glaze mixture.) This glaze formula dries quite slowly, takes impressions very distinctly, and dries with a sheen; but it can look somewhat heavy handed used with strong colours. To play down the 'sticky' effect, add a few spoonfuls of white, oil-based undercoat to the glaze. This will make the colour cloudier, and gives a softer result.

The glaze can also be thinned further with white spirit (mineral spirits), as much as 75% to 25% glaze. This gives a more delicate colour and a lighter, matt look, but it also means the glaze will dry faster and be harder to control.

## Colourwashing

This technique creates a lively, soft, luminous surface which looks perfect in small, dark or rustic rooms. It is most effective with mellow colours – warm ochres, pinks and russets – but can be used with almost any colour, bearing in mind that its distinctive patchiness will be more emphatic in a dark or strong shade.

To create a gentle, textured surface, use several coats of a very thinned-down water-based colour over two coats of matt emulsion (latex) base. The glaze can be thinned as much as three parts to one with water. Brush it on in loose, bold strokes that leave their brushmarks still visible (see diagram). The very thin glaze will allow the base colour to show through behind it, and you may decide one coat of glaze is enough. For stronger contrasts, heavily thinned oil-based paint can be brushed in the same loose irregular style over two coats of oil-based, eggshell paint. In both cases a soft clean brush, such as a painter's dusting brush, is useful for smoothing heavy brushmarks or drips.

Colourwashing with water-based paints (not oil-based) should be sealed with a clear matt acrylic glaze or varnish to make it washable without spoiling its freshness.

## Wood graining

This is now a very popular finish on all woodwork, but is especially good to add warmth and dignity to modern materials like blockboard (lumbercore board) and plywood; you could even fake wood panelling, with panels of a cheap material attached to a framework of wooden strips and extensive graining. Wood graining is, however, especially fashionable in modern bathrooms for bath surrounds, cabinets and doors and gives an Edwardian air of solid comfort.

It takes no great skill merely to suggest woodiness. Stop at fig. 3, and you will have already arrived at an impression of straight, even grain. If you want to attempt something more ambitious, more carefully imitative of real wood, begin by studying the natural material itself. Take a long, close, careful look at as large as possible a chunk of the real thing to see what you are aiming for. Pay some attention to the ordered accidents of the genuine material.

For a first attempt at creating a truly illusionistic effect you will need a serrated piece of stiff card or a rubber or steel graining comb, a selection of paintbrushes, a sable paintbrush, a soft dusting brush, and a cork, some blotting paper or a soft rag to simulate wood knots.

Don't worry if you make mistakes, a rag moistened in the appropriate solvent will clear away what you have done; just practise until you feel confident. Sealing the base coat with a quick-drying coat of shellac means you can wipe off your attempts many times, without leaving a trace.

*Method* (see diagrams) The paler woods, with a grey or blond cast, are grained over white, off-white or buttermilk base colours. Medium-toned woods are grained over a buff

### COLOURWASHING

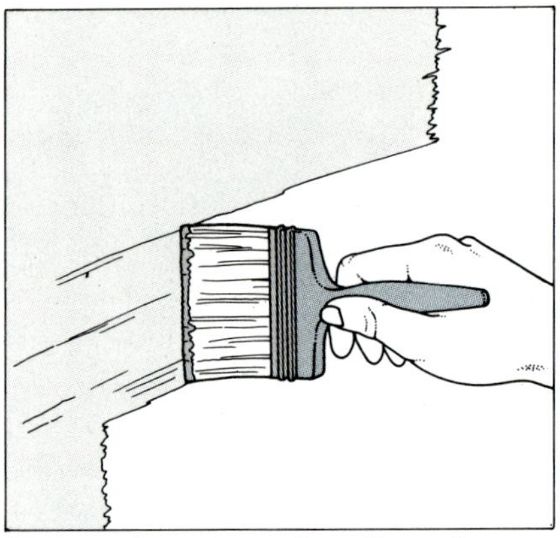

**1** Paint the prepared walls with two coats of base colour and then leave overnight to dry.

**2** Brush on several coats of very thin glaze or wash with quick, random strokes to achieve a 'brushy' finish.

*Colour-washed walls in sunshine yellow over white here form a luminous background to a simple and pretty stencil. Both techniques are handled with confident restraint, so that neither dominates.*

| | |
|---|---|
| PAINT TYPES | 98 |
| PAINTBRUSHES | 100 |
| TRANSPARENT OIL GLAZE | 115 |
| STENCILLING | 118 |




or biscuit shade. Reddish woods such as mahogany or rosewood can be grained over a pinkish-brown. Use an eggshell or lustre-textured paint for this base – a gloss type would be unsuitable – and apply two coats. Leave to dry. Next, lay a transparent or semi-transparent wood-coloured glaze over the top. For this graining colour, try to buy a ready-mixed wood glaze if you can. Alternatively, dissolve a little artist's colour – burnt umber, black, brownish red, yellow, ochre, even blue – in white spirit (mineral spirits), and add to an oil-based paint gradually, testing until you get the right colour. Thin further, if necessary, and make a note of your 'recipe' so that you can repeat and match it.

Distress the glaze with a graining comb or serrated card while still wet. Draw the tool steadily downwards, revealing streaks of the base colour. 'Fidget' these lines with a dry dusting brush to a greater or lesser extent, depending on the effect you want to achieve. You may want to stop here, with just the ruffled, rippled look of mahogany or maple. Alternatively, paint in the elongated, featured circles of the wood grain, known as heartwood. This heartwood is the figuring found where timber has been quartered and sliced thinly to make symmetrical patterns. Paint it in with a fine sable brush in a darker colour, a thinned black or burnt umber, working over a still wet glaze. 'Fidget' the lines as you go, and ruffle them with a dry brush while still wet: the markings should be irregular and naturalistic. Knots can be added using a cork, a soft rag or a crumpled-up piece of blotting paper.

When dry, the grained surface should be finished with at least two coats of semi-gloss or high-gloss clear varnish for protection and to give depth to the surfaces.

## WOOD GRAINING

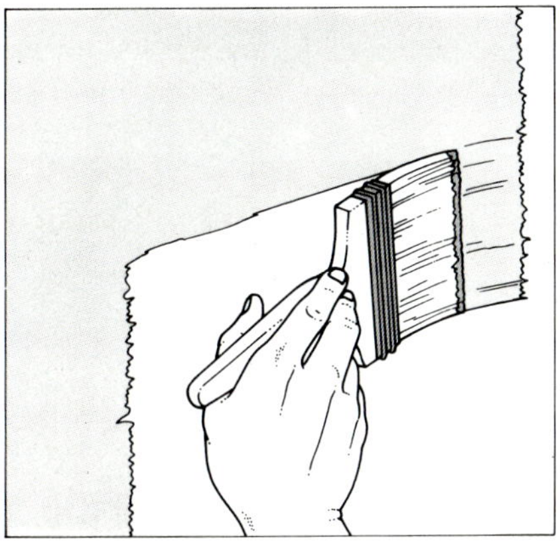

**1** Apply a base coat of oil-based, eggshell finish paint to the prepared surface and allow to dry thoroughly.

**2** Mix up a glaze of the wood colour and apply it to the whole surface with a small brush.

**3** Run the serrated edge of a piece of stiff card or graining comb over the glaze to create the grain pattern.

**4** Soften the ridges of the grain by lightly brushing along them with a dry, soft-bristled brush.

**5** Mix up a darker coloured glaze and paint in the darker streaks of grain with an artist's paintbrush.

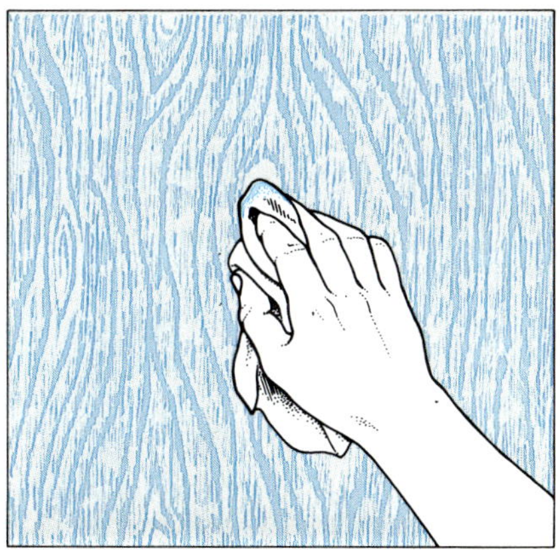

**6** Make knots by dipping a rag or cork in dark glaze and twisting it onto the surface.

# Stencilling

Stencils are the ideal way to add interest and individual personality to painted or papered rooms. Stencilled borders, crisply angular or softly floral, are a popular way of 'finishing' a room scheme, adding colour and pattern as well as underlining the shape and proportions of the room. Wide borders stencilled at ceiling level seem to lower high ceilings; a narrow border stencilled around a ceiling, skirting (baseboard), doors and windows adds crisp definition to a small dull box of a room; one motif repeated over walls can look rich and personalized. Any surface can be stencilled – not merely walls, but floors, furniture or fabric; and nothing adds more distinction to a room, particularly one that lacks any outstanding features.

The basic stencilling technique is very easy to do. A stencil is a decorative cut-out made from a thin sheet of oiled card, clear acetate or metal through which colour is brushed, sponged or sprayed on to the surface beneath. A good range of pre-cut stencils is available at specialist shops. Enterprising people may prefer to design and cut their own stencils using something like a fabric motif or a patterned china plate as inspiration. There are books of Victorian stencil designs available which can be scaled up or down and traced off on to stencil card: photocopying or graph paper are two easy methods. Cut stencils accurately over plate glass or a wood offcut.

The simplest stencils to use are one-colour stencils. These can look effective, especially painted in a darker shade of the wall colour. Mid-blue over pale blue, for instance, looks as fresh as blue-patterned china. Broadly speaking, stencilling vivid blocks of colour over a strong ground gives a lively countrified effect, reminiscent of the bold patterns of the English Blooms-

**STENCILLING**

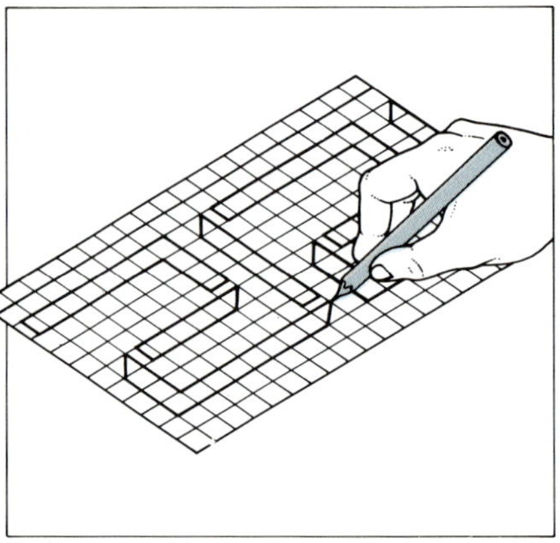

**1** Draw out the pattern on squared paper, or trace an existing one, and draw on a guideline.

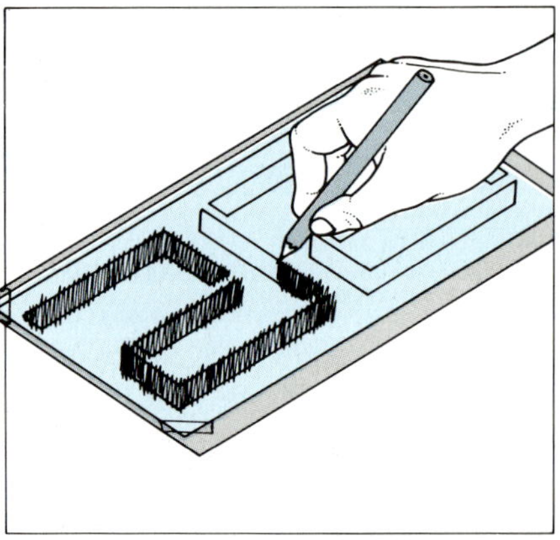

**2** Tape the pattern onto a sheet of oiled stencil paper or acetate and transfer pattern and guideline to it.

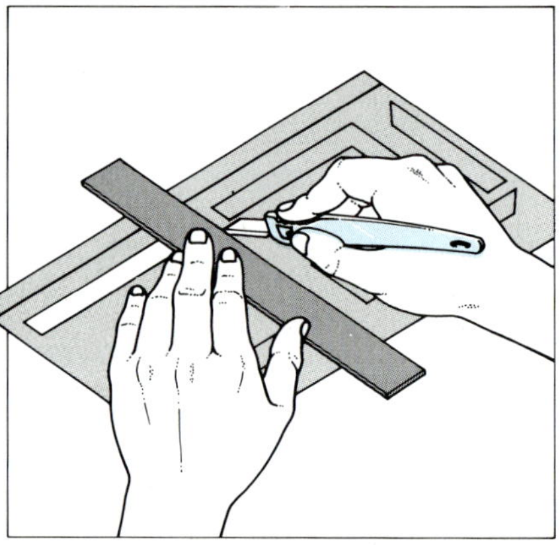

**3** Cut out the pattern with a craft knife against a metal straightedge, avoiding your fingertips!

**4** Align the stencil guideline with one drawn on the wall and 'pounce' paint through it with a stencil brush.

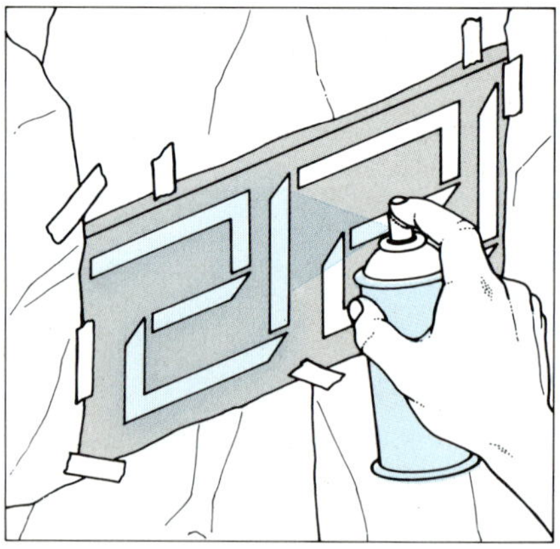

**5** Alternatively, spray on with aerosol paint after masking surrounding areas with newspaper.

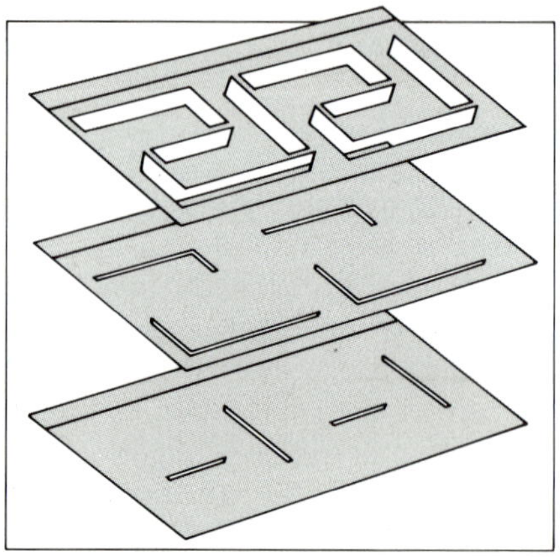

**6** For several colours, cut a stencil for each colour: the guidelines will enable you to match the edges.

*Left: For an all-over stencilled treatment, simple designs in one or perhaps two colours are often the best choice. This bedroom smacks of cool Scandinavian simplicity, and its white blind prevents the walls from becoming irritating.*

*Below: A border design can afford to be rather more complex. Add to the effect by using related motifs on the walls and other surfaces.*

bury group of the thirties.

A stencil using two or three colours, for example pink and blue flowers and green leaves, is more complicated as a separate cut-out is needed for each colour. Each paint coat must be left to dry and care is also needed to align cut-outs on top of each other. Most commercial stencils have accurate registration holes in each stencil, and pencilling a dot in these allows other stencils to be located precisely over the dots. To make your own, lay cut-outs over each other, then punch through them all at once; or draw or score a straight line over all your cut-outs, positioned accurately in relation to the design, and align this with a horizontal chalk line on the wall. For a border, this is an easy and foolproof way of getting a straight line of perfectly-registered stencils.

Stencilling can be applied over gloss, eggshell or matt paints. Wall surfaces do not have to be perfectly smooth; stencilling on rough plaster can look appealingly rustic. For maximum contrast stencil over a smooth, flat, base colour, but colour-washing and sponging can also make good backgrounds.

## Paints

Modern stencillers have the advantage of many suitable paints. Fast drying paints are good as they help prevent smudging. Artists' acrylic colours are popular because they dry quickly and come in a huge colour range. Signwriters' colours also dry fast and are cheap and durable. Imported Japan colours are expensive but excellent. Plain emulsion (latex) paint, perhaps tinted with universal stains, can be used too but can 'creep' under the stencil and smudge when lifted off. Spray paints are fast and give a soft-edged stencil, but

mask off the surrounding area with newspaper to stop it going on the wall. Use several coats, and work with the windows open.

Whatever paint you decide on, experiment first with the stencil on sheets of paper to check that the colours fit your design scheme.

Use as little colour as possible when stencilling. Heavy-handed colour is more likely to smudge, and also looks cruder.

*Method* Mark the position of stencils carefully in pencil or chalk your cut-out first. Friezes need to be marked out with a spirit level, straightedge and chalk to mark horizontal lines. Vertical lines can then be done with a T-square. Remember walls are rarely true, so align stencils visually. For rug-type stencils on the floor, make a plan on squared paper first, then square off the floor in chalk. Attach stencils with masking tape.

Traditionally, stencillers used blunt-ended stencil brushes to 'pounce', that is dab or stipple, paint colour through the stencils. This gives very fine control and can create a shaded effect, but is slow and laborious and probably most suitable for stencilling furniture where an impeccable finish is required. On walls or floors a small sponge or felt pad makes a convenient tool and one that adds its own texture. A soft brush, such as an artist's fitch, used in a brushing motion covers the ground fast but take care not to overload it with colour. When the colour has been applied, leave for a short time before lifting off the stencil and moving on. Clean stencils regularly and when work is finished remove any pencil or chalk marks.

On woodwork or if using water-based paint, apply two coats of varnish to seal the colour.

*Stencils can make a powerful stylistic statement, while the simplicity of the technique allows you to bring a painterly expertise to your decoration. Traditionally, stencils look pretty and countrified, and highly*

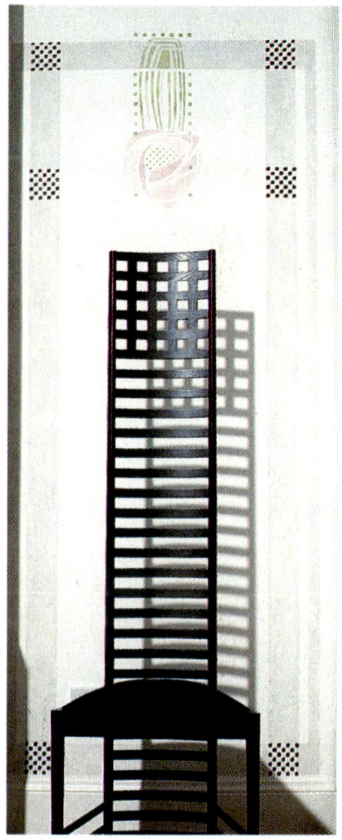

*appropriate to a bedroom with many period architectural features (opposite) – such as the linenfold panelling around the bed. Stencils can also look bold and contemporary: those around the walls (left) are treated variously, but unified by the fan that echoes their shape; while the designs of Charles Rennie Mackintosh are the inspiration for this stylized rose (above).*

# WORKING WITH WALLPAPER

The range of wallcoverings available is extensive. They come in different textures, weights, patterns, colours, lengths and widths. Some are stuck to the wall by using paste, some come pre-pasted and some have an adhesive and removable backing so that you just peel and stick.

Fabrics can be pulled taut over wooden strips or draped from curtain track, pole or wires attached around the tops of the walls.

## Buying wallcoverings

Hanging instructions are sometimes included when you buy your rolls of wallpaper, and you will find a 'batch' number so that you can buy rolls which have been produced together: you should always decorate a room with paper from the same batch, otherwise the colour could be slightly different.

Measure up your room before buying wallcoverings, ignoring door and window openings. Use the chart on page 125 to estimate the number of rolls you will need – this allows for any pattern-matching.

Before you choose, decide on the style you want to achieve in a room as a patterned paper, in particular, can be a very strong influence. You will also need to be practical – expensive silk and grasscloth papers will not suit a family bathroom and a washable vinyl is probably not suitable in an elegant living room.

## Types of wallcovering

The two most readily available types are printed wallpapers and vinyl wallcoverings which are paper-backed. Both come in a huge range of patterns, colours and textures. There are also special wallcoverings available with exotic finishes.

**Embossed/relief wallcoverings** are embossed to give a patterned, textured surface to walls and ceilings. They are ideal to cover uneven or

| | |
|---|---|
| FIXING TRACKS AND POLES | 50 |
| SURFACE PREPARATION | 74 |
| QUANTITIES REQUIRED | 125 |
| ATTACHING FABRIC TO WALLS | 126 |

*Making rooms out of awkwardly-shaped areas, often the legacy of converting houses, flats and apartments to a different arrangement, requires careful decoration. One solution, used to powerful effect here, is to paper the surfaces with designs from a co-ordinating range. The shape of the motif on all the walls is the same, a triangle; the variation is in the colour, size and arrangement, and in the background colour. The black of the furniture and floorcovering gives stability to the whole effect, yet has a drama of its own; and the accessories, from the Matisse painting to the flowers on the table, are the finishing touches that pick out the colours in the wallpaper.*

## TYPES OF WALLCOVERING

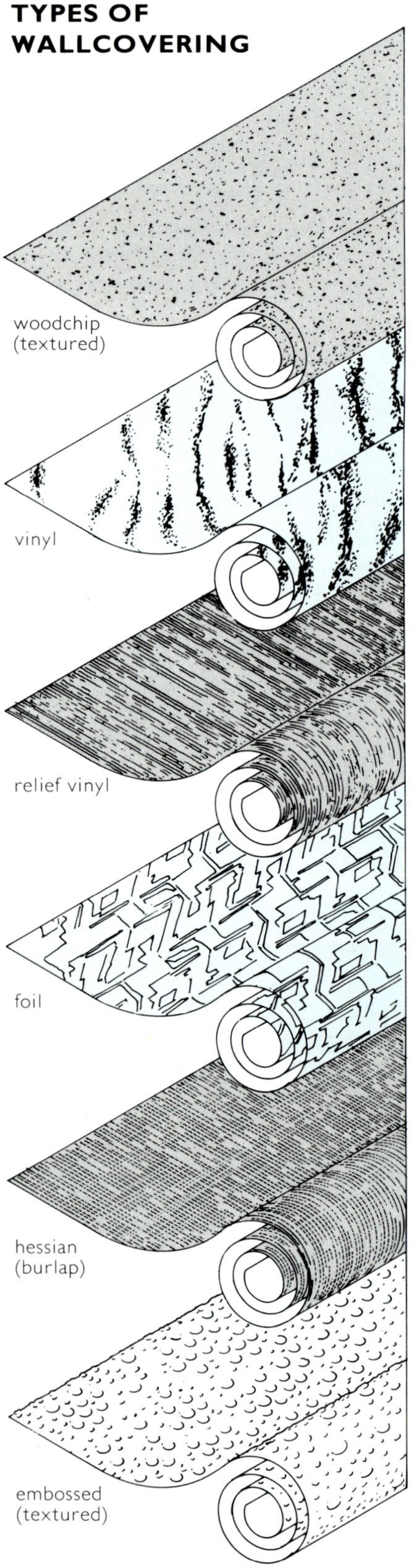


poor wall surfaces. Paint over them with emulsion (latex). Hang the papers with all-purpose adhesive, or a fungicidal paste for the vinyls.

**Ingrain/woodchip papers** are very inexpensive papers. They have a textured surface, but are not as heavy as the embossed/relief type, so can be used on poor, but not too uneven, wall surfaces. They are always painted, usually with emulsion (latex). They are easy to hang with an all-purpose adhesive, although they can prove difficult to strip as the wood chips stick to the wall.

**Foil wallcoverings** have a metallized plastic film bonded on a paper backing and a shiny, reflective surface. They are usually printed with very striking patterns. Do not fit this paper behind a light switch; simply butt it up and trim around the switch plate. Avoid using foils on uneven walls, too, as every bump will be exaggerated. Always cross-line walls with lining paper first. These are difficult papers to hang, and will need a fungicidal PVA adhesive. They are available as ordinary paper or come pre-pasted.

**Flock wallcoverings** have a characteristically velvety texture in a relief pattern on a silky ground. The backing can be paper or vinyl, so hang using an adhesive suitable to type.

**Lining paper** is ordinary, flat, unprinted paper, which is used to line ceilings and walls, prior to painting or hanging a wallcovering. (Hang horizontally if doing the latter.) Use an all-purpose adhesive.

**Standard printed paper** can be screen, roller or, more expensively, hand printed, in a wide range of different patterns. It is absorbent, so is not suitable for kitchens or bathrooms. Use an all-purpose adhesive and take care not to get paste on the front of the paper.

**Special wallcoverings** come in many different materials. Grasscloths are made from natural grasses, woven with cotton and glued to a paper backing. Hessian (burlap) is available with or without a paper backing. Silk is luxurious and lasts a long time:

*Small prints on wallpaper are often easiest to hang for the beginner, as slight mis-matches will not matter. Try to continue the pattern elsewhere, such as on the cushions.*

| | |
|---|---|
| STRIPPING SURFACES | 80 |
| CROSS-LINING | 134 |




## ESTIMATING QUANTITIES OF WALLPAPER

*The measurement around the room includes such items as doors and windows.*

**British wallpapers** (Table for calculating number of rolls required)

| Metres around room | Height of wall 2.0–2.2m | 2.2–2.4m | 2.4–2.6m | 2.6–2.8m | 2.8–3.0m | 3.0–3.2m | 3.2–3.4m |
|---|---|---|---|---|---|---|---|
| 10 | 5 | 5 | 5 | 6 | 6 | 6 | 7 |
| 11 | 5 | 5 | 6 | 6 | 7 | 7 | 7 |
| 12 | 5 | 6 | 6 | 7 | 7 | 8 | 8 |
| 13 | 6 | 6 | 7 | 7 | 8 | 8 | 9 |
| 14 | 6 | 7 | 7 | 8 | 8 | 9 | 9 |
| 15 | 7 | 7 | 8 | 8 | 9 | 10 | 10 |
| 16 | 7 | 8 | 8 | 9 | 9 | 10 | 11 |
| 17 | 7 | 8 | 9 | 9 | 10 | 11 | 11 |
| 18 | 8 | 9 | 9 | 10 | 11 | 11 | 12 |
| 19 | 8 | 9 | 10 | 11 | 11 | 12 | 13 |
| 20 | 9 | 10 | 10 | 11 | 12 | 13 | 13 |
| 21 | 9 | 10 | 11 | 12 | 12 | 13 | 14 |
| 22 | 10 | 10 | 11 | 12 | 13 | 14 | 15 |

**American wallpapers**

| Feet around room | Height of wall 8ft | 9ft | 10ft | 11ft | 12ft | 13ft | 14ft |
|---|---|---|---|---|---|---|---|
| 28 | 7 | 8 | 9 | 10 | 11 | 11 | 12 |
| 32 | 8 | 9 | 10 | 11 | 12 | 13 | 14 |
| 36 | 9 | 10 | 11 | 12 | 13 | 14 | 16 |
| 40 | 10 | 11 | 12 | 14 | 15 | 16 | 17 |
| 44 | 11 | 12 | 14 | 15 | 16 | 18 | 19 |
| 48 | 12 | 13 | 15 | 16 | 18 | 19 | 21 |
| 52 | 13 | 15 | 16 | 18 | 19 | 21 | 22 |
| 56 | 14 | 16 | 17 | 19 | 21 | 22 | 24 |
| 60 | 15 | 17 | 19 | 20 | 22 | 24 | 26 |
| 64 | 16 | 18 | 20 | 22 | 24 | 26 | 28 |
| 68 | 17 | 19 | 21 | 23 | 25 | 27 | 29 |
| 72 | 18 | 20 | 22 | 24 | 27 | 29 | 31 |
| 80 | 20 | 22 | 25 | 27 | 30 | 32 | 34 |
| 84 | 21 | 23 | 26 | 28 | 31 | 33 | 36 |
| 88 | 22 | 24 | 27 | 30 | 32 | 35 | 38 |

**Symbols**

These international performance symbols are now beginning to appear in wallpaper pattern books and on product labels. They are designed to help you identify the qualities which are attributable to the wallcovering on which they appear.

- Spongeable
- Washable
- Super-washable
- Scrubbable
- Sufficient light fastness
- Good light fastness
- Strippable
- Peelable
- Ready pasted
- Paste-the-wall
- 50 cm / 25: Design repeat Distance offset
- Free match
- Straight match
- Offset match
- Duplex
- Co-ordinated fabric available
- Direction of hanging
- Reverse alternate lengths

*Reproduced by courtesy of The Wallpaper Paint Wallcovering Retailers' Association*

avoid staining the material with water or paste by applying the paste to the wall. Jute, wool weaves, cane papers and even silica and granite chippings on a backing are also available. They are often sold by the metre or yard, and some are very expensive. Hang according to the manufacturer's instructions. It is often a good idea to cross-line the wall before hanging these types.

**Vinyl wallcoverings** are available in a wide range of patterns, printed on vinyl and then paper-backed – which makes them easy to strip. They come in a variety of different textures and can be embossed to create fabric look-alikes. They are very hard-wearing, washable and impervious to water. Most types are easy to hang. Use a fungicidal adhesive to prevent any mould developing from contact with water. Also use a latex adhesive if you have to overlap a join in a corner. Butt-join any seams.

**Washable wallpapers** are the same as standard papers, but with a waterproof coating which can be matt or shiny. These can be sponged but are not as easy to wash as vinyl and scuff fairly easily. Hang in the same way as standard paper.

**Foamed polyethylene** is a very light, slightly 'waffled' wallcovering. It is tough, can be sponged, and is warm to the touch. It is particularly suitable for kitchens and bathrooms. Hang by pasting the wall with heavy-duty paste, then slide into position over the paste, straight from the roll: there is no need to cut lengths, or to soak with paste first.

**Expanded polyethylene** coverings are used for their insulating properties, which are considerable. Hang with PVA adhesive, leave for two days then cross-line and paint or paper over the top: a dry-strippable type of paper is a good choice for this second layer. Stripping expanded polyethylene leaves a film on the wall: soak this in water, then peel off.

### Attaching fabric to walls

Several fabrics come paper-backed ready for pasting to the wall like other wallcoverings. With some nonbacked fabrics, pasting the wall with a heavy-duty paste is often advised, but great care must be taken not to stain the front of the fabric. Hessian (burlap), for example, can be used unbacked. Paste the wall in blocks as wide as about two widths at a time, then push the hessian (burlap) into place taking care not to stretch it. Flatten each piece firmly with a roller, overlapping each join. Complete the room before trimming to allow for any shrinkage. Cut along the top and bottom of the wall with a sharp handyman's knife against a metal straightedge, then cut through both layers of the overlapping joins in the same way. Peel away the excess and push the edges of the join firmly down. You can then go over them with a seam roller for a perfect finish.

Fabric can also be attached to the wall by means of wooden strips or battens. You can fit the strips to the wall first, as described on page 162, but use slimmer (25 × 6mm – 1 × $\frac{1}{4}$in) strips. The fabric can then be tacked, pinned or stapled to the wood. Start at the top of the wall and work down and across, stretching the fabric taut as you go. Use pins with decorative heads or cover the fastenings with ribbon or braid.

If you are worried about the process of attaching wooden strips to your walls, or want the fabric to be less permanent, hang the fabric on curtain wires stretched between hooks on the wall. These wires are the same type that are commonly used for sheers; and you will similarly need a lightweight cotton or other fabric. Measure the walls and buy curtain wire long enough to fit along the top and bottom of the walls. Drill, plug and then screw in cup hooks at the four corners of each wall. Stitch lengths of fabric together to achieve a width that is twice the length of the wires, and

## WALLPAPERING EQUIPMENT

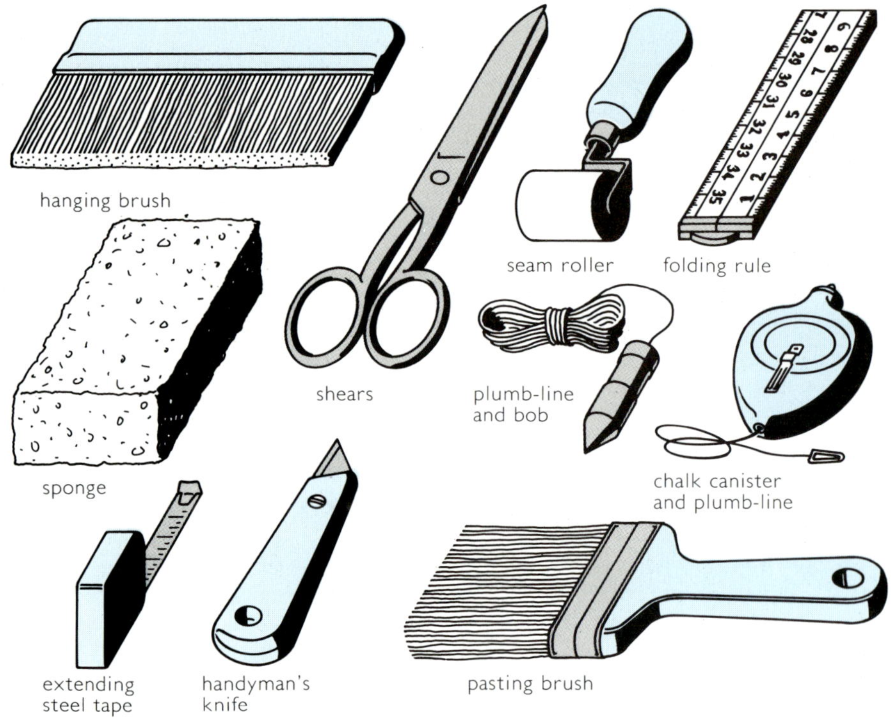


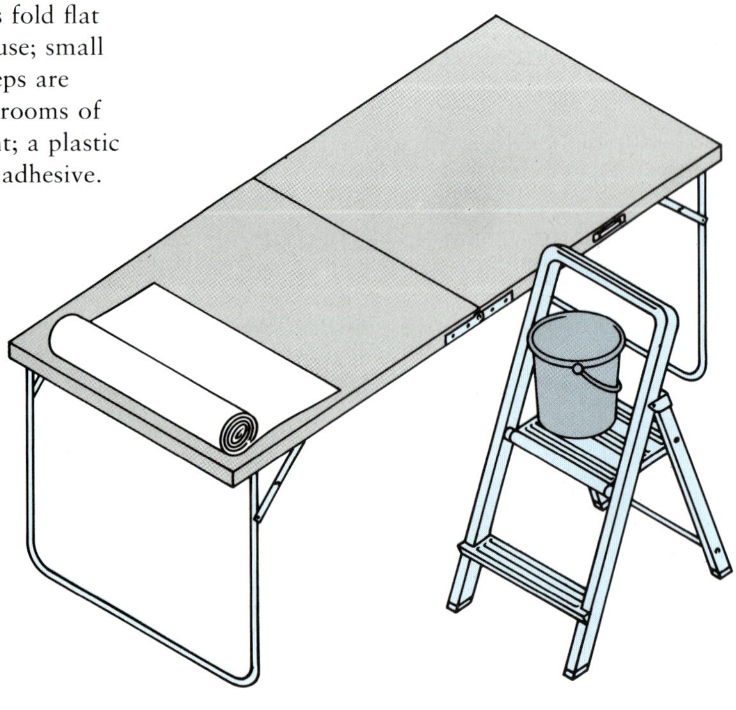

Pasting tables fold flat when not in use; small household steps are adequate for rooms of average height; a plastic bucket holds adhesive.

hem top and bottom making a casing 38–50mm ($1\frac{1}{2}$–2in) deep through which the wires can be fed. Make sure you allow for the fact that the fabric needs to be taut vertically. Cut the curtain wires to length with pliers or a hacksaw, insert a screw eye in each end, and feed them through the fabric hems. Then hang the cup hooks on the walls.

## Tools and equipment

As with all decorating and preparation, buy the best equipment for wallpapering you can afford. Major items like special ladders can be hired or rented. A pasting table is a worthwhile investment, but a large kitchen or dining room table can be used if covered with a heavy-duty polyethylene sheet to protect it. Do, however, buy a good-quality pasting brush which does not shed hairs; and tie a piece of string across the top of your plastic bucket to wipe any excess paste off the brush.

## The starting point

Before you can start wallpapering you will need to prepare the walls properly, stripping off any old wallpaper and filling any holes or cracks. Also make sure you remove such things as curtain tracks, and that you cover all floors and furniture with heavy-duty polyethylene or traditional cotton dust sheets. Wash the walls with hot water to remove any old paste, or if the walls have been painted wash with sugar soap or trisodium phosphate, then lightly sand with medium-grade abrasive paper to provide a key.

Newly-finished walls may require special treatment first. Don't sand down new plasterboard (drywall) surfaces but seal with a coat of emulsion (latex) paint before hanging the wallcovering. If your walls have recently been plastered, make sure they have dried out thoroughly: this can take as long as six months. Brush off any efflorescence (powdery areas) and sand lightly with medium-grade abrasive paper, then size the walls. You can use a proper glue size for this which prevents the plaster absorbing water from the paste, and also makes the wall slightly slippery so positioning the paper is easier. Alternatively, use a coat of thinned-down wallpaper paste, made up according to instructions. It is important to size walls which have never been papered, to make future stripping easier.

It is usual to finish any painting in a room before papering, and to start with the ceiling and work downwards. Paint the ceiling first, then take the paint down the wall about 25–50mm (1–2in) to conceal any gaps left by trimming the paper. Add a cornice (crown moulding) after you have painted the ceiling; if papering it, put the cornice up first.

### STARTING POINTS

With plain or small-patterned papers there are two alternative starting positions for wallpaper: either start in one corner of the main window wall, then paper along both side walls working away from the light (or towards the door), and finally the wall opposite the window; or, to avoid cutting full widths of paper round the window, start adjacent to the window, complete the window wall, and then continue as above. If using a paper with a large motif, centre the motif on a focal point in the room such as above the fireplace; either centre the first length or hang two lengths to join at the centre, depending upon which arrangement will leave a greater width at each corner, allowing for a 30mm ($1\frac{1}{4}$in) turn into the alcoves. Complete the fireplace wall, then paper the rest of the room, working away from the light to avoid overlaps appearing as hard edges.

# Papering Walls

Measuring the wall and cutting the wallcovering accurately is very important and remember, if your paper has a definite design on it you will also have to allow extra for pattern-matching: this is also relevant to heavily-textured and relief type papers. Some papers are matchless and the design does not follow on from width to width. A few wallcoverings have to be 'reverse hung' – this means you hang one length, then turn the paper round, hanging the next length upside down. This normally applies to textured or special wallcoverings where there may be colour variations from edge to edge.

If you are hanging a co-ordinating paper, perhaps in a scheme with curtains in the same fabric, make sure the design lines up neatly across the wall and window fabric.

As walls can often be an irregular size, measure the height of each wall at both ends and in the middle, and take the maximum measurement for all your lengths of paper. Allow an extra 100mm (4in) on each length for trimming at top and bottom.

Unroll the paper and check the pattern to see where the starting point at the top of the wall should be: avoid cutting through a design in such a way that you leave an ugly shape at the top. Measure, cut and paste several lengths at one time, so that some can be pasted and soaking while you hang another piece. Mark consecutive numbers on the back of

*Bedrooms require restful patterns and colours, and wallpaper will often give you the best choice of these. Fabrics chosen from ranges designed to co-ordinate will give you confidence that the whole effect will work as you intended.*

## MEASURING & PASTING WALLPAPER

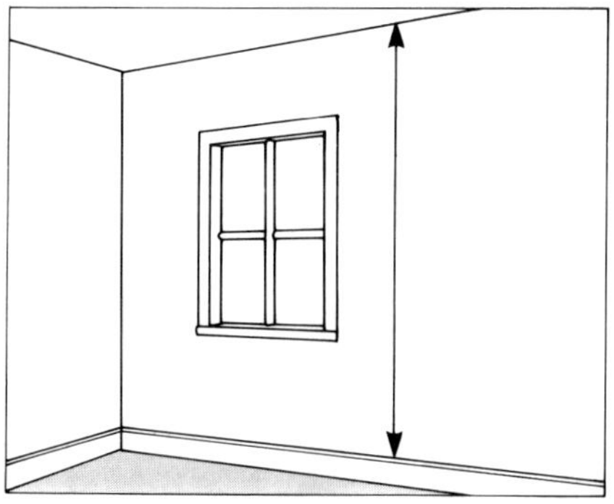

**1** Measure the height of the wall at both ends and in the middle, using a steel tape measure, and add 100mm (4in) to the greatest dimension to give the length of paper needed.

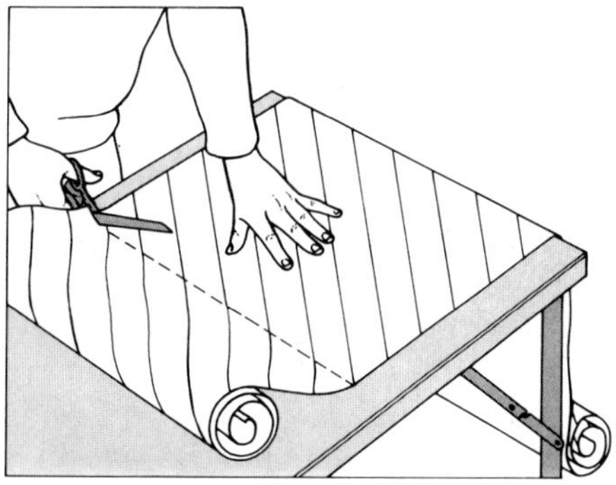

**2** Chalk TOP on the back of the free end of the roll. Measure the length of paper with a steel tape measure and cut squarely across, folding first as a guide if necessary.

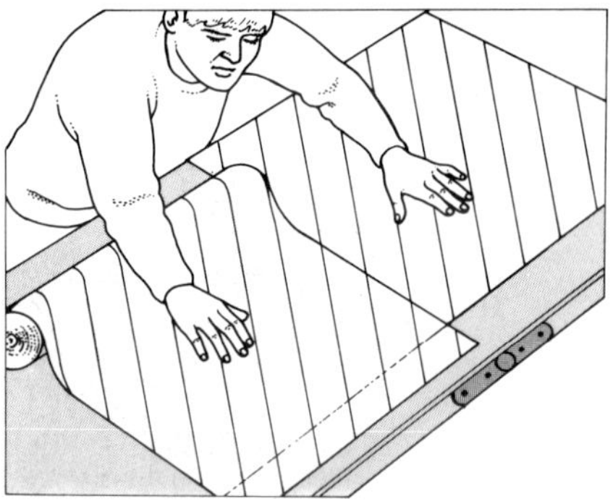

**3** Cut enough lengths of paper for one wall, matching the pattern on successive lengths, and trim excess from the top. Number and mark TOP on the back of each length.

**4** Brush the paste on in a strip down the middle of the paper, then push the paper slightly over the far edge and brush the paste herringbone-fashion over the far third.

**5** Without moving the paper along the table, pull it to overhang the near edge of the table slightly and brush the paste out towards you to complete the nearer strip.

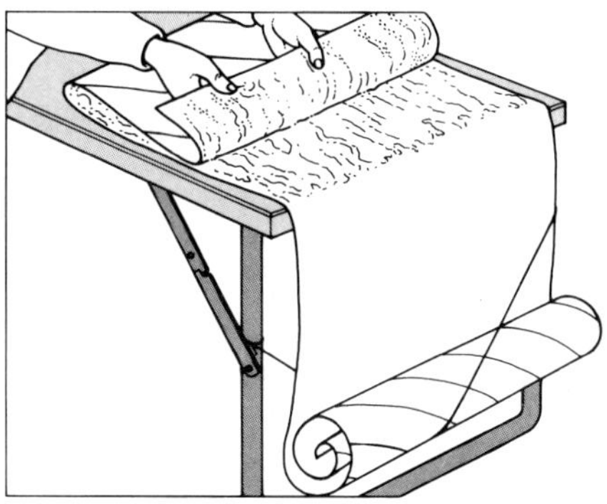

**6** Fold over the pasted end of the paper to the middle, pasted side inwards, then shift the paper along the table and paste the other half of the length in the same way.

each length in pencil, and also indicate which is the top. If your paper is a matchless one, work from one roll; if you have to match a motif cut lengths from two or three rolls alternately to minimize waste. Align the pattern carefully before cutting. Match a horizontal pattern by laying the roll end on top of a cut length and make sure the pattern runs across without any 'steps'. Measure off the next length and cut. With a drop pattern (see diagrams), lay the long edges of the length and the roll side by side, check the pattern continues across them, then measure off and cut the next length.

### Pasting and folding

Mix the paste according to the manufacturer's instructions, making sure there are no lumps, and allow to stand for about five minutes, or as directed. The diagrams show how to paste the paper without getting any on the front.

Normally, the paper will be longer than the pasting table and you will have to fold it. Paste the first half and fold this over lightly, end-to-middle and with pasted faces together: then paste the second half and fold in, taking care not to make creases. Leave to soak while you cut and paste more lengths, or hang a pre-soaked length. With a very long drop, fold pasted sections concertina-style. This technique is also used when papering ceilings or cross-lining walls.

Light and mediumweight papers should be left pasted for two to five minutes, heavyweight types for about ten to twelve. This process makes the paper easier to hang. Always let each length soak for the same time, or you will find the paper stretches in varying degrees.

If using pre-pasted wallcoverings, you will need to immerse the cut lengths in a special water trough,

## PAPERING FLAT WALLS

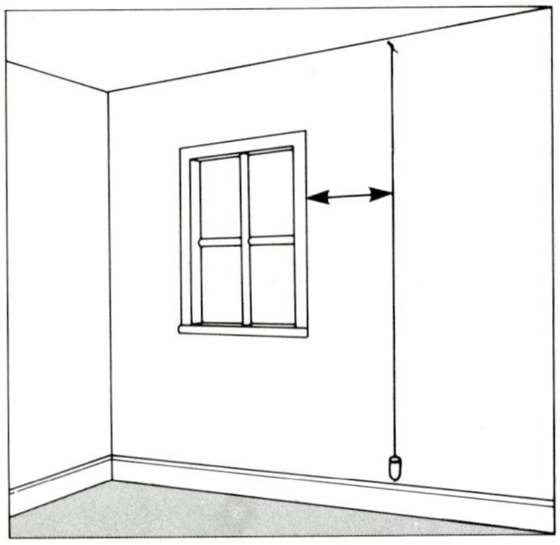

**1** Hang a chalked plumb-line and bob from a nail, snap it, and mark a guideline for the first length.

**2** After the correct soaking time for the paper, carry it to the wall and unfold the top half.

**3** Align the edge of the paper on the guideline, and so that the top edge overlaps the ceiling by 5cm (2in).

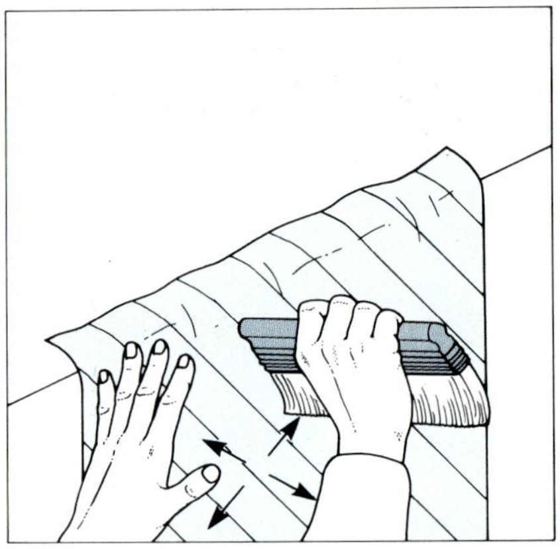

**4** Unfold the bottom half and brush the paper onto the wall, from the centre outwards, to remove any air.

**5** Crease the paper into the wall/ceiling angle by running the back edge of the shears along it.

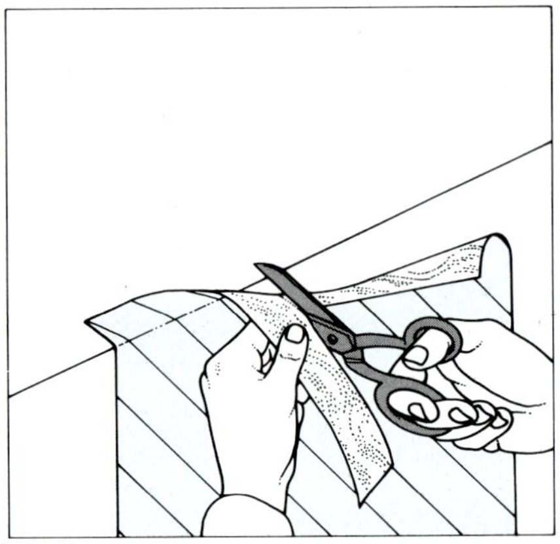

**6** Pull the top away from the wall and trim neatly along the crease line; repeat at the skirting (baseboard).

**7** Brush the paper back to butt up to the ceiling and skirting (baseboard) with no overlap.

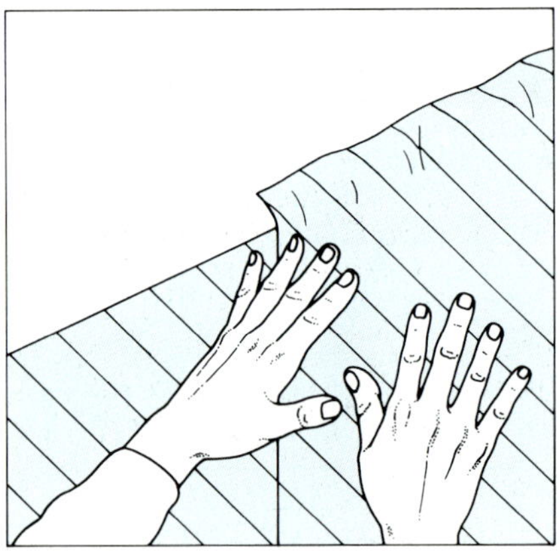

**8** Hang the next length of paper, butting up to the first and so that the pattern aligns exactly.

**9** After trimming at top and bottom, run a seam roller down the join, except on embossed papers.

which is sometimes provided with the paper. A plant trough can be used provided it is longer than the width of the paper. Soak the lengths for the required time (one to two minutes), then carefully lift the top edge, letting the water drain back into the trough, and hang in the same way as pasted paper.

## Hanging the paper

If you are going to be papering the ceiling, always do this first. Next, choose a starting point on the wall and hang a plumb-bob to establish a true vertical, marking this on the wall: a self-chalking plumb-line will make this easy, otherwise chalk the string before hanging the bob, hold the weight against the wall once it's stopped swinging, and snap the string on the wall. If you are starting beside a window or in a corner, position the line to allow 12mm ($\frac{1}{2}$in) of the paper to turn round the corner and overlap the next wall.

Measure, cut, paste, and fold the paper, and drape it over your arm with the right side facing outwards and what will be the top edge uppermost. Mount the ladder, grip the top edge of the paper and align the first length against the vertical chalk line, letting the length drop down the wall naturally. Leave about 25mm

*Right, above: The combination of partial wood cladding to dado- (or chair-) rail height and wallpaper is an unusual and smart one. The period furniture is covered in neutral colours to focus the attention on the walls themselves.*

*Right: The decoration of this elegant dining room exploits the straight lines of the stripes in the paper, and uses a potentially strong green with restraint. Striped papers need careful hanging, as mistakes and near-verticals will show.*

(1in) overlap at the join between ceiling and wall. Starting at the top, brush out the paper towards the edges with broad, sweeping movements of the wallpaper brush, to remove any air bubbles.

Crease and trim the paper at the top, then trim at the bottom (see figs. 5–7). Repeat with the next length of paper, butt-joining it up to the first length. Make sure you have a perfect pattern match where necessary. Check the verticals with the plumb-line after every two or three lengths, and draw a new guideline when you turn a corner. When the whole wall is papered, go over the seams with a seam roller (unless the paper is embossed) to flatten them.

Pre-pasted paper is hung on walls in the same way, although it may not be necessary to cut lengths before activating the paste.

You may find some air bubbles appearing after you have hung your wallcovering. Small ones may dry flat, but do not go on papering if there are large bubbles and creases: peel the paper back while it is still wet, and brush flat. If small bubbles still persist, pierce with a pin when wet or slit them and stick the paper back when dry.

## Corners and obstacles

You will come up against obstacles when papering – corners, doors, windows, and arches – and you will also have to paper around light fixtures and switches. Follow the diagrams, and be patient and gentle with the paper to avoid tears in it.

For safety, *always* switch the electricity off at the mains before cutting round light switches and fixtures and ceiling centrepieces, and take care not to mark or score the fixture.

When papering arches, there may be some confusion about which paper to use. It is most practical to paper each side of the arch to match

**PAPERING AROUND CORNERS**

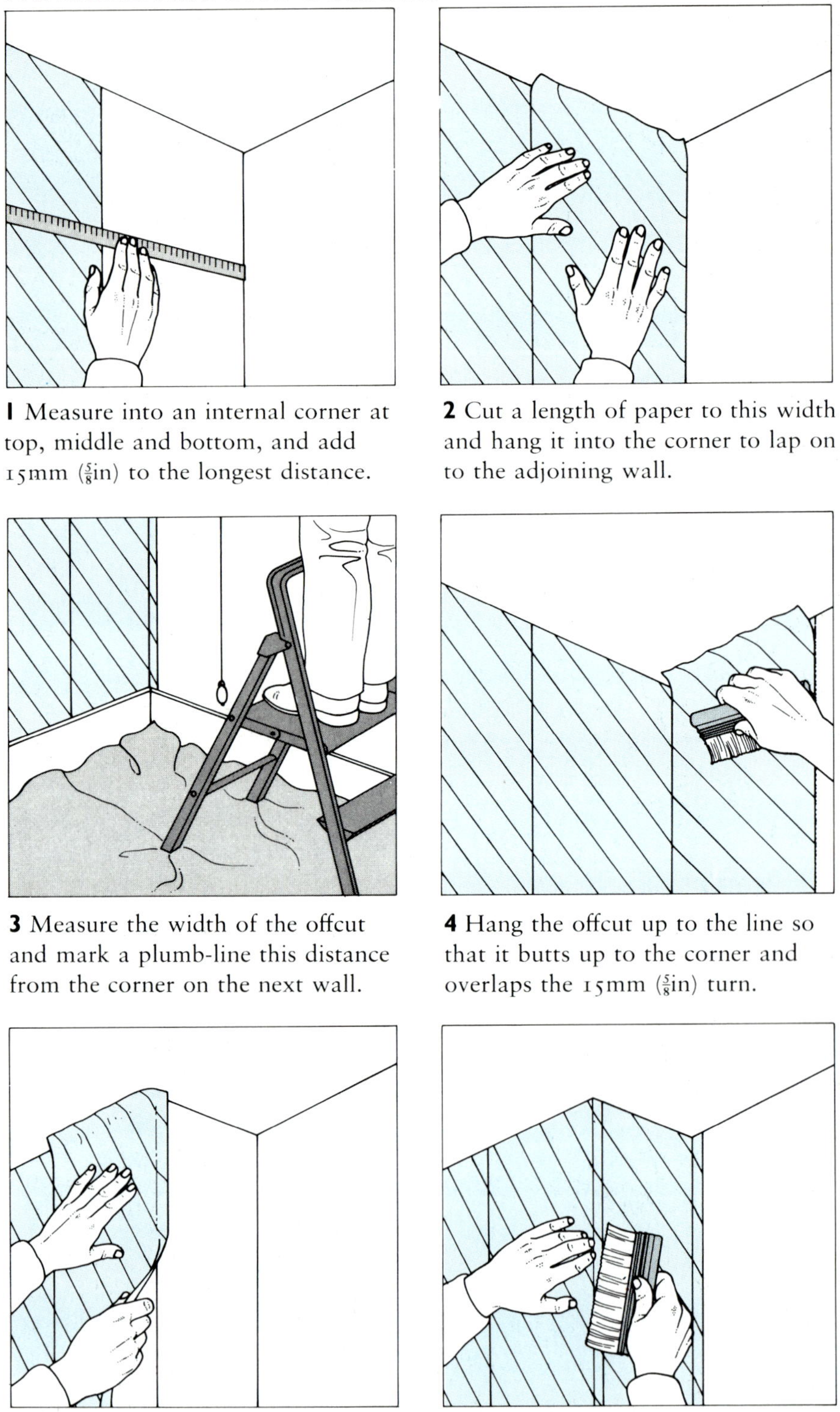

**1** Measure into an internal corner at top, middle and bottom, and add 15mm ($\frac{5}{8}$in) to the longest distance.

**2** Cut a length of paper to this width and hang it into the corner to lap on to the adjoining wall.

**3** Measure the width of the offcut and mark a plumb-line this distance from the corner on the next wall.

**4** Hang the offcut up to the line so that it butts up to the corner and overlaps the 15mm ($\frac{5}{8}$in) turn.

**5** Cut a narrow width to turn 30mm ($1\frac{1}{4}$in) round an external corner, but do not brush down the turn.

**6** Hang the offcut on the return wall to butt up to the external corner, and brush over the turn.

## PAPERING AROUND OBSTACLES

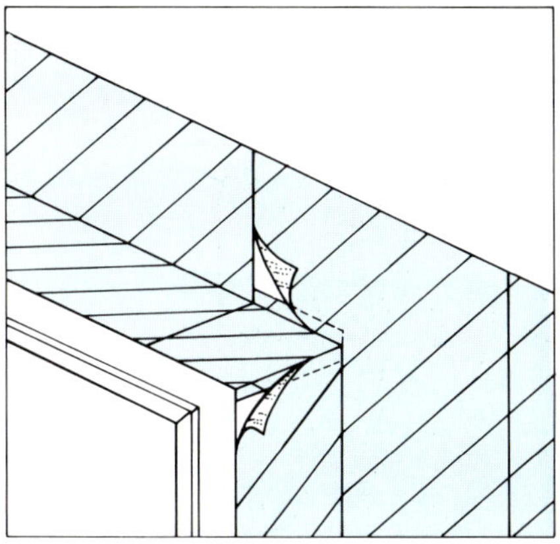

**1** Slit the paper flush with the front edge of a reveal, and butt the ends up to the frame. Patch the corner.

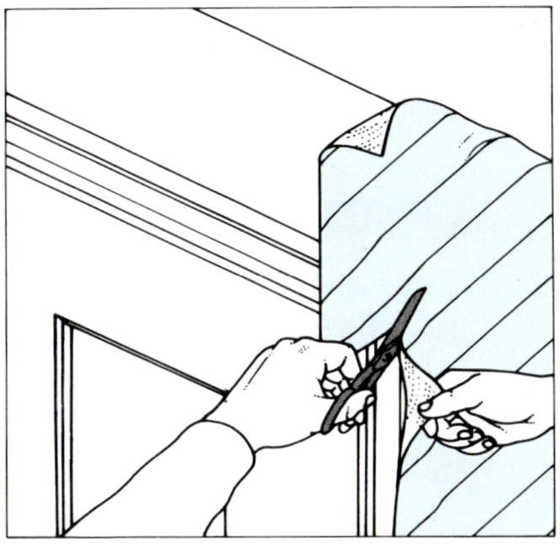

**2** Cut the paper at an angle towards the corner of a door frame and trim into the angle with the wall.

**3** Overlap a fireplace and make release cuts into the corners before trimming into the angles.

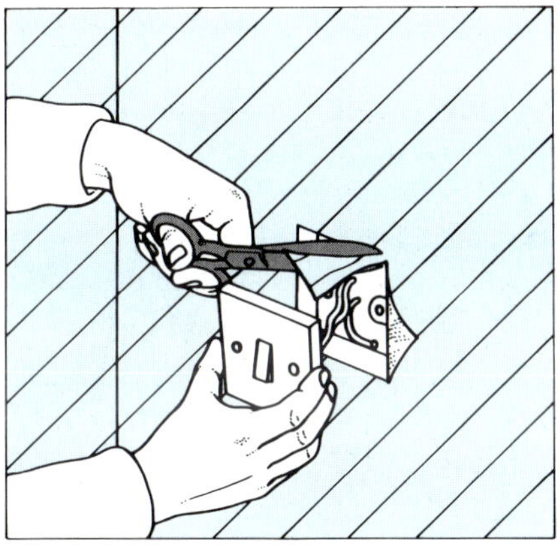

**4** TURN OFF ELECTRICITY at the main switch, make release cuts over a switch plate, unscrew, and trim.

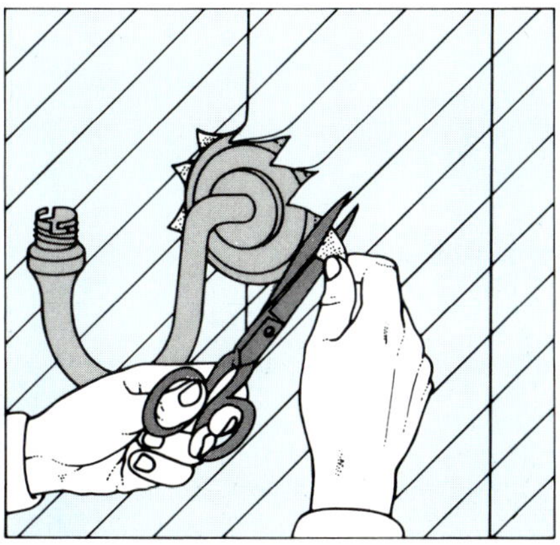

**5** Remove a wall-light shade, slit the paper to pass over the fixture and trim around the base plate.

**6** Hang paper over a radiator, cut up from the bottom in line with the brackets and smooth down behind.

the one used in that area of the room, then to use a lining paper on the under-side of the arch, painted to match the ceiling or woodwork. You will certainly have to do this where a picture rail or moulding continues round the arch: paint above the trim with the ceiling colour and paper below it to match the walls.

### Papering around radiators

Ideally, radiators should be taken off the wall and painted flat, then the wall behind can be papered with ease. However, this is not a job for the inexperienced since it involves isolating and draining down the radiator, which provides plenty of scope for disaster – it could result in more re-decoration than you anticipate! Far better to leave it in place and work around it, but be sure you turn it off before starting as the heat will cause the paper to dry too quickly. Wipe off any paste as you work as this can damage the paint.

The professionals use a full length of paper, and hang it on the wall above as normal with the remainder falling over the front of the radiator. Then slits are cut up from the bottom corresponding with the position of the brackets on which the radiator hangs. With a proprietary tool or bent wire coat hanger, the paper is pushed down behind the radiator and smoothed out perhaps with a radiator roller.

It can be difficult, however, for a beginner to manipulate a long length of paper and push it down a small gap without tearing or creasing it. An easier method is to cut off the bottom of the paper length, leaving you just a short piece to push down behind the top portion of the radiator. Cut the remainder of the length roughly in half and paper upwards from the skirting board (baseboard), producing the illusion of a continuous piece of paper down the wall.

# Papering Ceilings

Cross-lining and papering ceilings are usually done with a plain unprinted paper which can then be painted or papered over. This type of paper can stretch when pasted, so make sure you allow each length to soak for the same amount of time.

## Cross-lining walls

Lining paper is hung on walls in a similar way to ordinary paper, but horizontally. Start at the top of the wall which is at right angles to the window wall, and work across from right to left or left to right to suit you. Brush out each fold of your concertina as you work across the wall. The first length should overlap the ceiling by about 25mm (1in), before being trimmed. Also overlap into the corner by about 12mm (½in) to allow for any shrinkage.

Cross-lining is not the easiest of tasks for a beginner. If you are doing it to cover uneven or imperfect plaster, look to see if you can cover up just that particular area. If you can, line just that and leave the ends loose and unstuck. When dry, tear the excess off carefully and sand the edge well to remove any 'step'.

## Papering ceilings

Before you embark optimistically on this job, think twice. Papering a ceiling is not easy, and the beginner is well advised to get someone to help. If you can, paint the ceilings rather than paper them. Whatever you decide, always set up a safe working platform, using ladders and a scaffold board or part of a tower platform. If you are using lining paper as a basis for further papering, the lengths should be hung at right angles to the main window. Hang the next layer at right angles to this;

*Continuing a wallpaper up from the walls to the ceiling unifies a room and 'dissolves' the line between the two, particularly in an attic room.*

### LINING WALLS

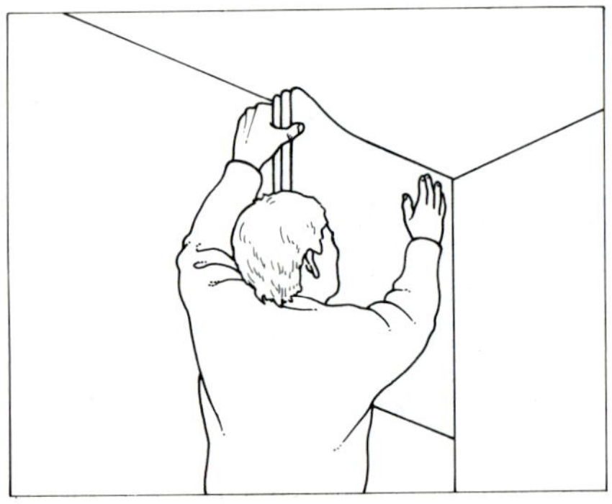

**1** Paste and fold the paper into a manageable concertina, and position the first end so that it overlaps both the ceiling and the next wall by 12mm (½in).

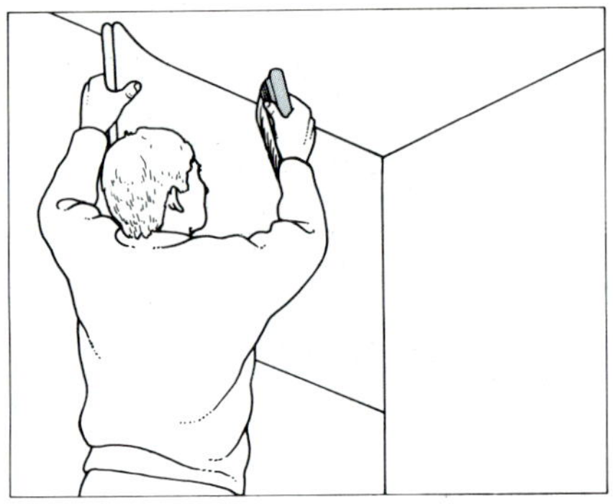

**2** Brush into the wall angle to remove any bubbles, then back towards the concertina. Open the paper out fold by fold, brushing bubbles out as you go.

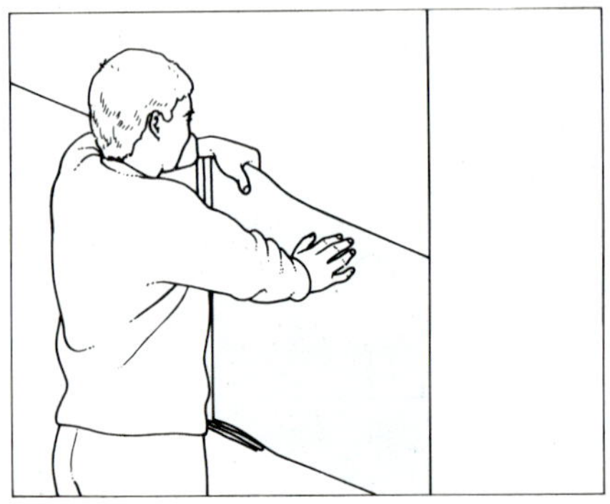

**3** Hang the next length to butt up to the first, overlapping the next wall as before. Trim all along the bottom of the last length when you've finished the wall.

| | |
|---|---|
| WORK PLATFORMS | 78 |
| PAINTING CEILINGS | 101 |
| SPECIAL WALLPAPERS | 124 |
| MEASURING AND PASTING | 129 |
| WALLPAPER BUBBLES | 136 |



## PAPERING CEILINGS

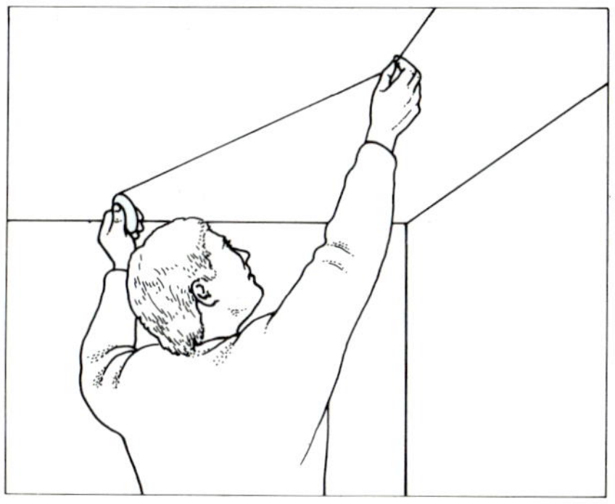

**1** Snap a chalked string onto the ceiling, or use a pencil, at a distance out equal to the paper width, or less 25mm (1in), depending on the wall treatment to come.

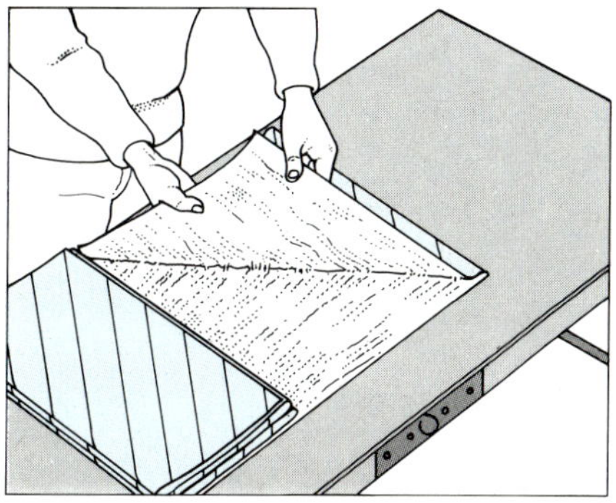

**2** Measure along the line and add 100m (4in) for trimming, cut the lengths to this and paste them as for wallpaper. Fold the paper into a manageable concertina.

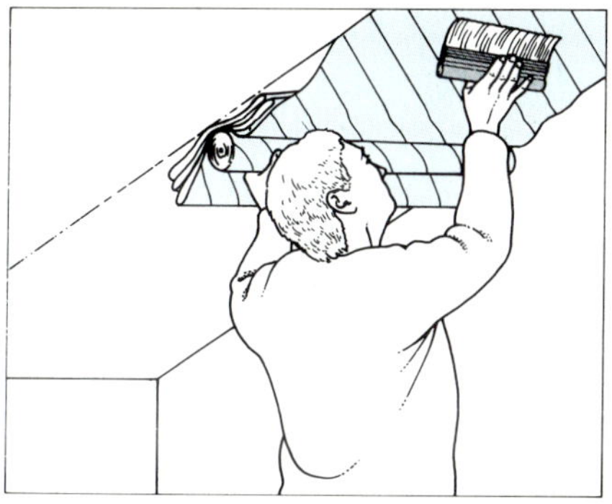

**3** Supporting the concertina, brush one end of the paper into the ceiling/wall angle, overlapping it on to the wall by 25mm (1in) along the long edge if appropriate.

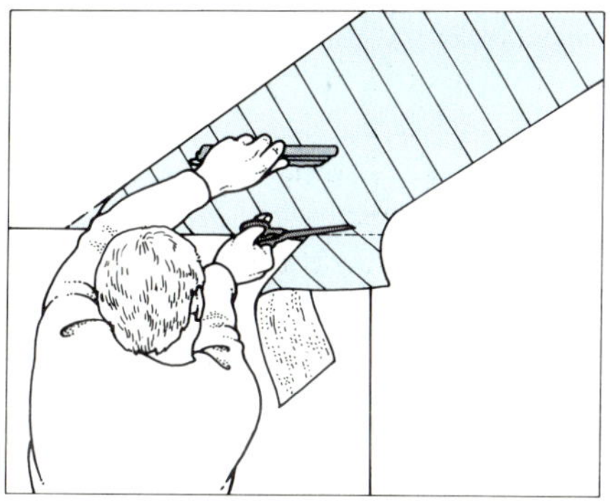

**4** Brush out any bubbles with the wallpaper brush as you go. Crease and trim both ends, leaving an overlap on the wall if required, and brush back carefully.

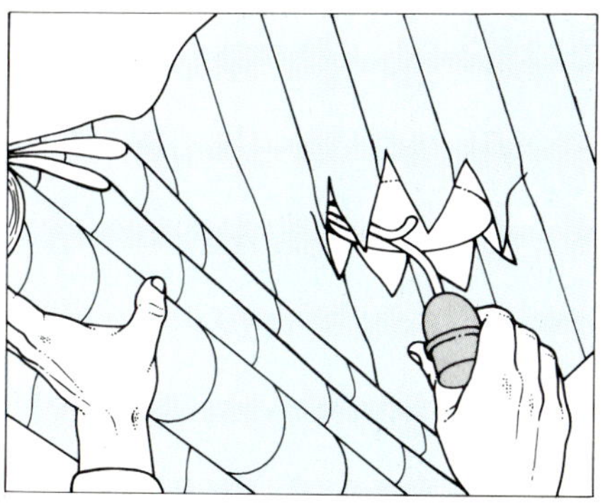

**5** TURN THE ELECTRICITY OFF. At light fixtures, pull pendant to one side and hold the paper up close. Stab with scissors, make release cuts and ease the cord through.

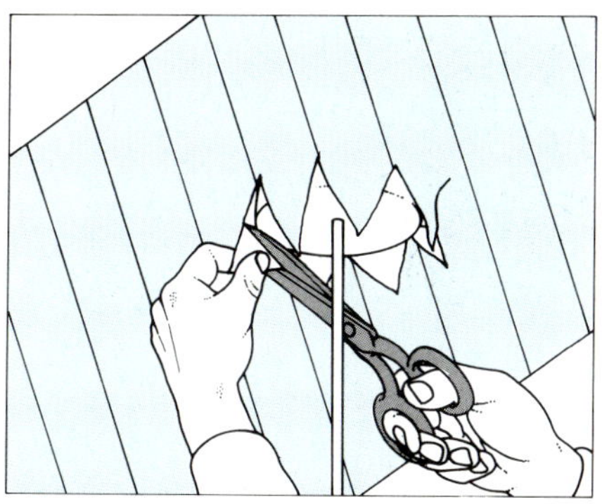

**6** Complete hanging that length of paper, brushing out air bubbles thoroughly. Trim off the flaps around the light fixture and brush the paper back neatly.

patterned wallcoverings should be hung parallel to the window, so the joins are less obvious. But don't give yourself the task of hanging paper parallel to the longest wall: the shorter the lengths the easier the paper is to manipulate.

You will need to mark a guideline on the ceiling for the first length, as far from the wall as the width of the paper minus 25mm (1in): this allows for you to overlap the paper on to the wall. If you will be painting the wall, you can trim this excess with a sharp knife. Use chalked string or a pencil, and measure at intervals to ensure the line is the same distance from the wall all along.

Measure, cut and paste the paper, folding it up concertina-fashion in an easy-to-handle size. Your task will be a great deal easier if you have someone to hold this as you attach the paper to the ceiling; otherwise support the concertina on a special holder, an up-turned broom or a spare roll of paper.

Gravity is against you, so work on one fold at a time, brushing it out quickly. Unfold the first piece of paper and align it with the chalked line on the ceiling so that 25mm (1in) overlaps on to the wall. Keep the rest of the paper as close to the ceiling as possible. Unfold and brush out the paper, fold by fold, all the way across the ceiling. Push the edges neatly into the wall or ceiling join. At each end mark a crease line and trim with a clean, sharp pair of wallpaper shears, allowing the paper to overlap the wall if you did this along the sides. Brush the edges of the paper back.

Hang the next strip in the same way, butt-joining the edge neatly up to the previous one but not overlapping it. When all the lengths are hung, smooth down the joins with a seam roller. (Do not do this with an embossed or textured paper.)

# Borders and Repairs

**WALLPAPER REPAIRS**

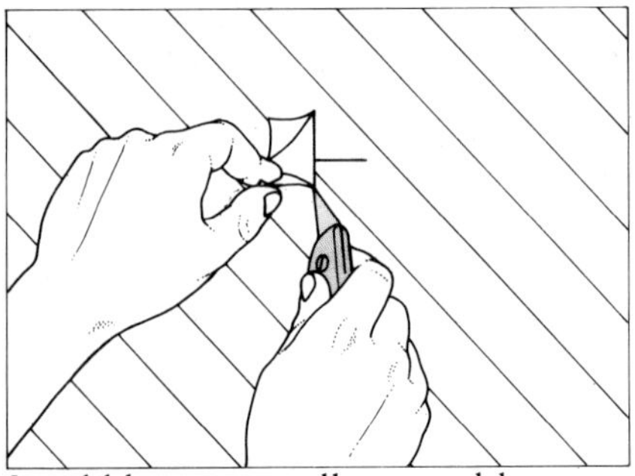

**1** Bubbles are usually caused by trapped air. If the paper has just been hung, lift the nearest edge and brush out the air. Otherwise, make two cuts across the bubble.

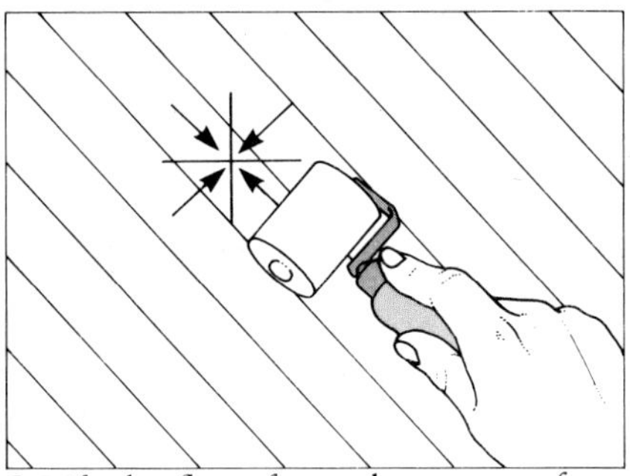

**2** Lift the flaps from the centre of the cuts, apply paste with a small brush, then press the flaps back on to the wall with a seam roller, working towards the centre.

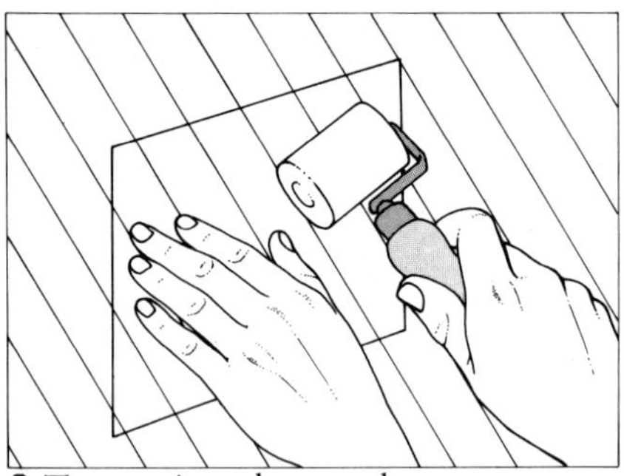

**3** To repair a damaged area, cut a matching patch through both thicknesses with a sharp knife – a scalpel or handyman's knife – remove the damaged piece and paste the patch in position.

## Wallpaper repairs

Bubbles or tears in patterned wallpapers can often be easily repaired, while plain papers may show your marks, so weigh up which will be most visually distracting, the imperfection or the repair.

Slit bubbles with a cross, using a handyman's knife. Paste with a little ordinary paste and roll down the flaps with a seam roller (press them down with your fingers if using an embossed or relief paper).

Patching a tear calls for a piece of left-over paper larger than the damaged area. Hold this against the wall, over the tear, and neatly cut round through both pieces of paper a short distance from the tear. Try to follow the edges of the paper design to minimize the chance of the patch looking obvious: cut carefully round a flower, for example. Remove the damaged piece of paper, soaking it if necessary, then paste the patch and position it. Go over with a seam roller if it is not embossed.

## Putting up borders

Decorative borders and friezes are very much in fashion. They can be used below the picture rail or to form an extra frieze just below the ceiling or cornice (crown moulding), or they can create the illusion of these features on a flat wall. They can be a powerful element in a decorative scheme, or a subtly pretty one.

Use a border to form a dado or chair rail, or to outline or emphasize an existing one. Borders can outline an attractive feature like a window or fireplace: even a bedhead or a built-in dresser can benefit from a border. They can help to trim a sloping ceiling or be used to form panels on a too-long or too-tall wall, to add interest or help adjust the proportions visually. To gauge the right effect, hold strips of paper against the wall as a trial run.

Borders come in different widths and in lots of different designs, and some may be part of a co-ordinated range of wallcoverings and fabrics. You can buy borders ready for use, or you may choose part of a full-width roll of paper and trim it yourself. Many have to be pasted, just like wallpaper, but there are also some self-adhesive borders. You could try creating your own personal border effects by using stencils.

Borders can be hung on top of painted or papered walls, but always make sure they are thoroughly dry before hanging the border. Mitre the corners properly and trim the curves (see diagrams). Borders with bold designs need to be centred on walls or projections such as chimneys, just like ordinary wallcoverings. You will need to draw guidelines using a try- or T-square to get the right angles correct and measuring assiduously between line and ceiling or nearest architectural feature (such as a window frame, floor, or fireplace), to make sure you have a true horizontal. Use a chalked string to mark the line. If you are hanging a border right up below a ceiling or cornice (crown moulding), you will need to compensate for any irregularities in the angle and line of these features: measure down in several places to the width of the border plus 25mm (1 in). Make marks with chalk, then join them up with a straightedge. Align the *lower* edge of the border on this guideline, thus giving yourself a gap of 25mm (1 in) to absorb discrepancies. This should prevent any problems with walls that are not true.

Use a seam roller sideways to press a border firmly into position. If you are hanging a border over a textured wallcovering, mark on the area to be covered, dampen this, then roll firmly with the seam roller *before* and after hanging the border.

## BORDERS

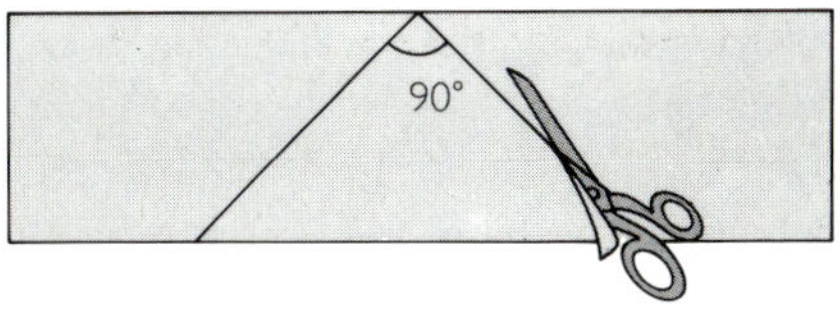


**1** Two mitre cuts at 45° to the edge form a right-angle corner.

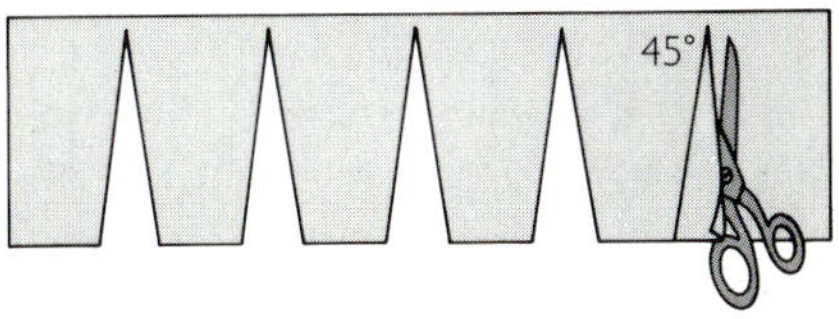


**2** A series of narrow V-shaped cuts will close up to form a curve.

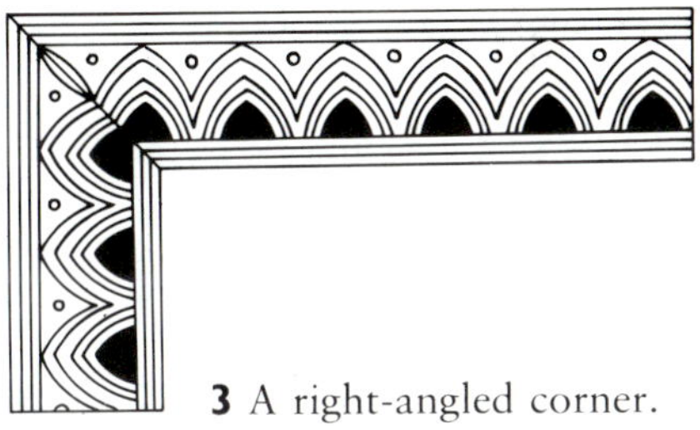

**3** A right-angled corner.

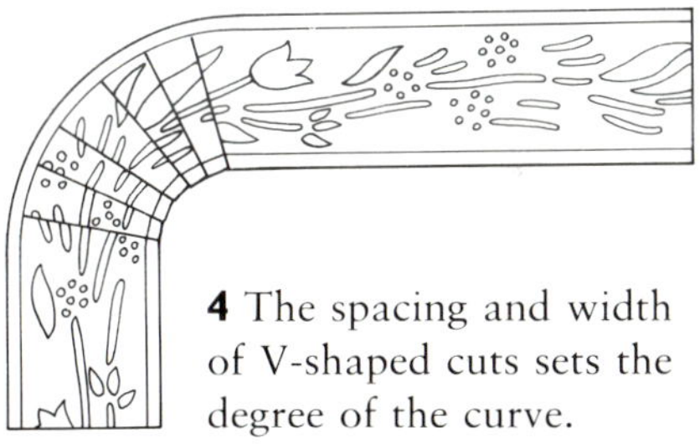

**4** The spacing and width of V-shaped cuts sets the degree of the curve.

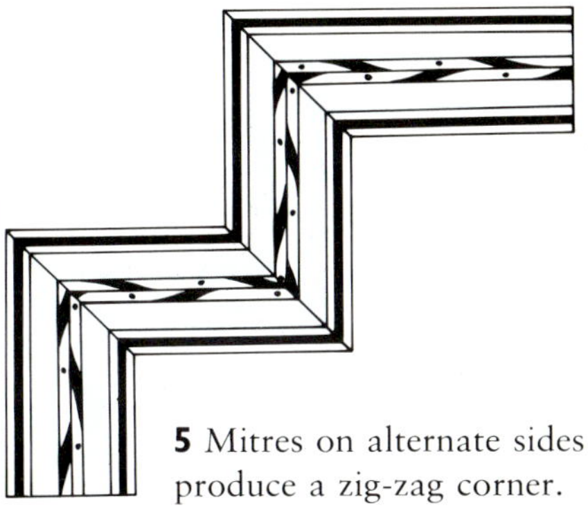

**5** Mitres on alternate sides produce a zig-zag corner.

*Borders can carry bolder, more highly patterned and more strongly coloured designs than you would want to risk on the wall itself.*

# WORKING WITH TILES

For texture, colour, pattern and practicality, tiles have enormous decorative potential for any interior designer, beginner or otherwise. They are hardwearing and can protect from water, heat and spillage from household chemicals; for these reasons they are commonly used in bathrooms and kitchens. But don't be constrained by convention. There is a wide range of tiles at your disposal – cork, brick, mosaic, mirror, vinyl, not to mention ceramic tiles in all their shapes and forms – suitable for any surface and almost any room in the house: the limit is your imagination and your pocket.

## Ceiling tiles

Only a few types are available: **Acoustic tiles** are designed to insulate a room from noise. They are heavily textured and are usually made from fibreboard for domestic use. **Polystyrene tiles** are the most popular embossed ceiling tile. They are lightweight, provide good insulation and can be ideal for kitchens and bathrooms where condensation can be a problem; some tiles are now fire retardant. Attach to sound ceilings with polystyrene tile adhesive and never paint with oil-based paint as they become a fire risk.

## Wall tiles

Many different effects can be achieved with wall tiles: **Brick tiles** are thin slivers of real or reconstituted brick used to face a wall to give a genuine brick-wall effect. These are attached with special adhesive. **Ceramic tiles** are the most popular, most common and potentially most gorgeous of all tiles. They are stuck to the wall with adhesive, then grouted to seal in the gaps. **Cork tiles** can be attached to a lined wall with adhesive but do not attach to a bare plastered wall as they can prove difficult to remove. The unsealed

*Far left: Bold tiles are mixed with plain ones to create walls that are lively and original as well as being extremely practical.*

*Above: Small coloured triangles on these tiles produce an effect of crisp, clean prettiness.*

*Left: Elegant tiles create a feature out of an otherwise ugly alcove, and help to cool down a potentially overheated space.*

types are best for walls. **Mirror tiles** are usually square or rectangular tiles made from plain or tinted mirror glass or plastic: see page 179. **Mosaic tiles** are small ceramic tiles that come on a mesh backing and are stuck with adhesive or embedded in mortar: see page 148. **Vinyl and plastic tiles** are made for walls and floors; the flooring type can be used on walls when a co-ordinated look is required, but not vice versa. Both types can be stuck with adhesive or are self-adhesive.

## Floor tiles

These are thicker and generally larger than wall tiles, and must be put down on a firm, dry, smooth subfloor to get the best finish. If laying them on a concrete floor, ensure it is brushed free of any loose flakes and is free of any dampness (get a professional to check for you). Check there is no 'spring' to timber floors and line them with hardboard, chipboard (particle board) or plywood sheets, sanding down any uneven joins between the sheets.

*Right: These modern, glazed tiles with chamfered edges give the faint look of brick – but in a very classy, highly polished incarnation. Their shape is echoed on all the surfaces in this bathroom, including the floor and the mirror, and all in unadorned black and white.*

*Opposite: Tiles in the faintest, softest of pinks are a similarly luxurious treatment in this bathroom. The simplest way to hang tiles diagonally is to nail a wooden strip along the bottom of the wall, as normal, a tile's width from the floor. Lay the tiles diagonally and fill in round the edges with half tiles, cut diagonally. Lay a row of uncut tiles at the bottom, square to the floor.*

Concrete or timber floors may occasionally benefit from a floor-levelling treatment, applied overall or just in the deepest hollows: use a cement- or latex-based one on a cement floor, and a latex-based one over plywood sheets (remember to prime them first).

The different types of tile available are: **Carpet tiles**: see page 172–3. **Ceramic floor tiles** are always thicker than wall tiles to cope with heavy use. They are virtually unbreakable, and have a non-slip surface. They can be glazed or unglazed (seal this type before use). Lay with either special ceramic floor tile adhesive, or embed in cement mortar. **Cork tiles** are warm and bouncy underfoot. The best type to buy are pre-sealed, although you can seal cork tiles with several coats of polyurethane varnish after laying. Always use sealed tiles in bathrooms or kitchens as they can push up when wet. Leave tiles in a room for two to three days to condition them, then stick with adhesive. **Linoleum tiles** come in a range of subtle colours and marbled effects. Stick to the subfloor with a special adhesive. **Quarry tiles** are unglazed ceramic tiles. They come in a range of warm, natural 'earth' tones. They are very durable and should be laid on a bed of mortar or special adhesive, then sealed with varnish or polish. **Vinyl tiles** come in two types – the solid vinyl sort or the more bouncy cushioned vinyl. They are laid with a special adhesive, and can be sealed or polished as recommended for extra durability.

## Tools and equipment

To achieve good tiling results the right tools and equipment are extremely useful. Soft tiles can just be cut with a straightedge and a handyman's knife, but you will need some specialist equipment for cutting hard tiles. Plastic spacers or matchsticks space ceramic wall tiles out from each other, unless they already have the spacer lugs incorporated.

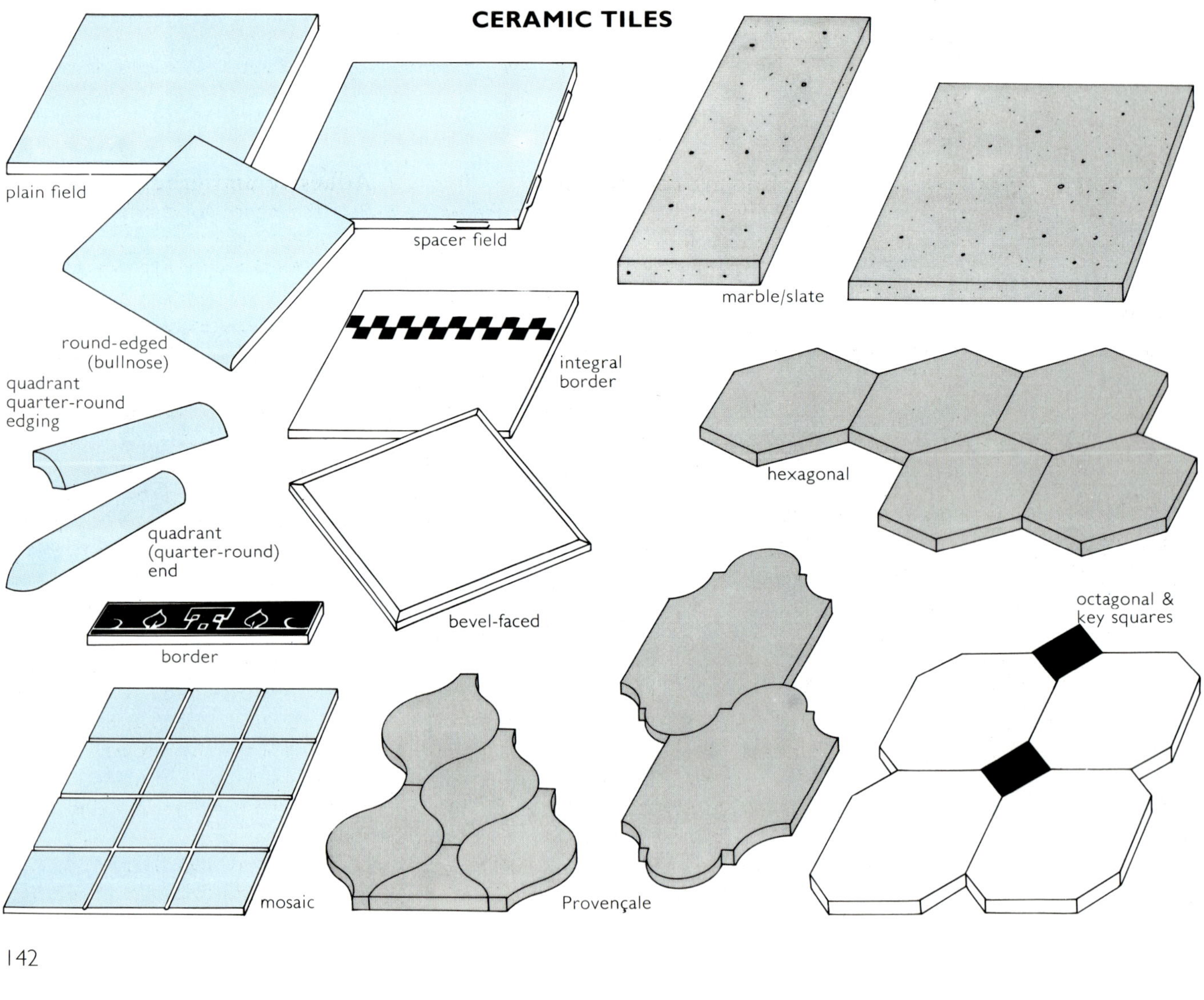

| | |
|---|---|
| GENERAL TOOLS | 76 |
| LINING FLOORS | 86 |
| CUTTING TILES | 144 |



## TILING EQUIPMENT

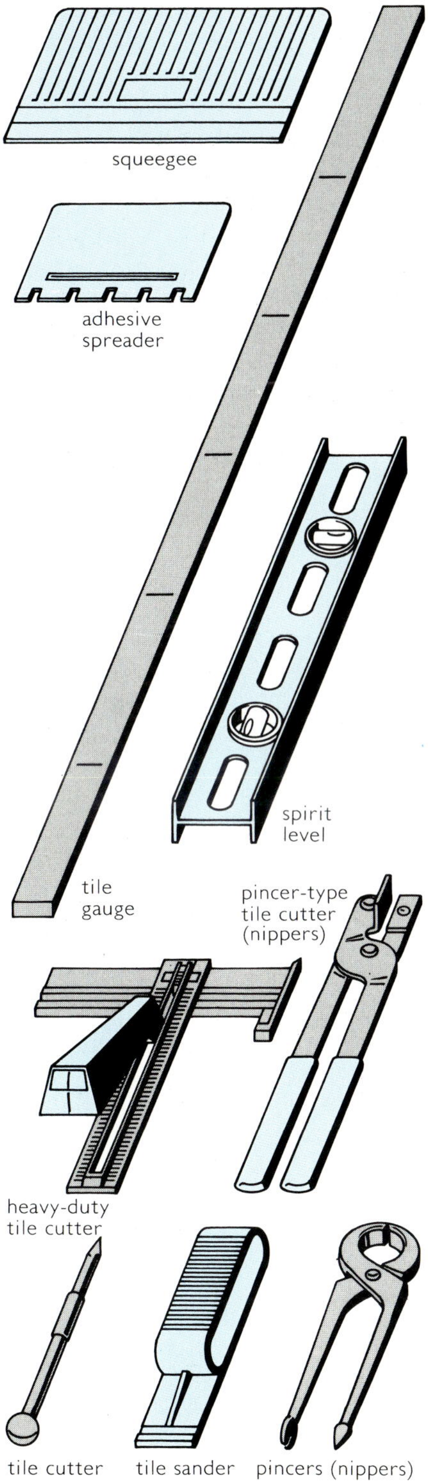


## ESTIMATING NUMBERS OF TILES

You can estimate all types of tiles in the same way. Make a plan of the room to be tiled and measure carefully, then work out how many tile widths you will need. For example, a 3 × 3m (10 × 10ft) room divided by the 30cm (12in) tiles needed works out at 10 tiles along both 3m (10ft) walls, so 10 × 10 = 100 tiles that are needed in all. Where obstructions occur, just divide the room into smaller areas and then work out the total. Always buy an extra five per cent to allow for areas which are not a whole number of tiles in either direction, and for some breakages.

| **Area to be Tiled** | | **Number of Tiles Needed** | | | |
|---|---|---|---|---|---|
| (SQ M) | (SQ FT) | 10 × 10cm (4¼ × 4¼in) | 15 × 15cm (6 × 6in) | 10 × 20cm (4 × 8in) | 30 × 30cm (12 × 12in) |
| 1 | 10½ | 100 | 45 | 50 | 12 |
| 2 | 21½ | 200 | 89 | 100 | 23 |
| 3 | 32 | 300 | 134 | 150 | 34 |
| 4 | 43 | 400 | 178 | 200 | 45 |
| 5 | 54 | 500 | 223 | 250 | 56 |
| 6 | 64½ | 600 | 267 | 300 | 67 |
| 7 | 75 | 700 | 312 | 350 | 78 |
| 8 | 86 | 800 | 356 | 400 | 89 |
| 9 | 97 | 900 | 400 | 450 | 100 |

### Cutting ceramic tiles

Different hard tile cutters are available – a simple cutter with a sharp tungsten carbide tip will be adequate for thin wall tiles. Another type scores the glaze with a cutting wheel and has jaws to hold the tile. When squeezed the tile breaks along the line. Other heavy-duty cutters are available which score and cut in one operation; some suppliers will also cut tiles for you. Wear protective gloves to cut tiles, and smooth with a file or carborundum stone.

For awkward cuts use a tile clipper, pincers, nippers or a tile saw. A tile file is a useful gadget for smoothing rough edges.

To fit tiles around pipes, draw the hole on the tile then cut the tile in two through the centre of the proposed hole. Chip or saw away the arc on each side of the tile. Apply adhesive to the backs of cut tiles round pipes or in awkward corners, rather than the wall.

### Adhesive and grout

Buy the correct proprietary adhesive to stick tiles to the wall or floor. For ceramic wall tiles this comes mixed or in powder form to mix yourself. Choose a waterproof type of both adhesive and grout if the tiles will be splashed regularly: the adhesive needs to be spread without ridges to prevent water seepage. Normal adhesive will need to be ridged with a notched spreader so that the tiles will stick firmly to the wall; it must be a uniform thickness if the tiles are going to lie flat. Press the spreader firmly against the wall, making the height of the ridges exactly the same. Leave tiles to set for 12–24 hours before removing the spacers; some types stay in place.

Grout comes pre-mixed or can be mixed yourself. It is used to fill the gaps between tiles. Coloured dyes are available to tint grout, perhaps to use with white tiles, or you can buy coloured grout pre-mixed.

# Tiling Walls

## TILING WALLS

Lay tiles only on a sound, level surface. Level small bumps with filler; if they are bad, you will have to replaster the wall or line it with plaster (gypsum) board. Seal bare plaster with a masonry sealant. Old tiles are a good base for new tiles if still firm.

Set out the wall with a tile gauge to give equal cut tiles each side of a window, for instance. Measure upwards from the lowest point of the surface to give a full tile at the top and temporarily nail a supporting strip of wood below the lowest whole tile mark. Mark a vertical guideline at one end.

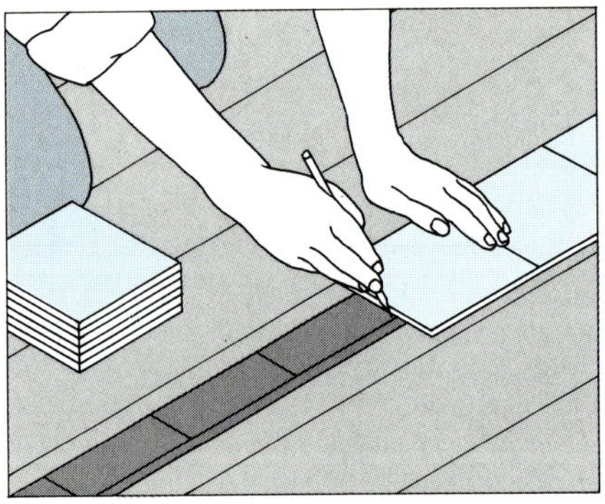

**1** To make a tile gauge, lay tiles along a strip of wood and mark; then allow a 1.5mm ($\frac{1}{16}$in) space between each.

**2** Measure with the tile gauge to arrange tiles symmetrically around fixtures, and mark across tiling row using a spirit level.

**3** Spread adhesive over an area of about 1sq m (10sq ft) at one time with a notched spreader or trowel.

**4** Lay the tiles with a twisting motion in horizontal courses, inserting spacers between each.

**5** To cut tiles, score the glaze using a tile cutter against a straightedge or tile to make straight even cuts.

**6** Place a match below the scored line and press down hard on both sides to snap the tile.

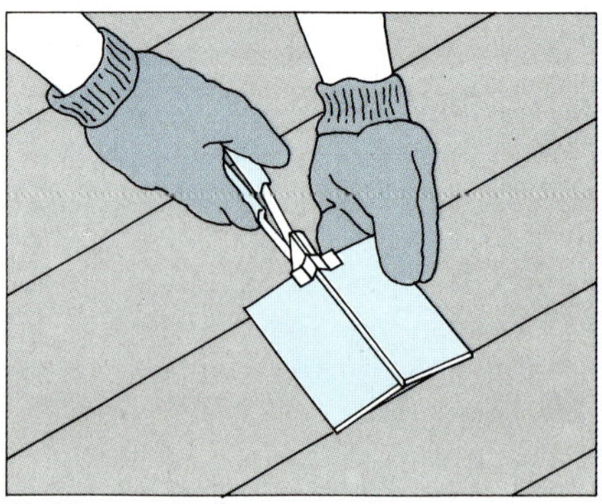

**7** Alternatively use a pincer-action tile cutter by scoring, and then snapping the tile in the jaws.

**8** Allow adhesive to set for the specified time, then apply grout with a squeegee, point joints and clean.

| | |
|---|---|
| REPOINTING | 22 |
| SURFACE PREPARATION | 74 |
| TOOLS AND MATERIALS | 143 |
| TILING COUNTERTOPS | 146 |

First, measure up the area to be tiled and calculate the number of tiles and the materials needed.

Many modern tiles have spacer lugs incorporated into the tile itself or bevelled edges: these allow you to get all the tiles evenly spaced one from another. Other types will need spacers pushed into the adhesive at the intersections, or you can push two spacer pegs or matchsticks along each edge of the tiles. Set corner and edging tiles to one side.

Prepare your surface, then plan your design carefully so that you end up having to cut as few tiles as possible. Your most helpful tool at this stage will be a wooden strip marked out with tile widths plus a 1.5mm ($\frac{1}{16}$in) gap between each tile all along its length. Use this to plan the way the tiles will fall: work from the centre of a wall or a fixture – perhaps a window – and plan so that cut tiles will come at the edges of your tiled area and not in the middle. Arrange tiles symmetrically around fixtures, ensuring that tiles around their edges will all be cut to the same width or depth. If you are incorporating tiles with border designs, perhaps following the line of a fixture, plan the wall vertically and allow for a row of cut tiles at the bottom, if necessary. Your main objective is to avoid having to cut small pieces out of your tiles – larger chunks are much easier. Hand-made ceramic tiles are different shapes and will need to be laid by eye.

*The drama in this bathroom comes from the choice of black and white for both tiles and towels, the row of black tiles at the top, and the co-ordinating glass in the window.*

With your wall planned out, nail a fresh wooden strip along the bottom of the area to be tiled, with its upper edge aligned on what will be the bottom edge of your lowest row of complete tiles. Make sure it is horizontal. Do this for tiling any small areas, such as above basins, too. Use a plumb-line to establish a vertical line at each end, and mark on the wall. Check the vertical rows frequently as you tile across the wall.

## TILING LEDGES

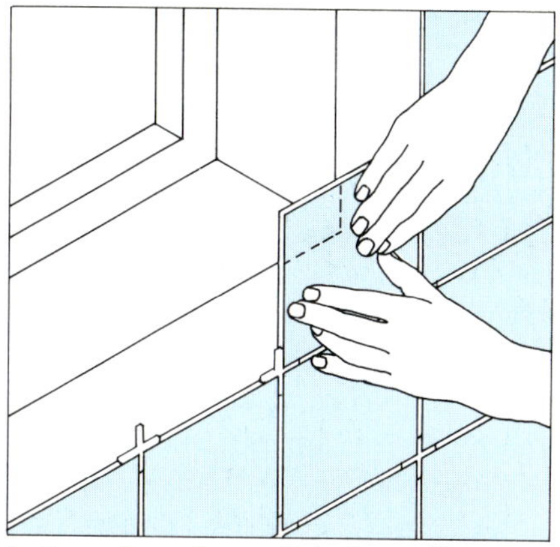

**1** Complete the wall before tiling a ledge. Hold corner tiles in place to mark the cutting lines needed.

**2** Score through the glaze along the lines with a tile cutter and nibble away the tile with pincers (nippers).

**3** Tile the ledge from front to back so that the round edge of the front tiles overhangs the wall tiles.

# Tiling Countertops

Tiled countertops in kitchens and bathrooms are both practical and decorative. Use ceramic tiles to continue a theme introduced on the walls or elsewhere: perhaps pick up a colour from a border tile, or even incorporate more border tiles in your countertop. If your walls are highly decorative, a plain countertop may make an elegant contrast. Quarry tiles are a popular alternative, and can be most attractive if used on the floor too. They are an unusual and effective choice for bathrooms. Mosaic tiles are another common and practical option. Edge them with a wooden strip, as described below.

Use flooring-grade tiles suitable for countertops; tell the supplier what you need them for. Tiles used near a cooking surface should be heat-resistant, or at least 9.5mm ($\frac{3}{8}$in) thick. A waterproof non-toxic and stain-resistant grout needs to be used for tiling countertops, in both bathroom and kitchen. It should also be used for tiling coffee tables, or similar items. The best is a two-part epoxy grout which dries hard. (Avoid skin contact.)

Edge your new tiled surface with a wooden strip or special curved 'nosing' tiles that will give a professional-looking finish. Edgings must be flush with the tiled surface.

You can tile over an existing laminated countertop, but remove any edging trim. Cover other finishes with a firm surface suitable for tiling, such as a layer of chipboard (particle board): prime porous surfaces with diluted PVA adhesive first. Always do a dummy run with dry tiles before spreading any adhesive.

If you are using wooden strips at the edge of the countertop, nail temporary guide strips in place of these first. Position your first row of tiles close to this strip and work from front to back so that any cut

## TILING COUNTERTOPS

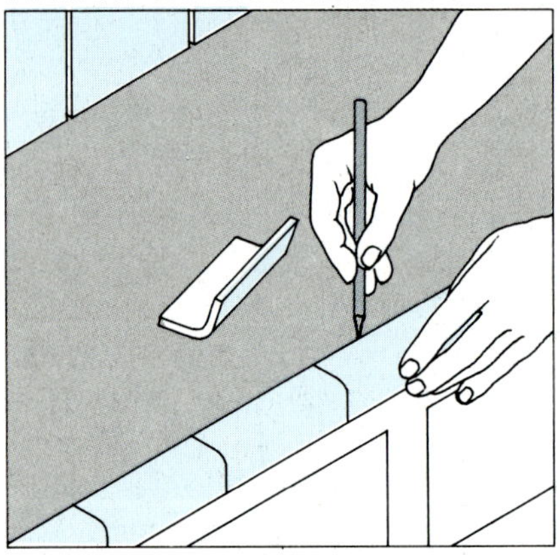

**1** Loose-lay quarter-round edging tiles along front of countertop and mark along inner edge.

**2** Remove the edging tiles, nail a temporary strip of wood outside the line, and tile backwards from it.

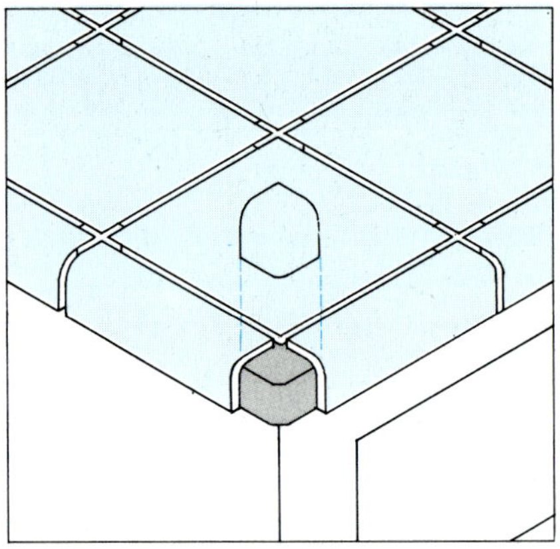

**3** Remove the strip and lay the edging tiles. Trim off an external corner and lay the corner piece.

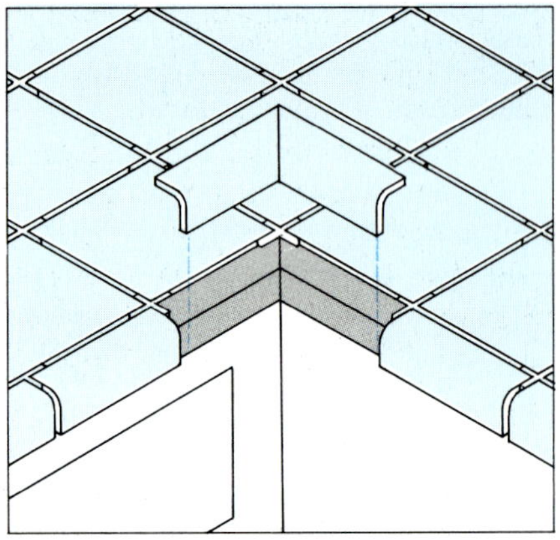

**4** Internal corners require two mitred corner pieces. Grout all joints to complete the job.

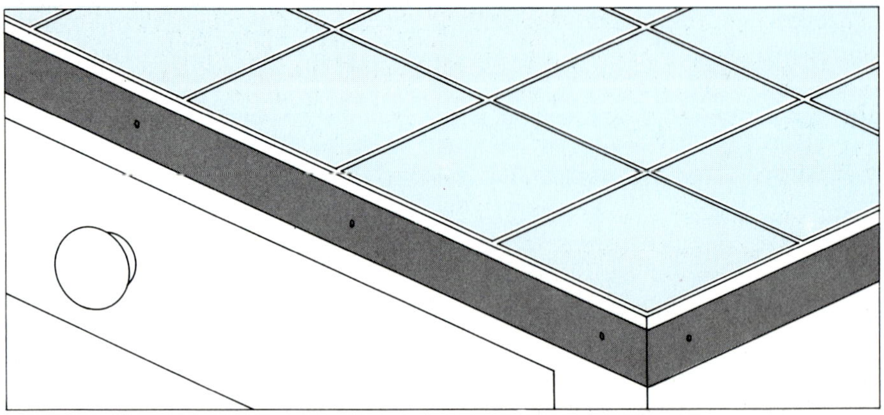

**5** To edge tiles with hardwood, nail guide strips to the edges of the countertop, protruding above it. Tile back from these and then replace them by hardwood strips mitred at the corners and flush with the top.

tiles fall at the back of the countertop. Make sure that the short edges of a countertop have whole tiles at the free end and cut ones against the wall. (Don't cut them yet.) Once you are satisfied with the tiles laid dry, spread your adhesive and lay them properly, cutting the tiles at the back.

If you are using curved nosing tiles, place these in position, dry, along the edge of the countertop. Mark the line with a pencil to give you your first row of complete tiles and then do a complete dry run. Fit a wooden strip up to your pencil line and nail this in position. Spread the recommended adhesive across the countertop, and lay the first row of tiles along the longest edge. Cut tiles should fall against the wall.

When the tiles are all stuck down and spaced carefully, remove the wooden strip, spread adhesive along the edge and set the edging tiles in position. Make sure you align these with the tiles already stuck down so that you will get continuous grout lines. Finally position any corner pieces, both internal and external, at the end – it may be necessary to cut away the corner of an existing countertop underneath to get a really good fit on an external corner.

If you are using wooden strips to finish the edges, remove your temporary ones when the tiling is done and nail on a hardwood strip with its top edge flush with the tiles. If it is to be painted, do this first.

When the adhesive is completely dry, normally in 12 to 24 hours, remove the spacers, wipe the surface and apply the grout. Make sure it is well compacted and flush.

*Decorative tiles carried round the walls and onto the work surfaces give this kitchen its French look. Colours harmonize throughout the scheme, even on the serving dishes.*

# Speciality Tiles

## Mosaic tiles

Mosaic tiles are small and sometimes irregularly shaped colourful tiles, which may be used on walls and countertops. They are easy to work with, as they come in sheets on a mesh backing, sometimes as large as 33 × 50cm (13 × 20in). The backing is printed with little arrows for easy planning: they should all face the same way. Some types have protective paper covering the face of the tiles – leave this on until the tiles are set firmly.

As with other tiling, you need a firm, level, dry surface, and careful planning is, as always, essential. Work out the layout before spreading any adhesive or doing any cutting: use a marked tiling gauge as before. If you are using sheets of square mosaic tiles, you will also need to line them up from sheet to sheet at the corners and on any edges to match them. (This is not necessary with irregularly shaped ones.) Mark horizontal and vertical guidelines on the wall or countertop, and nail a horizontal wooden strip at the bottom of the area to be tiled. Spread the adhesive and lay the complete sheets first, then the cut ones around the edges.

To fit edges, corners and awkward shapes, cut to fit or make a template with card and then cut through the mesh backing from the front, using a straightedge and a sharp handyman's knife. You may find it difficult to fit them accurately; if so, peel one or two individual mosaics off the mesh backing and slip them into small or narrow spaces. They are very difficult to cut, so fill gaps with grouting.

Complete the job by peeling off any facing paper and grouting between the joints, using special epoxy grout or the type recommended.

*Mosaic tiles can provide powerful details in stark, unadorned rooms. The recessed shelf in this bathroom picks up the mosaic tiled floor.*

**MOSAIC TILES**

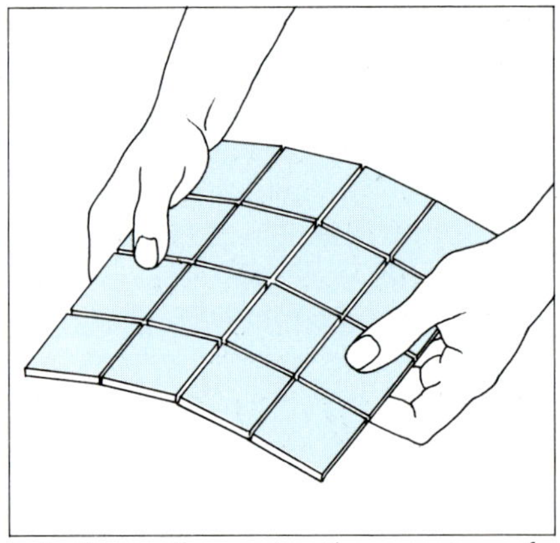

**1** A sheet of mosaic tiles consists of a number of tile squares fixed to a mesh backing.

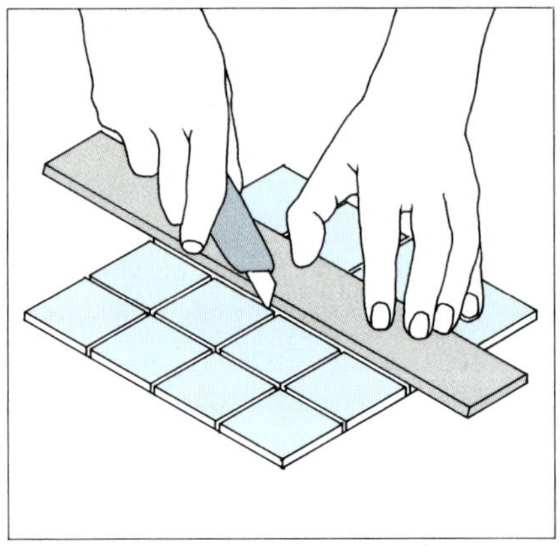

**2** Cut through the mesh with a sharp knife for borders, cutting from the front with a straightedge.

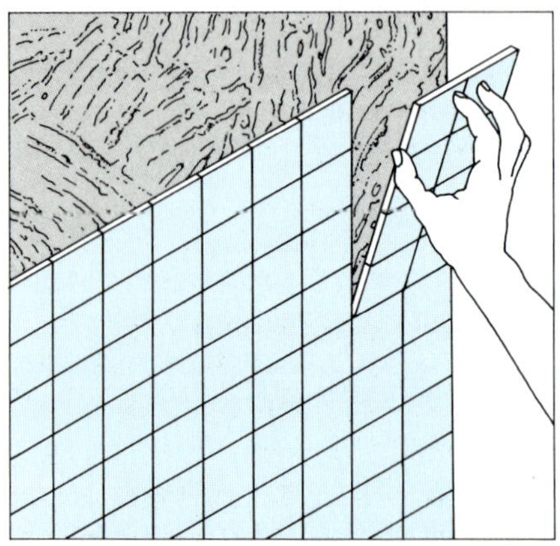

**3** Spread adhesive on the wall and lay the sheets, leaving the mesh backing in place, then grout.

| | |
|---|---|
| PLASTIC PLUGS | 42 |
| TOOLS | 76, 143 |
| CUTTING TILES | 143 |
| TILING COUNTERTOPS | 146 |
| WOOD CLADDING | 162 |



## Mirror tiles

These sometimes come as square tiles in the same sizes as ceramic wall tiles, although there are rectangular and larger types available. Mirror tiles can help to bring reflected light into a dark corner and can appear to magnify the size of a room or the surface on which they are placed. They are much easier to cut and attach than sheet mirror, and are less expensive, but be wary of using them in a steamy bathroom where they can cause condensation. They look very effective combined with ceramic wall tiles but make sure the thicknesses are the same. In a bathroom without a window they can be arranged in a rectangular panel to suggest one.

Like all other tiles they should be attached to a firm, dry and level surface, as any bumps in the plaster will cause distortion – this will be very distracting. If necessary, cover the wall first with chipboard (particle board) or plywood to get a perfectly flat surface. Mirror tiles are usually fixed by means of self-adhesive sticky tabs, so always let any newly-plastered walls dry out thoroughly first. Strip off any wallpaper and seal porous surfaces with a coat of oil-based primer.

The tiles should be perfectly aligned, so mark the wall with guidelines and pin a wooden strip to the bottom of the wall. Some tiles come with the sticky tabs stuck to the back and protected with a facing paper; with other types the tabs come separately: use four on a square tile and six on a rectangular one. Peel off the protective paper from one tile at a time, and stick in place in horizontal rows from the bottom of the wall upwards. Leave a narrow gap between each tile but make sure you align them perfectly. No grouting is necessary with mirror tiles. Press them into position over the tabs, not in the middle of the tile. Check the verticals regularly with a plumb-line, and the horizontals with a spirit level. Check also for any distortion as you go along, and if necessary take off any tiles and replace them. If you have to cut any of the mirror tiles, use the same technique as for cutting ceramic tiles, but use a glass-cutter and a straightedge. Always protect your hands with gloves. (Alternatively, you can have tiles cut by your supplier.) To attach larger sheets of mirror you can use special screws or fasteners (see fig. 3), in which case ask a glazier to drill four corner holes and provide nylon sleeves for inserting the screws; or secure a mirror without holes with fixed and sliding clips (see fig. 2).

*Mirrors always give the impression of extra space, and tiles break up the reflections, making the illusion less obtrusive.*

**MIRROR TILES**

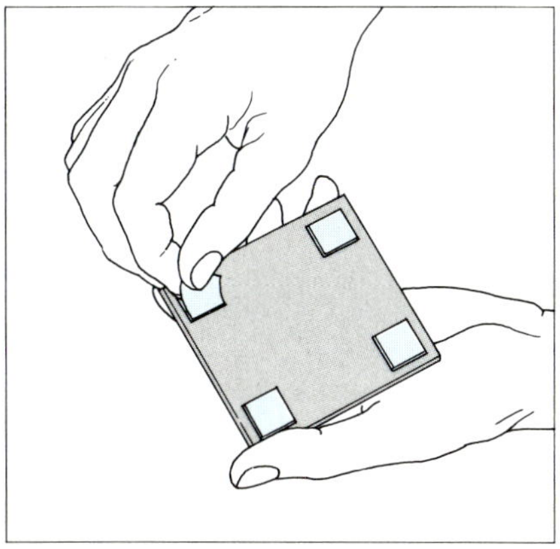

Stick a self-adhesive pad to each corner of a mirror tile and press it on to a perfectly flat surface.

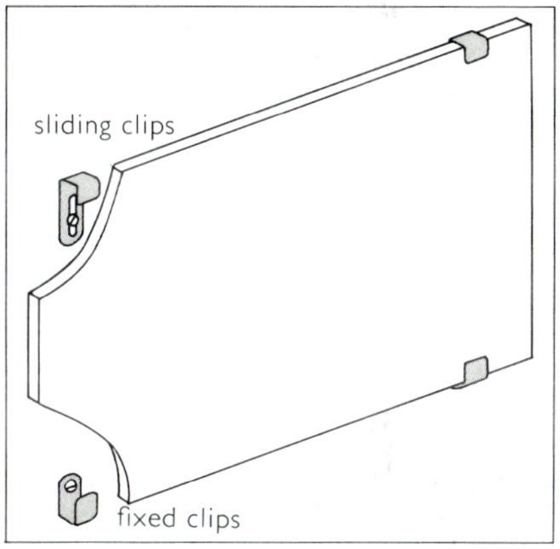


Screw four clips to the wall, place the mirror in the bottom clips and slide down the top ones to hold it.

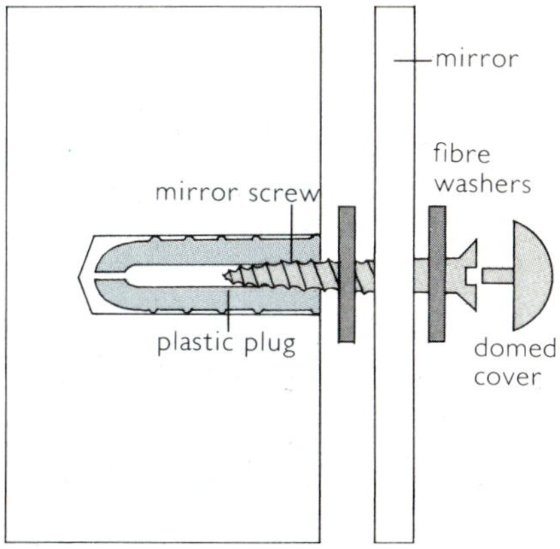


Secure a drilled mirror with domed-head mirror screws through plastic sleeves. Do not overtighten.

# Tiling Floors

There are various different types of floor tile available, from simple loose-lay carpet tiles to interlocking ceramic ones. All floor tiles need to be laid on a properly prepared subfloor which is level, smooth, rigid and damp-free.

## Marking out the floor

With all floor tiles you must first plan properly and square up the floor. Plan your layout of tiles from the middle of the room and work outwards towards the edges: this will give you a smooth fit in the centre, and equal-sized (cut if necessary) tiles at the corners and around the edges. With soft floor tiles you will be planning the layout of the tiles in this way too.

Find the centre points of two facing walls by measuring, nail a chalked string line across the room between these, and snap it. Do the same for the other dimension, and where the lines intersect in the middle is the centre of the floor.

Once the centre is established, try a dummy run to see how the tiles will fall. Place the first tile in the right angle formed by the intersecting lines. Lay tiles across the room, working outwards and following the guidelines, until you reach the wall. You will then see whether you have to cut tiles all around the edge, and by how much. You don't want to have to cut small fractions off tiles, so

*Floor tiles can be a flexible and powerful decorative element. Arrange vinyl tiles to delineate one area from another (above, right), or carry them over onto other surfaces to unify the whole scheme, as in this cork-tiled bathroom (right). Ceramic tiles are often overlooked as a medium for living rooms, but softened with a few colourful rugs they can make a clean and dramatic statement (opposite).*

| | |
|---|---|
| PREPARING FLOORS | 86, 140 |
| MARKING OUT THE FLOOR | 152 |
| RUGS | 178 |

adjust the guidelines with fresh chalked string to give you a reasonable fraction of a tile at each edge. Don't cut any tiles yet: walls are rarely perfectly true.

Always lay tiles working towards the door so you do not get trapped.

## Laying soft floor tiles

Whichever type of soft floor tile you are using, the basic laying principles are the same; you may, however, need to seal, stain or polish them as appropriate when in position.

Always work out your laying plan first and test the height of the tiles you are using against the door: you might well have to plane the bottom of the door slightly to fit over the tiles if they are quite thick.

A level floor is important, as always, but you can get away with very minor discrepancies with soft floor tiles. Cover floorboards with hardboard panels, rough side upwards, and prime with an oil-based primer. Check for unevenness by moving a wooden strip across the surface and noting if it rocks; correct if necessary.

**Lino, vinyl and plastic tiles** Some of these, particularly vinyl ones, may be self-adhesive and covered by a protective backing paper. Do not remove this until you are ready to lay the tiles, then peel and stick one at a time. If you are laying tiles with an adhesive, use whatever type is recommended.

Square up and mark out the way the tiles will fall. Starting at the centre, spread the adhesive over an area of about 1 square metre or yard using a serrated spreader, and push the tiles firmly down on to the adhesive, butting the edges up closely. Then lay the next section. Work outwards, laying all the whole tiles first before cutting tiles to fit around the edges of the room.

If making a straight cut, place the

### LAYING SOFT FLOOR TILES

**1** Mark the mid-point of opposite walls and snap chalk lines between them to find the centre of the floor. Loose-lay tiles from the centre outwards: if this leaves a gap of less than half a tile at the edge, make a new centre line half a tile width further from the wall.

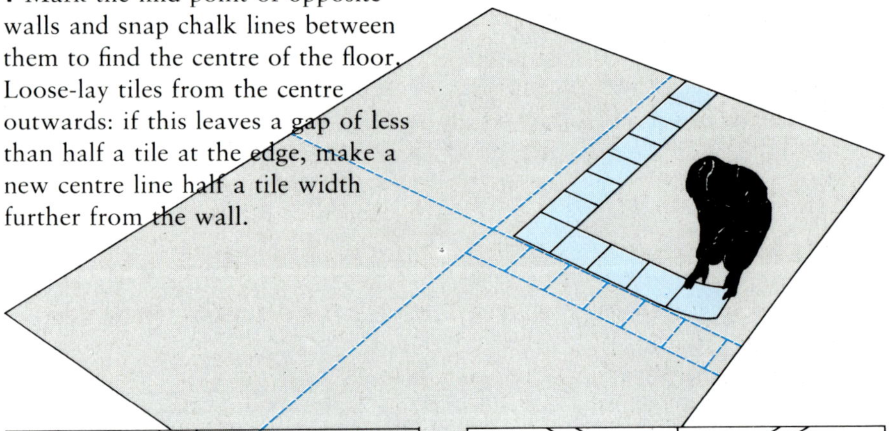

**2** Start tiling from the new centre outwards. Spread adhesive over an area of 1sq m (10sq ft) at a time and lay the tiles to align exactly with the chalk lines.

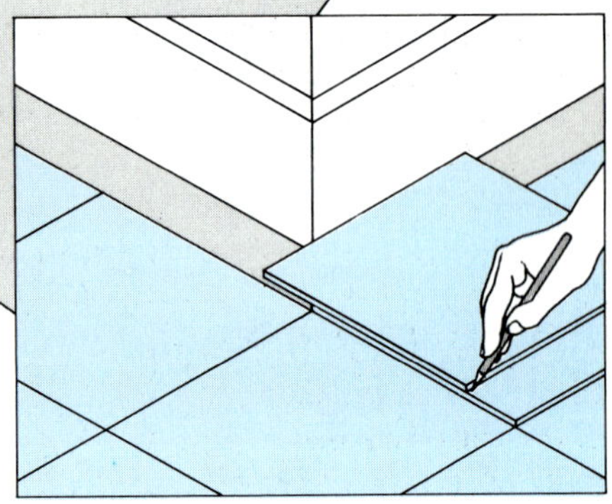

**3** At corners, lay the tile to be cut over the last full tile. Partly cover this with a full tile butting up to the skirting (baseboard) and mark a line along the tile to be cut.

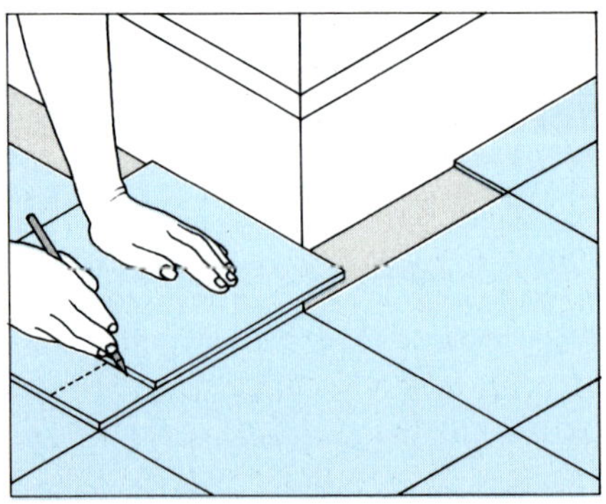

**4** Without turning the tile to be cut, move it to cover the last full tile on the other side of the corner and repeat the process. Cut away the waste with a sharp knife.

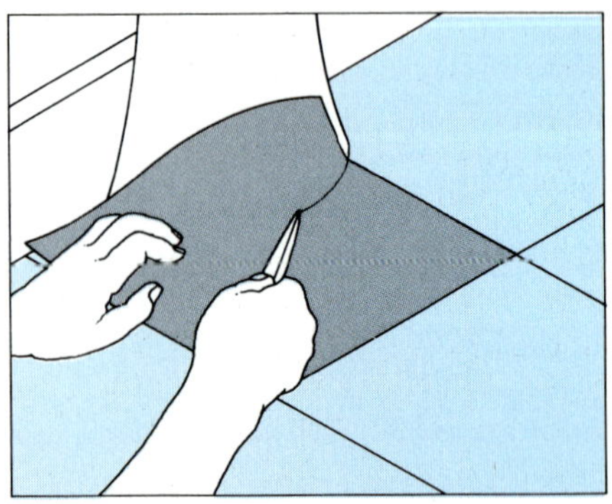

**5** To fit tiles around an awkward shape such as a washbasin pedestal, first make a template from stiff paper, pushed into the angles, and use this to mark the cutting lines.

| | |
|---|---|
| PREPARING FLOORS | 86, 140 |
| TYPES OF TILE | 140 |
| TOOLS AND MATERIALS | 143 |
| THE TILING GAUGE | 144 |
| THE PROFILE GAUGE | 183 |



tile to be cut exactly over the last full tile, as with ceramic tiles. Use another uncut tile pushed against the wall as a template, and mark on the cutting line. You can cut flexible vinyl tiles with scissors, but lino and hard plastic must be cut with a sharp handyman's knife and a straightedge. Cut self-adhesive tiles with the backing paper still in position. If there are difficult projections to get round, like door mouldings, use a profile gauge with sliding metal rods that adjust when you push them against the wall. This will give you an outline to trace and cut. Alternatively, make a template from card. To fit a tile round a pipe, make a template, then cut out the hole on the tile and cut a slit from it to the tile edge. This should be nearly invisible when stuck down.

When the floor is laid, cover with a protective seal, if required, working backwards towards the door. Leave to dry as directed.

**Cork tiles** These are laid in exactly the same way as lino and vinyl tiles, but you will need to use a special adhesive. Take care not to get any adhesive on the face of the tile, and if it squeezes up as you butt the tiles together, wipe it away immediately. Always protect unsealed cork tiles with polyurethane varnish if laying them in a bathroom or kitchen.

## Ceramic floor tiles

Ceramic tiles for floors are best laid on a concrete floor. Make sure it is flat and firm, and free of any damp spots or flakes of loose matter. If it is very uneven (test with a long wooden strip and see if it rocks from side to side) you may need to apply a floor-levelling compound first. If you want to lay ceramic tiles on a wooden floor, it must be well ventilated and have no suspicion of dampness in the subfloor. Before you start, line your floor with hardboard, plywood or chipboard (particle board) sheets and sand joints for a flat surface. Prime with thinned PVA adhesive to stop the tile adhesive drying out too quickly, and if necessary fill any hollows with self-smoothing latex-based screed.

Choose tiles appropriate to your location: glazed surfaces can become slippery when wet, for example in a kitchen or bathroom – a matt finish is better. Begin, as for other tiles, by planning your design with a dummy run. Mark up the floor with the aid of a tiling gauge marked out in tile widths – allow for 3mm ($\frac{1}{8}$in) between each tile. Check the final height, and adjust doors if necessary by planing a little off the bottom.

With the centre of your room established, and the width of the space for cut tiles round the edge adjusted, nail a wooden strip right along one wall, with its innermost edge along the line of what will be the last row of complete tiles. Do the same along an adjoining wall, and check that the angle between them is exactly 90°. The 'frame' will ensure straight rows of tiles in both directions. Start tiling in the corner of the 'frame': you have already planned the tiles to ensure they are centred on the floor.

Ceramic floor-tile adhesive normally comes in large plastic buckets, and should be prepared to the manufacturer's instructions and stirred if necessary. Spread adhesive on the floor over a small area at a time – about 1 square metre or yard – and use a special notched trowel to ensure a uniform thickness. Use spacers or matchsticks between the tiles if they are not the self-spacing type.

*Vinyl tiles are the perfect option if you are looking for a practical but decorative floor. Hallways are one good place, (above), kitchens another (left).*

Check the tiles are level frequently as you work using a spirit level.

When you have laid all the tiles, cut the border tiles to fit. Place the tile to be cut over the last whole tile and place another whole tile on top of this, butting up to the wall. Mark a line 3mm ($\frac{1}{8}$in) outside the edge of the top tile on to the middle tile. Cut the tiles in the same way as wall tiles, wearing gloves. Spread adhesive on the cut tiles, not on the floor.

As you complete sections of tiling, remove any surplus adhesive from the face of the tiles and keep the joints clean. When the whole floor is finished, leave the adhesive for at least 24 hours to set before grouting. If you cannot grout without standing on the tiles, leave the floor to set for about 48 hours.

Use a pre-mixed or powder floor grout. Apply as for wall tiles and make sure the grouting is flush with the tiles. Leave for about two hours until the grout has set and then wipe over the tiles with a damp cloth. Leave for a further 48 hours before walking on the floor.

### Laying Quarry Tiles

Thick quarry tiles should be laid on a very firm, concrete floor, and are embedded in mortar rather than glued to the floor. Lay a sharp sand and cement screed between battens to ensure the surface is level.

Plan the tiles as before, centring them on the floor and adjusting the space at each edge for cut tiles. Make sure your measuring strip includes a 3mm ($\frac{1}{8}$in) gap between each tile if they are not self-spacing.

Nail 50 × 25mm (2 × 1in) wooden strips along the lines of the last rows

*The warmth and texture of quarry tiles is unbeatable, whether you are looking to tile a bathroom – as here, where practicality is also at a premium – a kitchen or a hallway.*

## QUARRY TILES

**1** Lay the tiles in bays, four tiles wide, set out with strips of wood fixed to the floor.

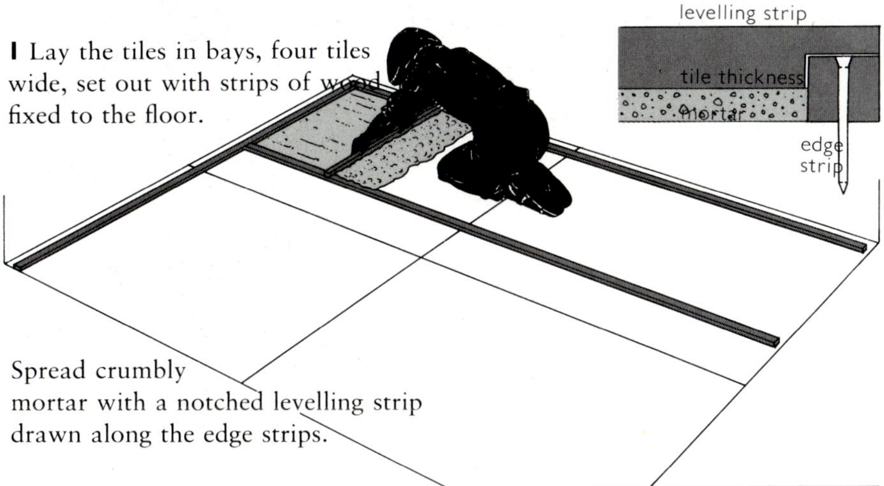


Spread crumbly mortar with a notched levelling strip drawn along the edge strips.

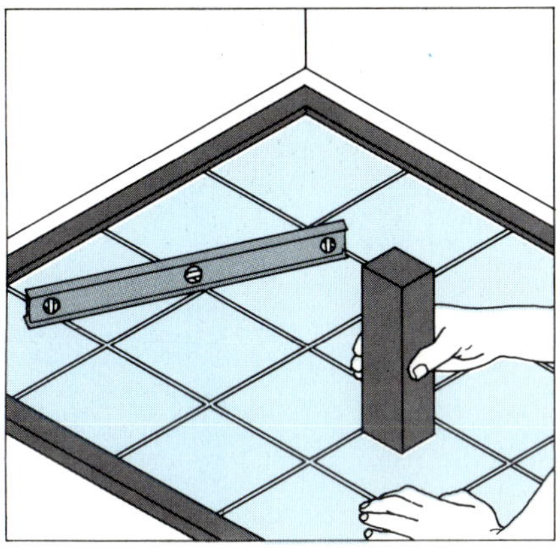

**2** After completing one bay, tamp down the tiles with a block of wood and check that they are level.

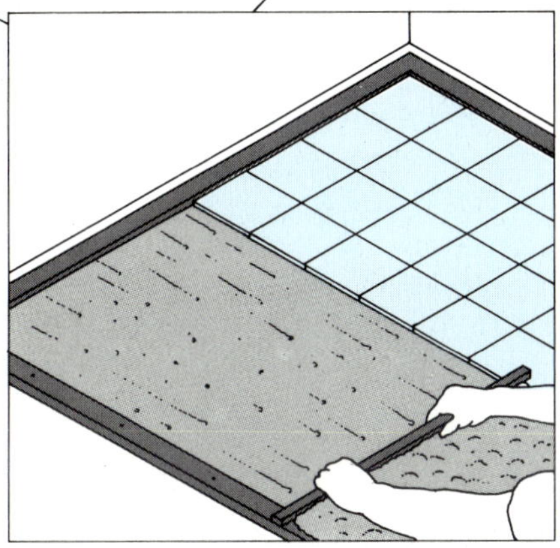

**3** Move one edge strip across to form a second bay, spread mortar, and continue in this way.

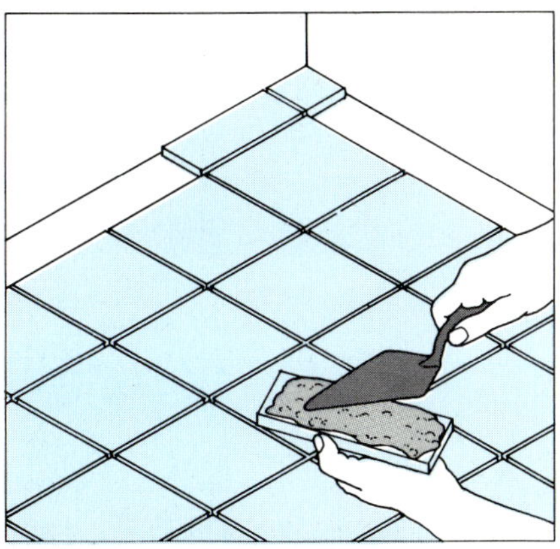

**4** When all the whole tiles are laid, butter the back of cut tiles with mortar to complete the edges.

**5** After at least 24 hours, mix up a creamy flooring grout and sponge it into the gaps between the tiles.

of complete tiles, and check the angle between them is 90° – this is as for ceramic tiles. Again, you will start to lay them from a corner, but this time you will work in strips four tiles wide. Mark this distance out from one strip, and nail down a third strip: check the two are exactly parallel and exactly flush. Into this space spread your mortar, about 13–15mm ($\frac{1}{2}$–$\frac{5}{8}$in) thick. To level this you need a further strip of wood. It should be wide enough to reach from the outside edges of your two parallel strips, and have a step cut into each end: this step must be as wide as the strips nailed to the floor and as deep as the thickness of the tile. Draw this along to level the mortar.

Bed the tiles in the mortar, tamping down with a small block of wood and checking the level with a spirit level. Wash off any mortar from the face of the tiles before moving your wooden strip along to do another 4-tile-wide strip. The border tiles should be cut last. (There are also tiles available for the edges, that do the job of a skirting board or baseboard for you.) Leave the tiles to dry for 24 to 48 hours and then grout with a cement-based grout.

Quarry tiles are harder to cut than ceramic tiles, and you will need to allow extra tiles as you may break a few. Score the front with a tile cutter, and tap the back of the tile along the score line with a small hammer. If you have a lot of tiles to cut it is a good idea to buy, hire or rent a heavy-duty tile cutter.

A quarry-tiled floor will benefit greatly from a polish with liquid wax floor polish; this if often specifically recommended in any case, as the tiles may be porous. Use a non-slip, transparent type, to let the natural colour and texture of the tiles show through. You can also use a proprietary quarry-tile sealant or perhaps a polyurethane varnish.

# WORKING WITH WOOD

Despite many recent innovations wood is still one of the most versatile materials used in house building. Its structural properties are well appreciated in construction work but its pleasing decorative value is often under-estimated. The natural look of wood can do much to enhance the appearance of any room, whether it is used in the furniture or the fixtures. If you already own some attractive old wooden furniture, such as bookcases, bureaux or tables and chairs, you will know what warmth they add to your home.

If some of your furniture has been damaged or badly neglected there is much that can be done to restore it to its former glory. Renovated pieces will add style and individuality to even the most uninspiring room, but you do not have to stop there. Often the theme can be continued into the general decorations by stripping painted doors and mouldings back to the wood, particularly if they are intricate and ornate. Windows, always an important feature, are often a key pointer to the character of a home. The range of protective finishes now available makes all these features suitable for stripping down.

The kitchen and bathroom can benefit from the introduction of bare, but well protected, wood. Wooden countertops can look superb in the right setting and make a refreshing change from man-made laminates. They must be sealed to improve their durability. Structural beams in a conservatory, for example, can be left exposed and highlighted by a glass roof. Knock-through openings and arches can be made striking features in themselves if you have the opening faced with wood panels; alternatively, you could leave some structural wooden beams uncovered, but always get a professional in to do the work.

*The natural warmth and colours of wood can be used in all sorts of ways in your decoration. In the kitchen (above and opposite, below right), it will soften and enliven a traditionally stark and hard-working environment, while making a suitable material for countertops. Don't forget that furniture plays a decorative role as well as a functional one (opposite, above): stripped and refurbished examples can be made into the central feature in a scheme. Wood has a practical function, too. The archway made by knocking two rooms into one (opposite, below left) could be faced with wood painted in a contrasting colour, giving you an exciting architectural shape.*

# Laminate Alternatives

Durability and ease of cleaning have long made laminates ideal to use for kitchen and bathroom surfaces.

Practically any surface will take a laminate but if it is smooth it must be lightly sanded to provide a key. Countertops and shelves, unless securely attached on to a kitchen cabinet or table, will gradually curl up if they are laminated on one side only. Attach a balancing laminate on the under-side, which can be of lower quality than that used on the top.

For the beginner, it is best to use a time-delayed impact adhesive when gluing laminates to the top surface: this gives you a minute or so to move the sheet around. Cut the sheets with a special blade in a handyman's knife, making them slightly larger than needed. Gently plane off the excess after the sheet is stuck – this can be quite a fiddly process and must be done accurately.

*Laminates are often best used in a way that seems to exploit the personality of the material itself: so bold, modern treatments in monochromatic colours (right and opposite) are somehow inherently right and appropriate. Pastel colours can be just as successful, however, and often more welcoming in a bathroom (above).*

# Equipment and Repairs

A good, basic set of tools is quite sufficient for the beginner to tackle simple woodworking jobs (see opposite). Always clean and oil them well and they will perform successfully.

These days it is possible to buy a good quality fine-toothed hand saw for very little money – choose a hard-tipped one that will not need re-sharpening. A general rule worth remembering is to let the saw do the work. Forcing a saw through a piece of wood will produce an uneven cut and ruin the saw. Make sure the material is dry before you cut it. If it binds or sticks, coat the saw blade with wax by rubbing it with a candle.

A surform plane with throw-away blades will save any re-sharpening. Never place a plane down on a work surface with its blade touching as you might blunt it. If you haven't used a plane before, practise first on a piece of scrap timber.

Always hold your wood or other material steady while you work. Ideally, you should use a workbench but an old table and a couple of clamps is a good substitute.

Finally, remember to measure twice and you will only need to cut once: it's a rule that even the most experienced carpenter follows.

## Old furniture

One of the joys of setting up a new home is snooping around second-hand furniture shops looking for bargains. Often this turns out to be furniture that needs restoring.

The results of your hard work will be very rewarding; but do take a good look to see what repairs may be necessary before you buy – and avoid anything with woodworm. Often all that is needed in the way of repairs is some glue to hold the joints together. Rickety dining room chairs are a good item for the beginner. The joints can be quite easily taken apart and reglued with white

**WOODWORKING EQUIPMENT**

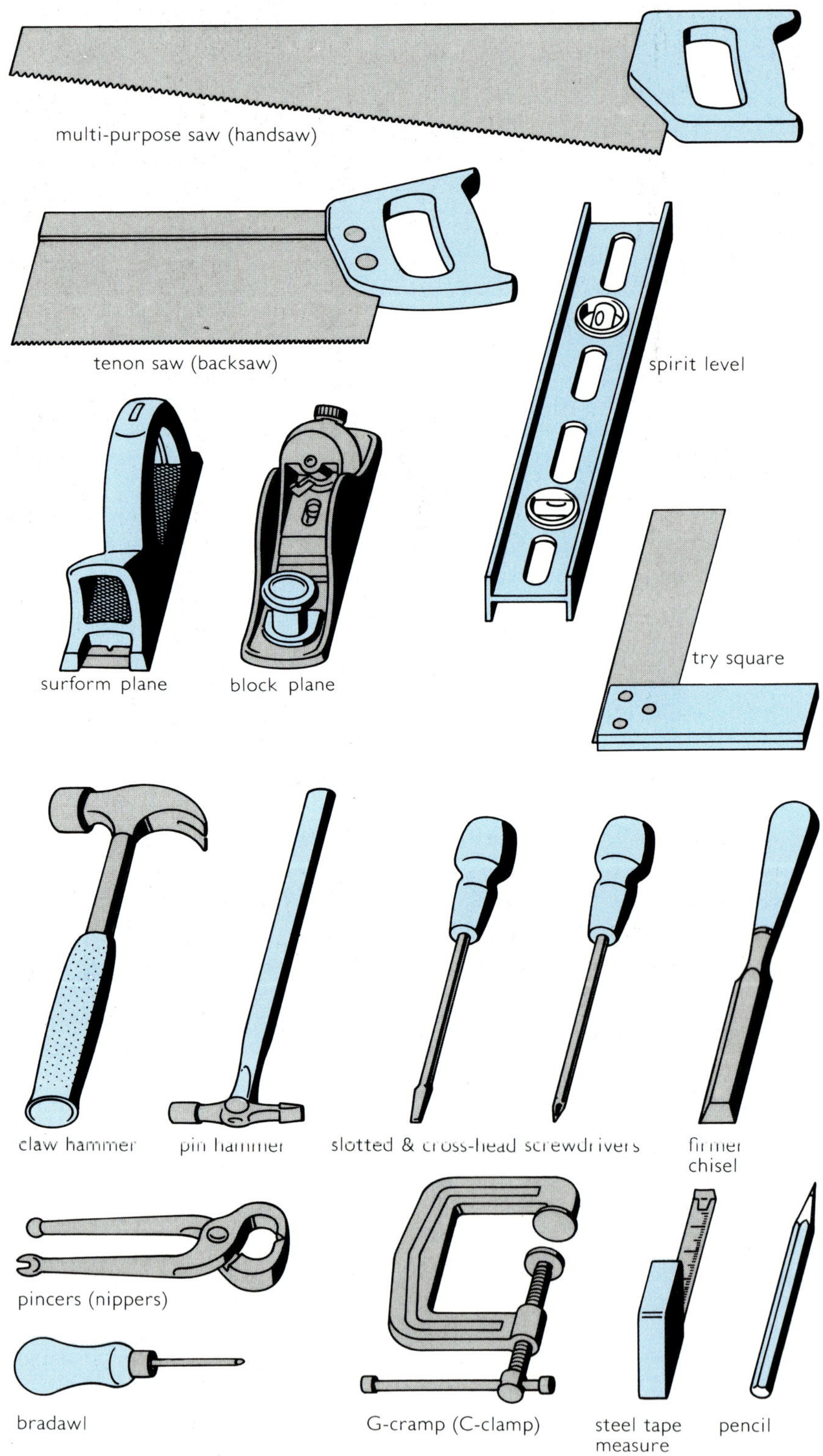

woodworking glue; a string tensioner will hold the whole thing together while the glue dries. Small wooden bracing pieces can be screwed invisibly to the under-side to provide extra reinforcement of the joints.

An old chest of drawers that has been painted can be a real 'find' if you are prepared to strip it. Beware of dipping it in a caustic soda tank as this can dissolve the glue and damage the wood. A chemical stripper is safer and easier, but do not use on veneer. Pine is the best wood to strip as hardwoods can tend to discolour.

Drawers which are held together with dovetail joints are easy to reglue. Wax the under-sides of the drawers to help them slide freely.

## Wood finishes

Anything that has been painstakingly restored then needs a protective finish to bring out the natural beauty of the grain.

If you are applying a coloured stain, do this before sealing the wood or use a combined stain/varnish. New softwoods can be toned down into mellow pine by applying a light oak stain.

Linseed oil mixed with an equal amount of turpentine is an inexpensive treatment for dark hardwoods. It penetrates the wood and helps to repel water. Rub it in with a rag, applying four coats and leaving two days between each. Teak oil also stops water getting in, and is quicker to dry. Apply with a cloth, allowing eight hours between coats. Finally rub down with fine steel wool and wax polish. Dispose of all cloths after use as they are inflammable.

Polyurethane varnish is the most durable sealing finish, giving resistance against heat and moisture. Paint directly on to clean sanded wood across the grain. Allow eight hours to dry and sand lightly before applying a second coat.

### REPAIRING JOINTS IN FURNITURE

**The secret of successful repairs to joints of all types is to remove thoroughly all traces of the old adhesive. To do this, you will have to dismantle the joint. Scrape off the old adhesive from all surfaces of the joint and clean it by rubbing lightly with coarse abrasive paper. Reglue with PVA woodworking adhesive and clamp the joint firmly; leave to dry overnight before removing the clamp.**

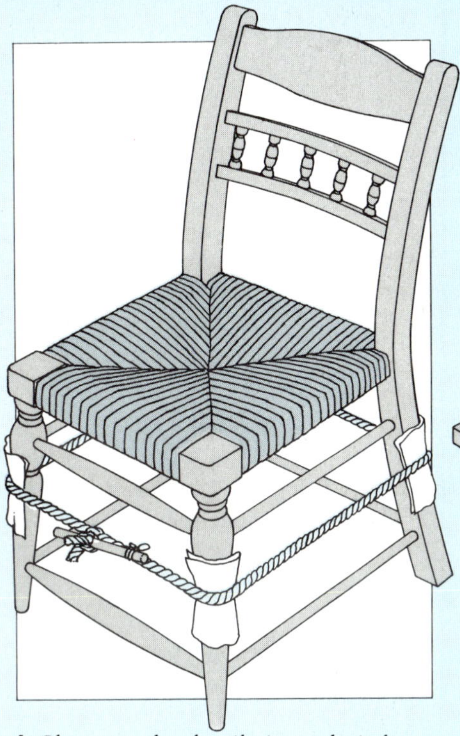

**1** Clamp reglued rails into chair legs with a rope twisted tight with a length of dowel; tie the dowel end to the rope to hold it tight.

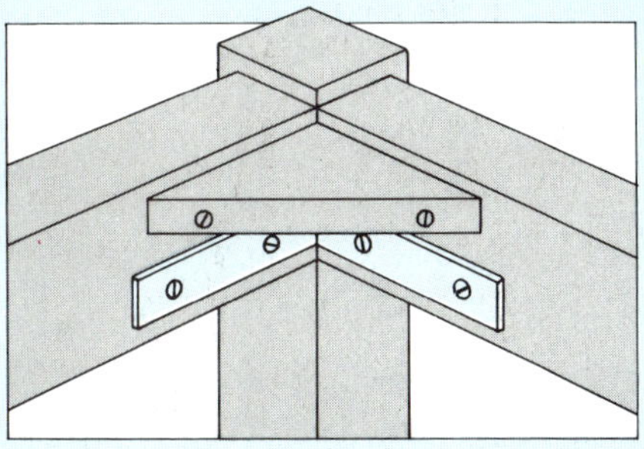

**2** Strengthen a chair frame with an L-shaped metal bracket screwed beneath the triangular seat block.

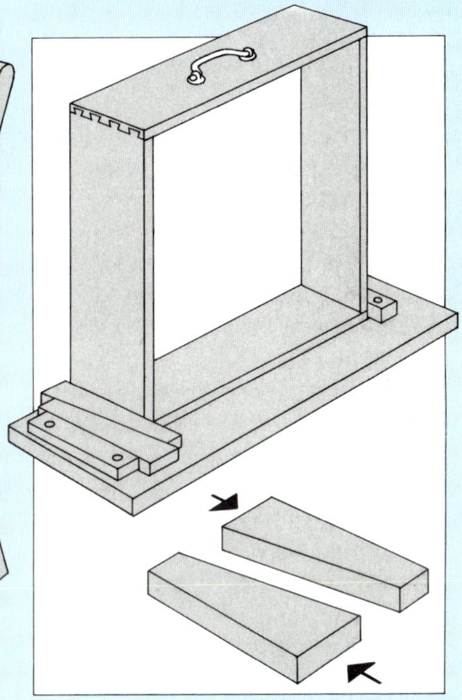

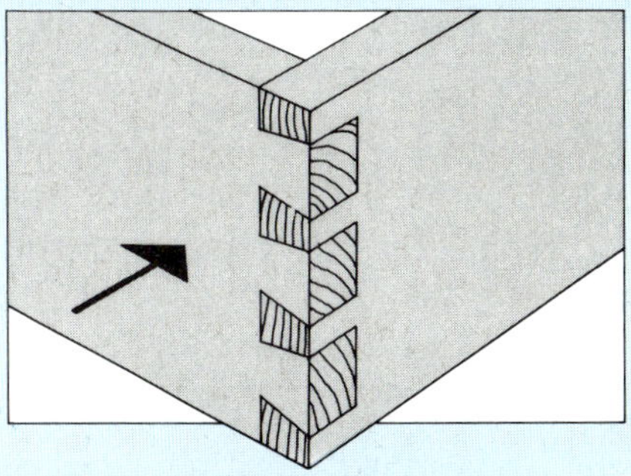

**3** To tighten loose dovetail joints in a drawer, nail two wooden blocks to a board and shape two wedges. Tap these in between the drawer and one block, applying pressure in the direction indicated. Apply PVA adhesive to the dovetails first.

# Wood Cladding

The natural warmth of wood makes it especially suitable as a decorative wallcovering and its durability is a practical consideration for areas subject to exceptional wear and tear. It can be used to cover up unsightly plumbing pipes, and is useful in kitchens and bathrooms, especially where clean lines and easily wiped-down surfaces are desirable. You can even cover a badly deteriorated ceiling with tongue and groove pine cladding: it will give a cosy air. The only difference is that the wooden strips will have to be attached directly into the ceiling joists.

Wood cladding is also an attractive and popular way of covering up poor plastering. However, it is often also used, wrongly, to cover up damp walls. Before covering any wall with wood cladding always check that it is structurally dry. If in doubt call in a damp specialist and have it checked with a special moisture meter. Moisture build-up caused by condensation is a different matter and here cladding a wall will help to make it warmer and eliminate any surface condensation. Trap a polyethylene sheet between the cladding and the framework of wooden strips.

Two or three coats of polyurethane varnish will seal the wood, or use linseed or teak oil. Treat any knots with shellac knotting first, to

*Right: Wood cladding is an unusual and dramatic treatment for a lavatory – which also provides a suitably small area with which to start. The glossy texture of the varnish, repeated on the lavatory seat, the floor and the ceiling, plays a powerful part here too.*

*Opposite: Cladding is often powerfully evocative of Scandinavian style, and this kitchen is no exception. Note the edging given to the window.*

prevent any resin 'bleeding' out. Any of the softwoods could, of course, be painted: a couple of coats of oil-based paint in an eggshell texture can give a fresh, clean look to cladding. Partial cladding could be finished with a paint effect, perhaps an impressionistic marbling. Staining is another alternative, and could be effective if you want to achieve a darker look to the wood.

## Types of cladding

There are two main types of wooden cladding generally available. One is shiplap board which is heavy and designed mainly for use outdoors: the shape will not allow water to seep between the joins. Use it vertically or horizontally indoors.

The other type is lightweight tongue and groove matchboarding, which also can be set horizontally or vertically. A traditional form of partial cladding is wainscoting. This is simply vertical wooden lengths of approximately 1m (3ft) laid up the wall. The top edge should be finished with a moulding which is best attached before the boards.

Whatever the type, a wastage figure of 10–20% is to be expected.

Before you begin nailing the boards make sure you store them inside the room where they will be used for at least three days so they take up whatever natural humidity there may be in the air.

## How to install cladding

Whichever type of cladding you choose, the basic installation procedure is the same. The job entails laying wooden strips around all four edges of each surface and around windows and doors, then adding strips at intervals in between.

Masonry nails or wall plugs and screws will give adequate support but watch out for any pipes and cables. Arrange the strips so that the ends of each board are supported

### BOXING-IN PIPES

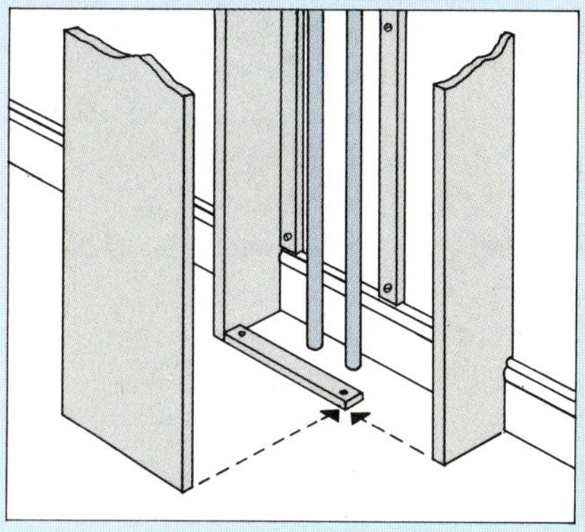

**1** Screw a wooden strip each side of the pipes, and one to the floor, and screw side and front panels to them.

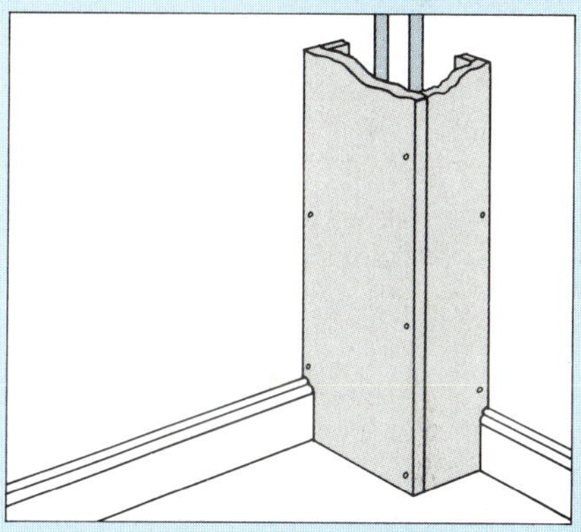

**2** In corners, screw the strips of wood to each wall and shape panels to fit around mouldings.

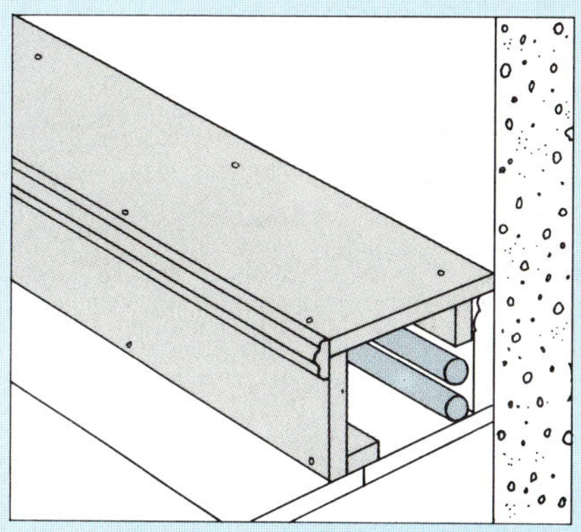

**3** Cover floor-level pipes with panels nailed to strips of wood on the floor and skirting (baseboard).

and place intermediate strips approximately 50cm (20in) apart.

The strips will run at right angles to the run of the boards. In this way a layer of air is trapped between boards and wall, while the strips are a suitable material into which the cladding can be nailed. The framework also provides an even surface for the boards. Bumps or irregularities can be overcome by packing any gaps behind the strips.

On stud partition walls, lay the wooden strips horizontally and nail into the stud positions.

The wooden strips to which the cladding is nailed should first be treated to prevent attack from rot and fungus. In any room where condensation may be a problem, lay a continuous polyethylene sheet between the wooden strips and the cladding to prevent airborne moisture getting to the wall.

Start with the first board laid into the corner and then proceed along the wall. If you measure how many boards are needed for a complete run you can trim the first and last board to obtain a symmetrical cut at each end. Outside corners should either be finished with trimmed boards to avoid an open tongue, or with wooden corner mouldings to provide a neat edge.

Lightweight tongue and groove boards are attached to the battens by 'secret' nailing through the tongue; or use metal clips (figs. 3–4). If you cannot use complete length boards make sure that the ends join midway over a wooden strip.

Shiplap boards (figs. 5–6) cannot be 'secret' nailed, so punch in the nails 25mm (1in) from the top edge and fill with filler or plastic wood.

Sockets and light switches can be left in place if you frame around them, or the light switch boxes can be brought out level with packing boxes by a qualified electrician.

## THE FRAMEWORK FOR WOOD CLADDING

Before cladding a wall with boards, you will need to supply support for the ends and middle of the boards, and around windows.

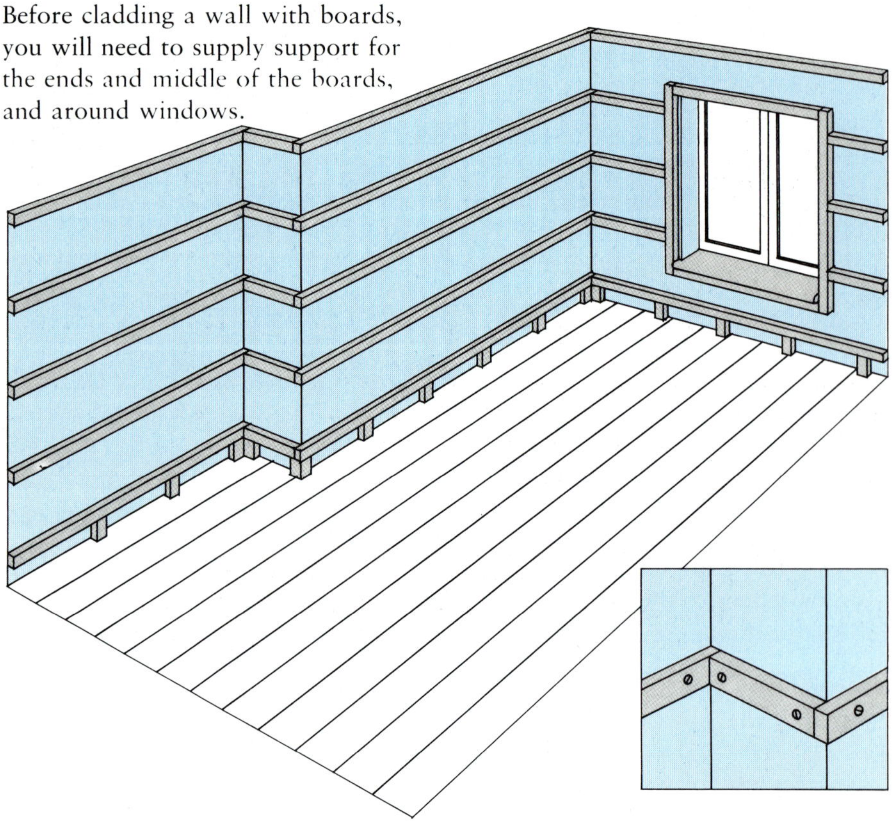

You can do this by nailing or screwing strips of wood to the wall. They should be spaced about 50cm (20in) apart, and run horizontally for vertical boards or vertically for horizontal boards. At windows, set the strips back from the edge of the reveal to allow for a finishing timber. You will also need short vertical strips at floor level to hold the skirting (baseboard). Butt-join the strips at corners (inset).

**1** With some wall plugs you can drill through the wood and wall together; or drill the wood and mark through it to give the wall drilling position.

**2** Countersink the hole in the wood slightly. Plug the masonry and insert the screw, hammer in, then finally tighten with a screwdriver.

| | |
|---|---|
| WALL FIXINGS | 42 |
| TOOLS AND EQUIPMENT | 76, 160 |



## WOOD CLADDING

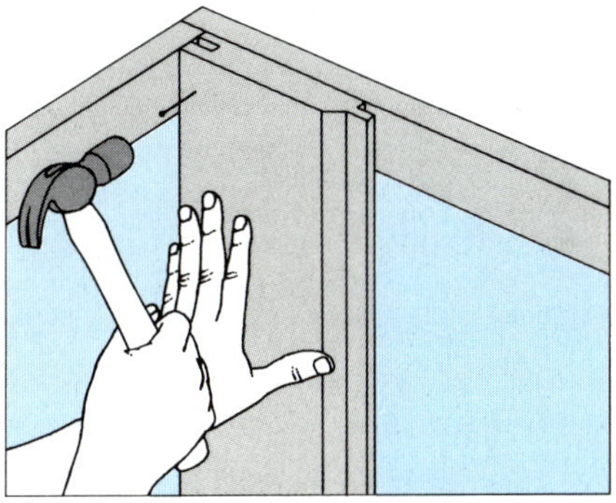

**1** To attach tongue-and-groove boards with nails, start with a groove butting into one corner and nail through the board into the wall strips, 6mm ($\frac{1}{4}$in) from the edge.

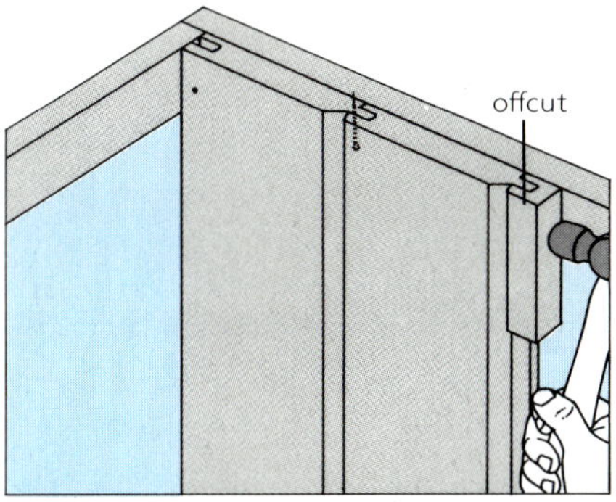


**2** Then nail at an angle through the tongue to secure the other edge. Tap the groove of the next board over the tongue, using an offcut or scrap, and nail through the next tongue.

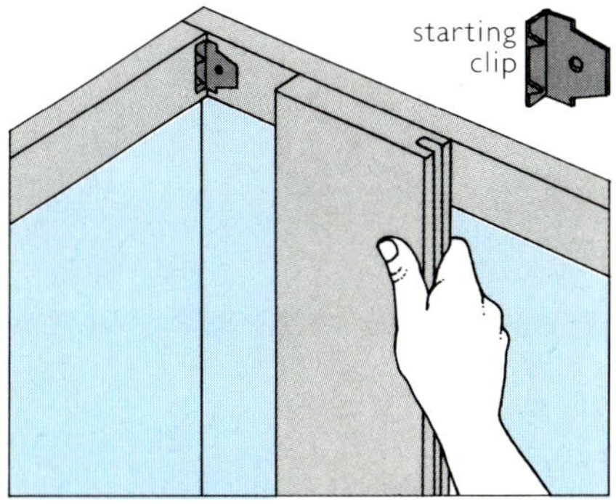


**3** If securing the boards with clips, nail a starting clip tight into the corner. Cut the groove off the first board and tap this edge onto the spikes of the clip.

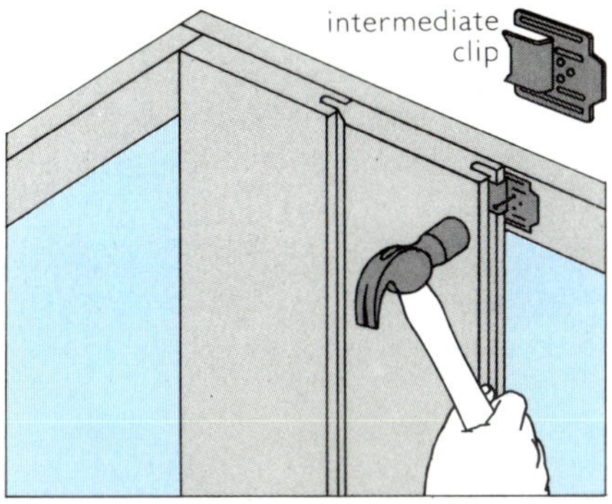


**4** Slide an intermediate clip into the groove of the board and nail it to the wall strip. Slide the tongue of the next board into the groove, and nail a clip in the next groove.

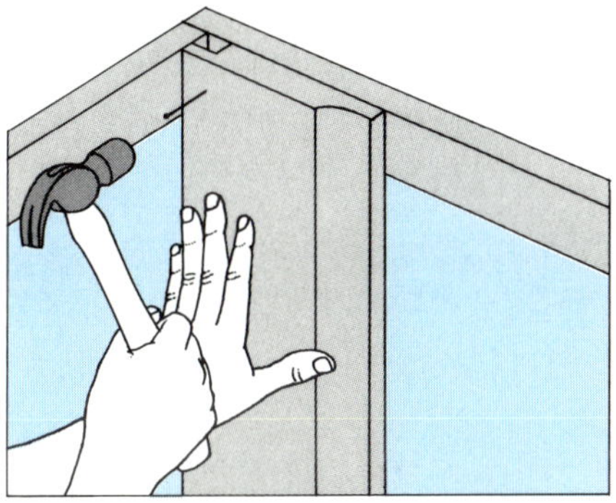

**5** Nail the first board of shiplap cladding with the rebate (rabbet) side into the corner. Nail through the whole thickness of the board, not just through the rebate (rabbet).

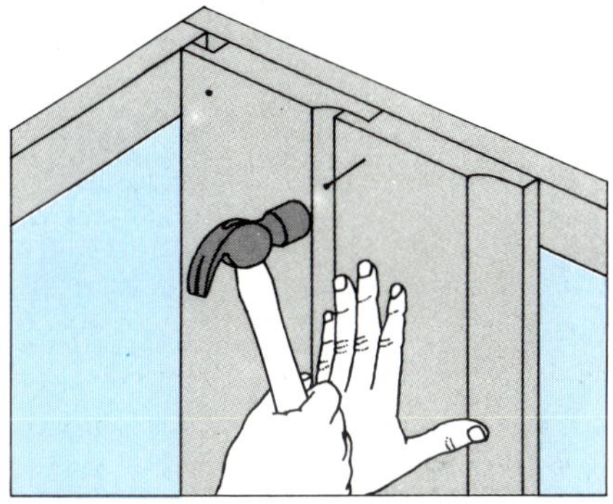

**6** Cover the curved edge with the rebate (rabbet) of the next board and nail through the double thickness. Punch the nails below the surface and fill with plastic wood.

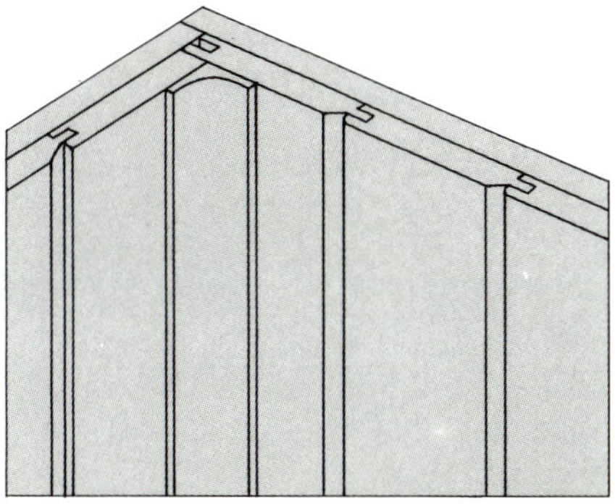

**7** Butt-join boards at an internal corner by cutting off the tongued edge and starting with the next groove pushed into the corner. Cover the joint with a moulding.

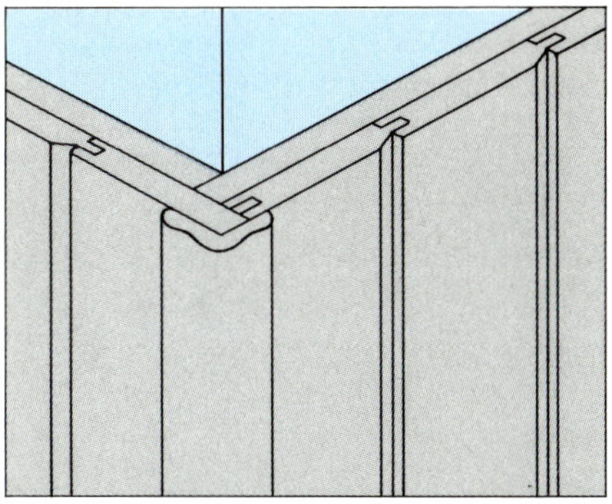

**8** At an external corner, cut off the tongue of the last board so that it will neatly overlap the groove of the first board on the next wall. Cover with a moulding.

**9** At windows, cut off the edge of the board and make a template for the shape of the sill. Chisel out this shape from the board, then fit in position. Cover with a moulding.

# Decorative Wood Mouldings

## TYPES OF WOOD MOULDING

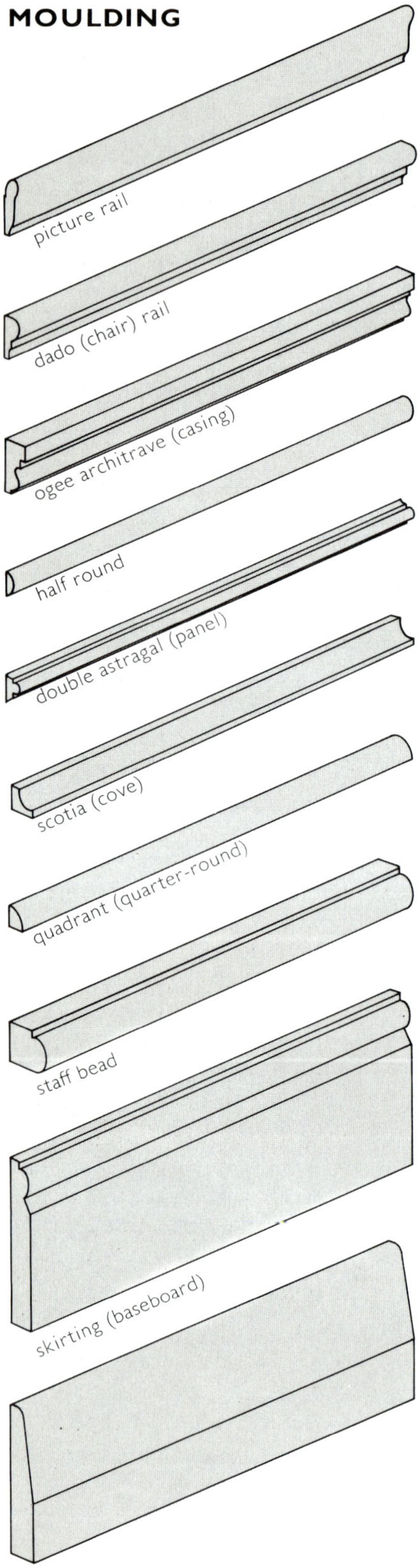


It is sad to see how many old homes have had their finest woodwork features covered over or removed in the pursuit of modernization. Anyone trying to restore such a home to its former glory will place the reinstatement of picture and dado or chair rails high on the list, for rooms with high ceilings can look cold and cavernous if the walls are not visually broken up.

Apart from aesthetic considerations, picture rails are also functional, although it is surprising how many people overlook this possibility when hanging pictures. Picture rail or moulding hooks are still available so there is no reason why pictures and mirrors should not be hung in this way. If you are not happy about the look of string, use transparent fishing line instead.

Dado or chair rails, positioned a third of the way up the wall, also have a function in protecting walls from knocks. Traditional places for them are the dining room, to stop the backs of chairs striking the wall, and the hallway, where they provide valuable protection from knocks in a busy space.

Stock mouldings are normally available from good timber suppliers but the range is likely to be limited to a few patterns. The likelihood of matching an existing broken rail is remote but it is possible to have some pieces machine-made, although this can prove an expensive exercise for small amounts.

When selecting picture and dado or chair rails, remember they are completely different in shape and cannot be happily interchanged.

*Picture rails painted to match the picture frames are used to dramatic effect in this hallway. The hooks and the wires are exploited for their visual effect.*

| | |
|---|---|
| DECORATIVE MOULDINGS | 24 |
| DISPLAY | 32 |
| WALL FIXINGS | 42 |
| TOOLS AND EQUIPMENT | 76, 160 |
| FILLING HOLES | 83 |




## ATTACHING MOULDINGS

Mouldings are traditionally attached to brick walls by nailing them with cut nails to wood 'soldiers' set into the mortar joints every 70cm (27in) or so. You can also use plastic plugs and screws. Nail to the timber studs of partition walls or screw into cavity fasteners. Corners are mitred.

Cut small mouldings in a mitre box after holding the two lengths at the corner of the wall to mark the angle. Place the moulding in the groove and saw through the slots.

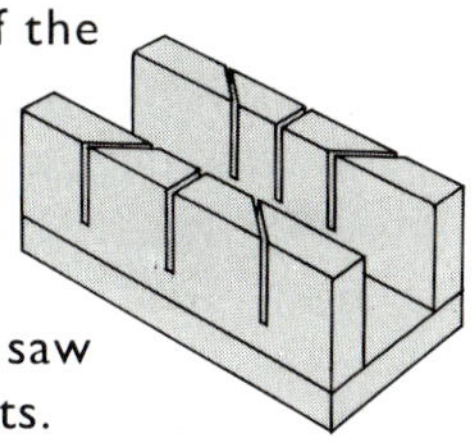

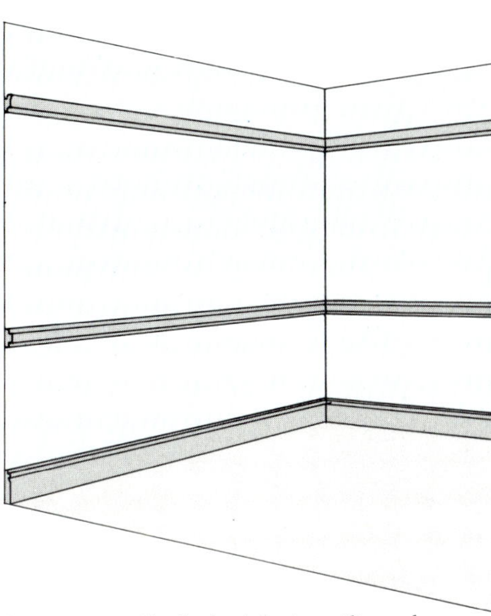

**1** Picture rail, dado (chair rail) and skirting (baseboard) are the different mouldings featured in a room.

**2** Attach with cut nails to 'soldiers'.

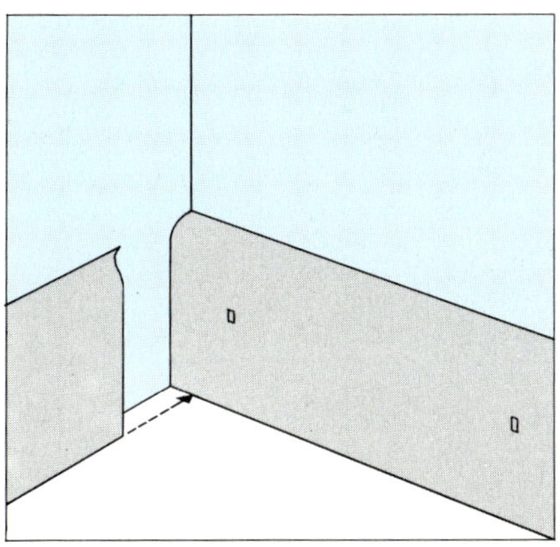

**3** To allow skirting (baseboard) to be removed, nail one length into the corner and fit the other over it.

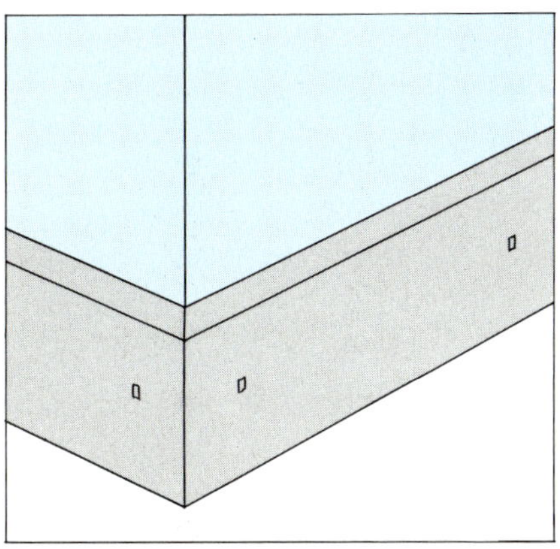

**4** Mitre external corners; skirting (baseboard) will not fit into a mitre box so cut it freehand.

## Attaching the mouldings

Attaching picture, dado or chair rails into masonry walls can be done in two ways, depending on the age of the house and your inclination. Picture rails used once to be nailed into wooden plugs or 'soldiers' sunk into the masonry of the wall, and you may be able to locate these if you are taking old rails down. If so, replace them with new wooden plugs and nail the new rails into these with cut nails. If you plan to leave the rails bare, use 'lost-head', ovalhead, masonry nails, punch them below the surface with a nail punch and fill over the holes with wood filler. More often, however, you will be attaching the rails by means of screws. Drill first through the moulding using a wood bit on your drill, countersink the hole, then mark the position on the wall through the hole and drill into the wall with a masonry bit. Insert a suitable plastic plug, then screw on the picture rail with countersunk screws.

Stud partition walls should have picture, dado or chair rails nailed into their timber frames: find these by tapping along and noting the differences in sound.

Start by stretching a chalked string line along the wall at the required height and check it is level by measuring against the nearest horizontal line (the ceiling or the floor), then snap the string to make a straight line. Nail the mouldings along this line; avoid making joins anywhere but the corners. Both internal and external corners must be mitred at an angle: use a mitre block for best results.

**Skirting boards (baseboards)** In practical terms these are similar to other wooden mouldings as they are both decorative and give protection against knocks.

The boards should be primed, then attached with cut nails which may be driven into small wooden blocks or 'soldiers' set into a masonry wall; or drill clearance holes through the boards, mark the hole positions, then drill and insert plugs into the masonry before attaching the boards with screws. On stud partition walls, nail them into the timber frame as described for picture rails.

In most cases irregularities in the floor can be overcome by just lifting the board slightly – carpet and underlay will cover the gap. Only in severe cases will it be necessary to shape the under-side of the board. Internal corners should be butted together by cutting the end of the second board in the shape of the moulding profile, so that it sits neatly over the first. Use a wood offcut to mark out the shape and then cut it with a coping saw.

## Decorative effects

It is still possible to re-create some of the panelling effects used a century or more ago. At one time hardwood panelling was extremely expensive, but now it can be 'faked' from plywood and various mouldings for a reasonable price. Visually, few rooms will take full length panelling but many will benefit from partial panelling. The plywood sheets can start from the top of the skirting boards (baseboards) and finish under the dado or chair rail. By gluing mitred mouldings to the face of the plywood, squares can be created. A coat of coloured stain will help to tone in the various wood shades when construction is complete. The effect may be further enhanced by some illusionistic wood graining.

If you are prepared to look you can find a great variety of different mouldings but the problem is choosing which are suitable for your home. When you are trying to match a certain type, take a sample with you or bring a small piece home first.

STAINS 98, 108
PAINT FINISHES 110

*Opposite: This room has the very traditional combination of wooden decorative mouldings, treated in a very untraditional way. Sponged walls seem to recede in comparison to the black-painted woodwork and cornice (crown moulding), while the tongue-and-groove wainscoting is marbled – surely the ultimate in unlikely illusions.*

*Above: A decorative floor will be greatly enhanced by an unusual skirting (baseboard). This example carries the eye upwards in a most pleasing way.*

*Left: Panelled wainscoting painted with high-gloss paint will be a dramatic feature in any hallway.*

# SOFT FLOORINGS

Most of the floorings covered in earlier sections are either permanent or semi-permanent, and are sometimes defined as 'hard floorings'. Carpets, rugs, carpet tiles, and sheet material like vinyl and lino are softer floorings and are easier to take up or change to suit a new colour scheme. They are also considerably easier to lay. The chart on pages 180–1 describes all the various types of floorings available.

## Measuring

With any sheet material, the first step is to measure and work out the amount of material required, allowing for as little waste as possible; your supplier can and will advise on the quantity required. If the room has alcoves and recesses, measure into these to give the maximum overall length. If you are having a carpet professionally laid, the installer will measure up and order the correct quantity for you, but do your own calculations initially so you know what carpet you can afford.

In a large room the flooring may well have to be joined. To make the seams virtually invisible always try to have them at right angles to the main window, as near to the wall as possible and never near the doorway. With carpet, always try to run the pile away from the light to avoid any uneven colour shading.

As with other decorating items, if you have to join material from two different rolls, or of two different widths, make sure the colours are identical, or the join becomes very obvious. Remember to allow extra for any pattern-matching.

## Carpeting

Carpets are made in three different ways, and from a range of fibres.

*Left: On a large expanse of floor, stone tiles can be dramatic and eye-catching; here they blend well with the architectural shell of the building. Nevertheless, they are an uncommon choice for a bedroom, and seem to demand something to warm them up literally and visually. Coconut matting is a cheap and suitable alternative.*

*Above: Stamped rubber lends a hi-tech feel to a decorative scheme, bringing with it an interesting texture as well as practicality. Daylight streaming through will make the most of its shiny surface.*

*Opposite: For comfort and warmth, the combination of carpet and rugs is still unbeatable. The soft furnishings in this bedroom have been chosen with a good eye for colour, texture and pattern, manifest in the extravagant folds of the curtains and also in the geometrically-patterned rug.*

**Woven** carpets are usually made by the Axminster or Wilton method, but there are other types, including hand-made oriental ones. Axminsters are woven a row of tufts at a time, and the U-shaped tufts are anchored firmly into the backing. They are usually patterned carpets as this weaving method allows a wide range of different colours to be used. Wiltons are more closely woven in one continuous length with some of the pile incorporated into the backing to give more strength and thickness to the carpet. They are usually plain or in limited colour combinations. The pile can be twisted, looped or 'carved'.

**Tufted** carpets are not woven; the yarn is stitched into a primary backing to give a looped pile. The backing is then anchored with a latex adhesive to secure the tufts.

**Bonded or non-woven** carpets are made by a relatively new process which involves bonding pile fibre on to a pre-woven backing. These types of carpet will not fray when cut but are only available in a limited range of colours. Carpet tiles are invariably made in this way.

The various fibres that are used to

*Wall-to-wall carpet is expensive, so choose the colour carefully. This room exhibits the perfect blend of soft pastels, enlivened by the patterning in the curtains that is carried cleverly onto the edge of the window seat.*

make carpets can be synthetic or natural fibres, or a mixture of both which combines the resilience of the natural material with the long-lasting and easy-care properties of the synthetic fibre. The pile content and method of carpet construction will determine the price – generally speaking, the higher the wool content the more expensive the carpet. Some broad guidelines on the quality and wearing properties are usually indicated on the label.

Carpet comes either in roll form (broadloom), in strips (body), in large squares or rectangles with bound or fringed edges, or as carpet tiles. Broadloom and carpet tiles are the easiest types to lay yourself, as narrow widths need seaming.

Most carpets benefit from an underlay, even those which are foam-backed, to improve comfort underfoot, improve heat and sound insulation, and increase their life expectancy. Hessian- (burlap-) or paper-backed rubber underlay are the best types to use, but if you have underfloor heating use a heavy felt underlay. Plastic foam underlay can be used in bedrooms, but it does tend to flatten easily and will need felt paper placed underneath it to stop the backing sticking to the floorboards. Do not lay a new carpet on top of old underlay, as the wear patterns will transfer themselves to the new carpet.

## Laying carpet

Once again you need to start with a firm, level and dry floor. Secure any creaking or loose floorboards and, if they are in very bad condition, cover with chipboard (particle board), plywood or hardboard (rough side up). On a solid but very bumpy concrete floor, it may be necessary to apply a floor-levelling compound first.

Laying carpet is hard work and is a relatively cheap job to have done professionally; you will also get a much neater finish. There are two main methods: hessian- (burlap-) backed carpets are fixed by tacks or gripper rods (strips of wood with pins sticking upwards) nailed or stuck around the edges of the room.

| PREPARING FLOORS | 86, 140 |
|---|---|
| LAYING CARPET TILES | 175 |


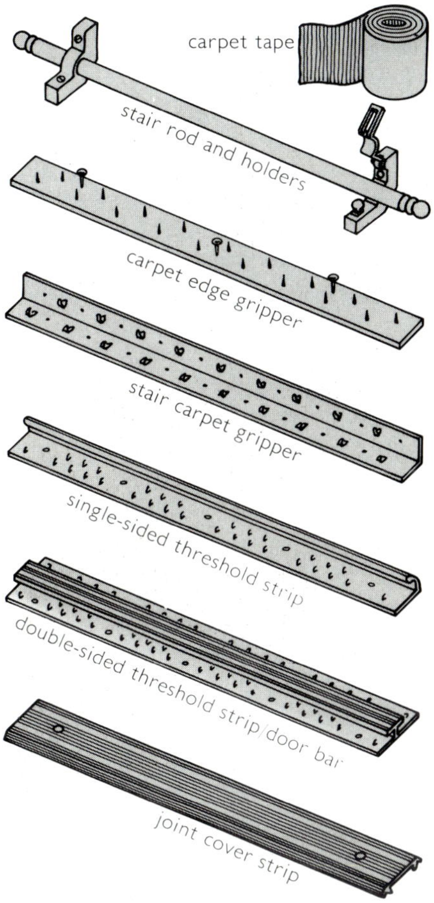


The carpet is stretched over these. Foam-backed carpets are stuck down using double-sided carpet tape.

Carpet underlay should always be fitted slightly smaller than the room and carpet. Felt can be loose-laid, stapled or tacked around the edge; felt-paper underlay is joined and stuck to the floor with double-sided carpet tape or adhesive; hessian- (burlap-) or paper-backed rubber is tacked or stapled, rubber-side down, all around the room, just inside the gripper strip.

Doorways are potentially dangerous areas when it comes to carpet, so make sure the ends are always secured into protective threshold strips. Different types are available for places where two carpets meet and where one carpet meets a harder floorcovering.

## CARPET LABELLING

Most woven and tufted carpets are classified according to wear. There should be a label on the back of the carpet giving the relevant details, or there should be information with the sample swatch. Some carpets are numbered, others simply graded. Always buy the best-quality carpet you can afford for a particular area in your home.

| Grade | Carpet Type | Location |
|---|---|---|
| **1** Light wear (F) | Light domestic | Bedrooms, bathrooms, secondary rooms with light traffic |
| **2** Medium wear (E) | Medium domestic | Domestic areas not subject to concentrated use |
| **3** General wear (D) | General domestic | Most domestic areas, but not ones with very heavy traffic |
| **4** Heavy wear (C) | Heavy domestic and medium contract | Heavily used areas such as halls, stairs and living rooms |
| **5** Very heavy wear (B) | Heavy domestic and general contract | Very heavily used areas |
| **6** Extra-heavy wear (A) | Very heavy domestic and contract | Locations where very good-quality carpet is needed |
| **L** Luxury | Long pile luxury | Locations which are not subject to very heavy wear |

### MEASURING FOR CARPET

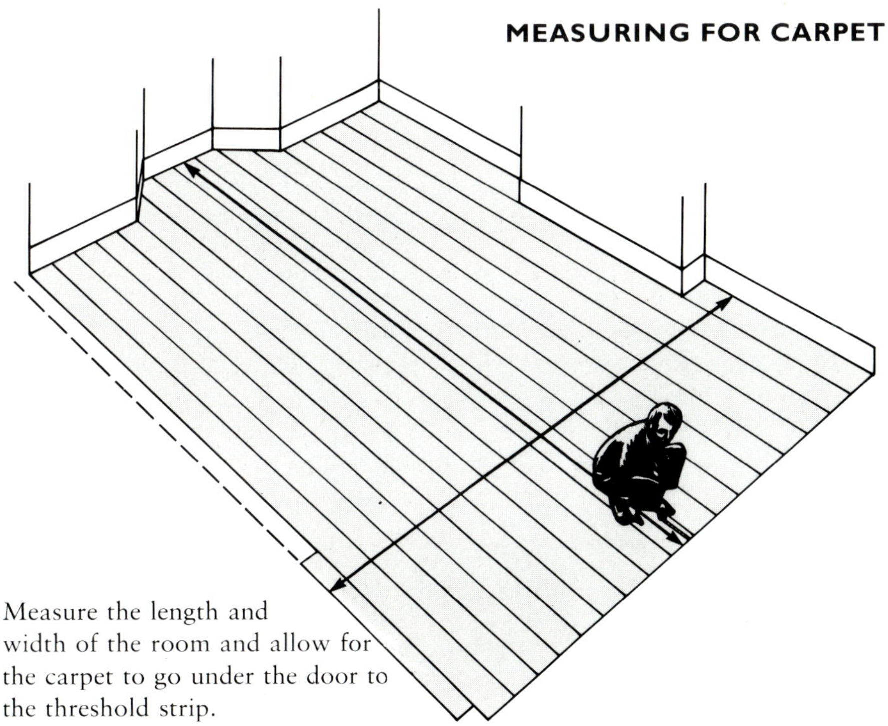

Measure the length and width of the room and allow for the carpet to go under the door to the threshold strip.

## Stair carpets

The stairs are an area where safety is very important, so make sure you choose a carpet that is not slippery in use and that it is secured properly. Sisal or some types of cord would just not be suitable as they are too easy to slip on.

Check the stairs carefully before you lay carpet and make any necessary minor repairs. If you notice any woodworm holes, treat the entire floor with a proprietary fluid. Loose nails should be pulled out or punched below the surface. Clean the stairs thoroughly and give the whole staircase a new coat of paint so that you won't have to go to the trouble of taking the carpet up again at a later date.

Always buy the best quality carpet you can afford for the stairs, hall and landing areas of the home, as these get very heavy use. Also think about the colour and pattern of the carpet in relation to all the neighbouring rooms and make sure the total effect is co-ordinated or toning. In a small house, an impression of greater space can be created by laying the same carpet throughout the ground floor, up the stairs and on to the landing. Toning floorings can then be laid in the bedrooms and bathroom. For a practical treatment, you could select a multicoloured patterned carpet for the hall, stairs and landing area, and then pick a plain colour to match each of the colours in this carpet for each room that leads off.

With stair rods or hinged clips laying stair carpet is relatively easy – as long as the staircase is a simple, straight one. (Remember the carpet should always be laid with the pile running down the stairs.) However, if you want edge-to-edge carpeting, or if there are some complicated turns and half-landings, perhaps even bullnose curved treads at the bottom of the stairs, it is strongly

### LAYING STAIR CARPET

**Measure the length of stair carpet with a piece of string. Hold one end at the back of the top tread and run it across the tread, into the angle of the next one, and so on to the bottom of the last riser. Add 50cm (20in) for turning under. It is usual to cover the top riser with the landing carpet.**

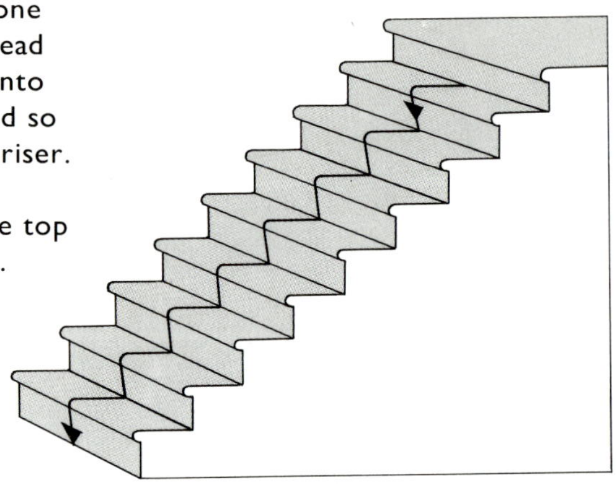

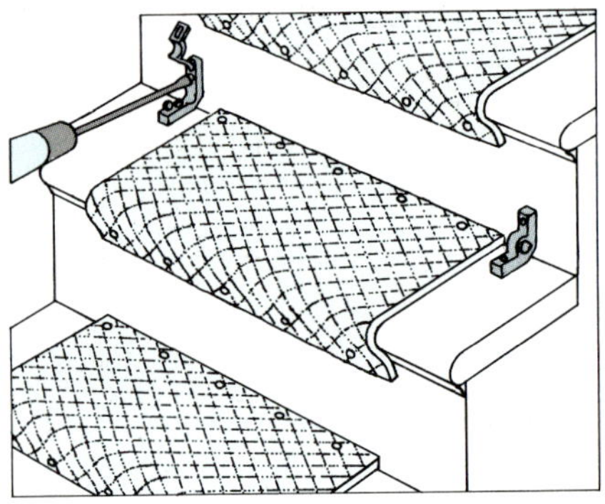

**1** Cut underlay pads 25mm (1in) narrower than the carpet and secure with carpet tacks. Screw a fixed and hinged rod holder to each tread with the carpet width between them.

**2** Tack the carpet to the second tread and run it over the nosing and between the rod holders. Slide the rod into the fixed holder, then secure it in the hinged one.

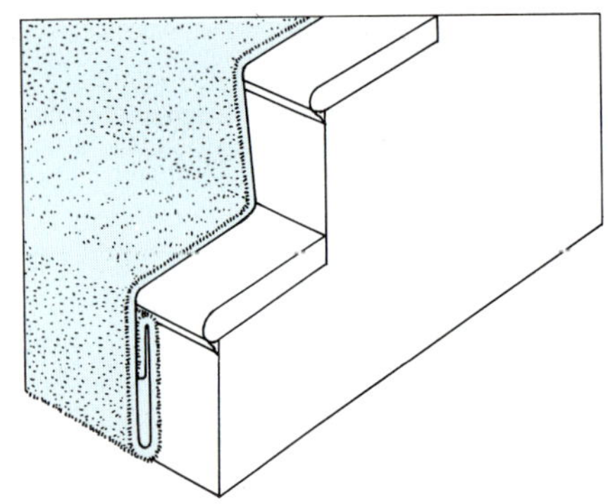

**3** To allow for uneven wear, turn the surplus carpet inside the length covering the bottom riser, and then tack through the double thickness at the folded edge.

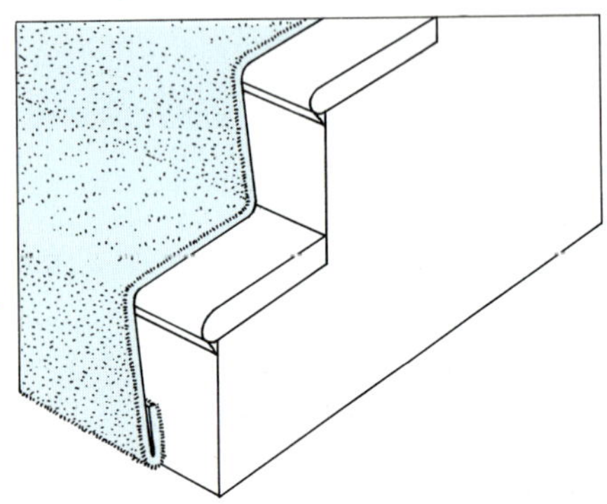

**4** Every twelve months or so, move the carpet one tread-width along the stairs (either up or down), concealing the surplus at the top behind the carpet on the top riser.

*An elegant hallway will be enhanced or spoilt by the stair carpet. Old-fashioned staircases can look good carpeted in the old-fashioned way, that is, with loose-laid carpet attached with rods (below) or hinged clips. These are easy to install and manipulate yourself. Gripper strips are your alternative (left). Notice the paint finish on the wall: it has been marked out to suggest blocks of stone, then given a light, quite gentle, marbled treatment in grey and white.*

recommended that you call in a professional to do the job for you quickly and safely. Remember this is a very vulnerable area of the home, and stair carpet must be laid well, and, above all, securely.

For carpet laid with rods or clips, always buy at least $\frac{1}{2}$m ($\frac{1}{2}$yd) more carpet than you need: the excess is tucked under at the bottom and top of the stairs, so that the carpet can be moved up and down the stairs to even out any worn patches that inevitably occur. This should really be done every twelve months to keep the carpet looking good, and the rods or clips make this an easy and quick task to do yourself.

If you are going to use the stair rod method, screw a rigid holder to the wall side and a hinged holder to the other side of each step (see fig. 1) before you begin, as wide apart as the width of your chosen carpet. Hinged clips are all the same and are likewise screwed to each side of the tread. Secure the underlay pads between the holders or clips so that they cover the tread nosing and lay the carpet from the top of the flight to the bottom with the pile running downwards. Position the rods in the rigid holes between the stair tread and riser, then secure in the hinged holders or close the clips. Work slowly and carefully down the staircase coping with one step at a time, making sure the new carpet is taut and running straight.

Landing and hall carpet should always be laid afterwards.

## Laying carpet tiles

Carpet tiles can be especially useful in areas which get heavy use such as kitchens and bathrooms. They are loose-laid which means they can be taken up and cleaned very easily –

making them ideal for kitchens and children's rooms; they can also be moved around to hide any worn patches. Buy enough so that you have a few spares.

Heavy bonded carpet tiles can be loose-laid and butted up together quite successfully, and do not move in use, but the lighter sort can push up when furniture is moved or the floor is vacuumed. If you think this will be a problem, you can secure the tiles on double-sided carpet tape, which is stuck to the floor on one side and to the back of the tile on the other. The carpet tile can still be lifted if necessary.

All the tiles need to be laid in the direction of the pile, unless you want the tiles to be very obvious. Arrows are printed on the back of the tile as a guide. Carpet tiles can also be laid to create interesting patterns or to make a border, which can be as simple or complicated as you like. You can create a Greek key pattern, for example, by cutting two different-coloured tiles to the required shape. Tiles can also be laid to create a chequerboard effect. Do this with two contrasting colours, or by using the same colours and then laying the tiles with the pile at right angles to each other.

As with all other types of tile, make sure the floor is smooth, clean, dry, level and free from dampness before you start tiling. Mark up the floor and work out the tile sequence in a dummy run. When you are satisfied lay the tiles, starting in the centre and cutting tiles at the edges and corners. If you are loose-laying, just butt the tiles up against each other and when you reach the edges cut the tiles to a tight fit with a sharp handyman's knife. If you are going to use double-sided tape, stick this across the floor following your initial guideline, position the tiles, then peel back the protective face from the tape and stick the tiles firmly and accurately in place.

*Carpet tiles can be useful in kitchen situations, where food is likely to be spilt: dirty tiles can be lifted and cleaned or replaced.*

## LAYING CARPET TILES

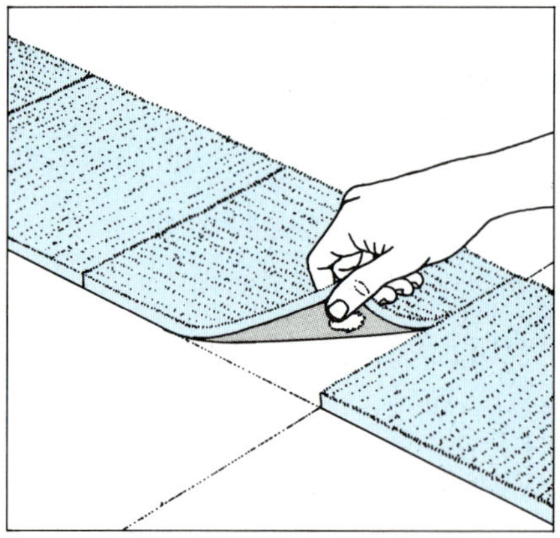

**1** Loose-lay tiles from the marked centre of the floor outwards and check edge width; adjust if needed.

**2** Stick double-sided tape along the chalk lines to secure the tiles; lay outwards from the centre.

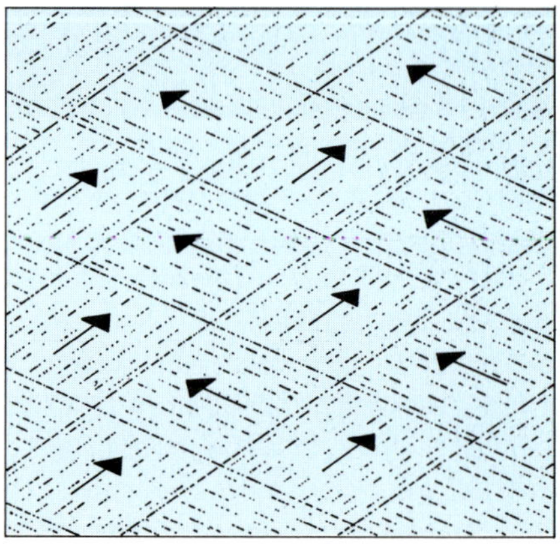

**3** Arrows on the backs of the tiles show the direction of pile. Lay at 90° for a chequered effect.

| | |
|---|---|
| PREPARING FLOORS | 84, 140 |
| MEASURING UP THE FLOOR | 152 |
| LAYING SOFT FLOOR TILES | 152 |




## PATCHING CARPET

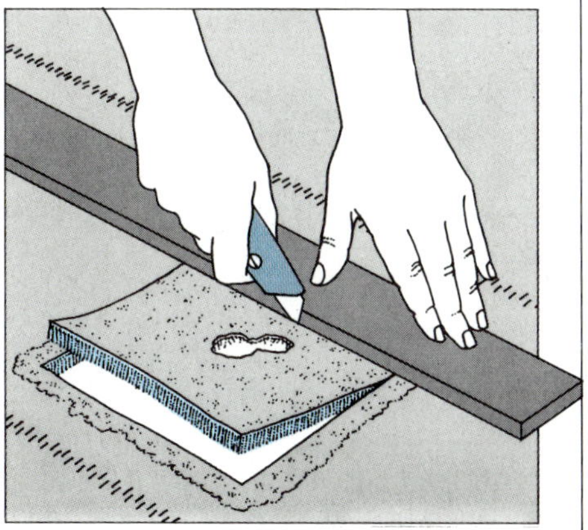

**1** Coat the back of the damaged area with carpet adhesive to prevent fraying, and cut out from the back.

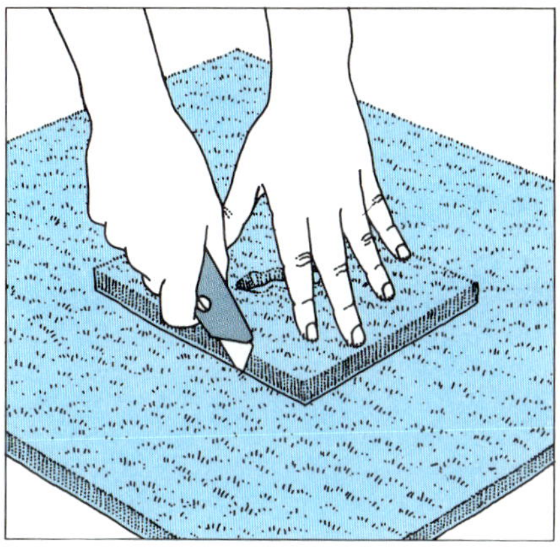

**2** Lay the piece, right side up, over a spare carpet piece, match the pile and pattern, and cut it out.

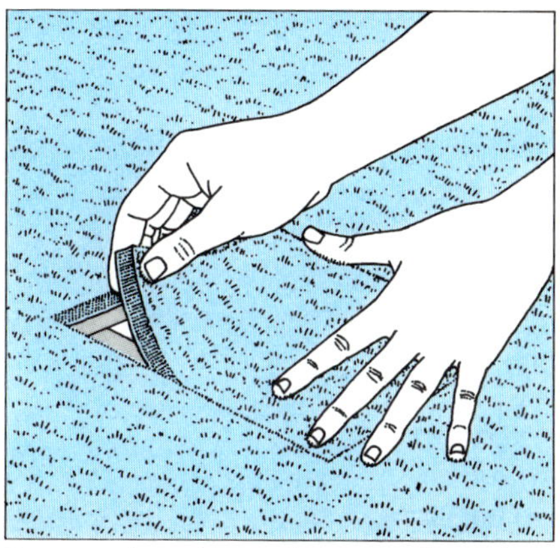

**3** Coat the edges of the patch with adhesive and stick it to the carpet with carpet tape.

## Carpet repairs

With time, carpets often develop loose edges or can become untacked. Always attend to these areas immediately to prevent accidents.

Spills and stains should also be coped with immediately to prevent any permanent damage to a carpet. If a carpet gets burnt or an accident occurs and it develops a hole, it may be necessary to patch it, so always keep some spare offcuts when laying a new carpet. When it is first patched in it may look a slightly darker colour from the main carpet, which may have faded if it has been laid for some time; but it should tone down to match in a short time.

If the carpet is a woven one with a hessian (burlap) backing, this will have to be coated with adhesive along the cutting line to prevent fraying. Lift up the carpet and spread latex carpet adhesive on the back of the carpet around the torn area, place a board underneath it then cut right through the backing to the pile along the adhesive line. Use the damaged patch as a template to cut a new piece, matching pattern and pile carefully. Again, coat the cutting line with adhesive first. Double-sided carpet tape stuck around the edges holds the patch on the floor.

## CARPET STAIN REMOVAL

First always scoop or blot up any spills, using soft paper or cloth; If the stain is urine, neutralize with soda water first. Shampoo carpet after treatment.

| Stain | Treatment |
|---|---|
| Beverages | Cold water |
| Blood | Cold water |
| Burn or scorch marks | Scrape lightly with fingers or coin |
| Butter | Dry cleaning fluid |
| Candle wax | Absorbent paper and a hot iron |
| Chocolate | Carpet shampoo |
| Cream | Carpet shampoo |
| Egg | Carpet shampoo |
| Floor wax | Dry cleaning fluid |
| Gravy and sauces | Warm water |
| Ink (pen) | Cold water |
| Ink (ballpoint) | Surgical alcohol |
| Lipstick | Carpet shampoo |
| Metal polish | Carpet shampoo |
| Milk | Warm water |
| Mustard | Carpet shampoo |
| Nail polish | Nail polish remover (acetone) |
| Oil and grease | Dry cleaning fluid |
| Furniture polish | Dry cleaning fluid |
| Paint (oil-based) | Turpentine or white spirit (mineral spirits) |
| Paint (water-based) | Cold water |
| Shoe polish | Dry cleaning fluid |
| Soot | Turpentine or white spirit (mineral spirits) |
| Urine (fresh stain) | Carpet shampoo |
| Urine (cold stain) | Hot water, detergent and bicarbonate of soda |
| Vomit | Cold water |
| Wine | Absorbent powder (Fuller's Earth) |

# Rugs

If you have used a hard floorcovering or have stripped, sanded and sealed your floorboards, these may well need to be softened visually with a rug or loose carpet. You can also lay a rug on top of the softer floorings, including carpet, for an extra luxurious touch. In a multi-purpose room, for example, a rug can help define the sitting or dining area. In a bedroom it can add that extra softness that will tempt you out of bed in the morning. Machine-washable cotton rugs can be a practical solution for a child's room.

'Floorcloths' can be unusual, decorative, and highly personal. Paint your design – perhaps with stencils – using gloss paint on to canvas tacked to a simple frame. When dry, remove from the frame, turn under the edges and stick them down with carpet tape. The cloth will give an original, stylish touch to a room, but do tack it to the floor if there is any possibility of someone tripping up. Use a cloth on a hard floor (if used on carpet, the paint will crack when the rug is walked on): a painted floor is probably the ideal surface.

Rugs come in many different types and sizes and are made from different fibres and blends of fibres. They are often machine-made nowadays, but many ethnic variations are still hand-made in the traditional ways. The bright, colourful Indian dhurries are usually handwoven in cotton and are very reasonably priced. The colours can sometimes bleed out on to carpet below, so line the back of each rug with fabric if the carpet is a precious one. Flokati rugs are inexpensive Greek shaggy-pile wool rugs in white or off-white colours. Kelims, mainly from Turkey and Iran, are bright tapestries woven with fairly harsh wool. Rag and braided rugs are made from strips of cotton or wool which is then braided or coiled from the centre out. Rag rugs date back to the seventeenth century and evoke the world of America's founding fathers. Stop rugs sliding on polished floors by using a special adhesive backing.

Many other different types of rug are available and you can choose, or make your own, to suit the style and atmosphere of your home.

FABRIC 46
RUGS WITH CARPETS 170

*Rugs are a most dramatic, flexible and colourful decorative element in your home. These two rooms suggest the possibilities open to you. Geometric, modern designs can be bold and dominating, excellent in a very designerly, architecturally exciting room (opposite). In a home with dominating paintings and traditional furniture (left), a rug with rich colours and a strong design can make a powerful counterpoint.*

# Floorcoverings

| Types of flooring | Suitable areas and uses | Cost | Ease of laying |
|---|---|---|---|
| BRICK | Conservatory, hall, kitchen (if sealed) | Medium to expensive, depending on type of brick | Need careful laying |
| CARPET (BODY AND TILES) | Most rooms. Tiles are good for kitchens or where spills are likely | Varies, depending on grade, fibres used and method of weaving | Squares and tiles are easy to lay. Fitted carpet needs professional laying |
| CERAMIC TILES | Bathroom, conservatory, hall, kitchen, shower room and utility areas | Medium to very expensive | Not too easy. Need accurate laying |
| CHIPBOARD (PARTICLE BOARD), FLOORING GRADE | Good cover for poor flooring. Not suitable for damp areas | Cheap | Fairly easy |
| CONCRETE | As subfloor on ground floor only | Relatively cheap | Heavy work but not too difficult |
| CORK (USUALLY TILES) | Most rooms. Seal with polyurethane varnish and use pre-sealed type for kitchens and bathrooms | Medium price, some can be expensive | Fairly easy |
| CUSHIONED VINYL (SHEET AND TILES) | Most rooms (not stairs) | Cheap to fairly costly, depending on type | Fairly easy, tiles very simple |
| HARDBOARD PANELS | For levelling floors. Not suitable for wet areas | Very cheap to medium (use suitable weight) | Very easy, and can be cut to shape |
| LINOLEUM (SHEET AND TILES) | Most rooms (not stairs) | Fairly cheap to quite expensive | Not as easy as vinyl, but tiles are easy |
| MARBLE | Ground floor rooms, bathroom or shower room | Expensive to very costly | Have professionally laid |
| PLASTIC (SHEET AND TILES) | Bathroom, children's room, hall, kitchen and shower room | Fairly cheap depending on type | Fairly easy |
| QUARRY TILES | See ceramic tiles | Usually cheaper than ceramic tiles | Not too difficult, but heavy work |
| RUBBER (SHEET AND TILES), SYNTHETIC RUBBER | Bathroom, children's rooms, hall, utility room or kitchen | Quite expensive to very expensive | Tiles much easier to lay than sheet |
| SLATE | Most ground floor rooms, but must be sealed in kitchen or utility areas | Fairly expensive | Not too hard, but heavy work |
| SOLID VINYL (SHEET AND TILES) | Most rooms (not stairs) | Inexpensive to medium | Fairly easy, tiles very easy |
| STONE | See slate | Quite expensive | Not impossible, but heavy work |
| TERRAZZO | See ceramic tiles | Expensive to very expensive | Difficult, best to have professionally laid |
| VEGETABLE FIBRE MATTING (SISAL) | Most rooms (not stairs), but avoid in kitchens as it is difficult to clean | Cheap to expensive, depending on type | Easy |
| WOOD (STRIP, PARQUET, BOARDS) | Most rooms, seal in 'wet' areas | Medium to expensive, depending on type | New boards need to be professionally laid |

| Durability | Comments |
|---|---|
| Good | Can prove harsh underfoot but provides an interesting texture. Bricks can be laid in a variety of patterns. Lay only on a solid base of concrete. Ideal for country-style homes |
| Depends on grade, fibres and method of weaving | Good quality carpet wears well and is warm and comfortable underfoot. Avoid buying very cheap grades; and always use good underlay. Carpet tiles are very flexible to use |
| Very good | Good range of different sizes, textures, qualities and colours. Can be cold underfoot but practical for kitchens or bathrooms. Check there is not too much 'spring' to timber floors and line with hardboard or similar. Subfloor must be damp-proof. Use frost-proof quality for sun rooms and conservatories |
| Good | Ideal for strengthening or levelling old wooden floors. Screw in position. Could be painted or stained but best if it is covered |
| Good | Can be used as a subfloor domestically, covered with a screed or levelling compound before the final finish. Can be painted |
| Good if properly sealed with polyurethane varnish | Good range of natural colours; can create some interesting coloured effects. Always need to be sealed in areas such as bathrooms |
| Depends on type | Wide range of colours, patterns and designs available. Very practical for utility areas and children's rooms. Tiles are very easy to handle |
| Not very hardwearing unless covered or tempered type | Like chipboard (particle board), best covered and just used as a floor leveller, but could be painted or stained |
| Good | Tougher than vinyl, can be cut and laid in interesting patterns. Rather restricted colour range, mostly marbled effects |
| Good | Good range of natural colours, can look very stylish and elegant. Can be rather cold and slippery underfoot |
| Quite good | Different types available, from plastic matting to simple sheet type. Good as quick, inexpensive flooring for limited time |
| Good, but seal in wet or greasy areas | Similar to ceramic tiles, but only earth tones or black colours available. Hard underfoot. Heavy tiles must be laid in mortar bed |
| Good | Colour range fairly restricted and no patterns are available. Come in interesting textures which give a hi-tech look but are difficult to clean |
| Good, but seal in wet or greasy areas | Colour range rather limited. When polished the tiles can look very elegant in the right setting |
| Quite good | More brittle than the cushioned type, but the tiles are easy to handle |
| Good if sealed where necessary | Not used much domestically except in conservatories |
| Good | Good range of colours and types, similar properties to marble |
| Quite good, but depends on type | Several different types available; coir and sisal very hard-wearing but can tend to be slippery |
| Good | Old and new boards can be stained, varnished or stencilled. Wood strip, tiles or parquet can be laid on wood or other subfloor |

# Linoleum and Sheet Vinyl

The two main types of sheet flooring material are linoleum and vinyl. The former is used less frequently these days. Both types are suitable for kitchens, utility rooms and bathrooms where a practical, washable surface is required, but they can also provide an inexpensive floor-covering for living areas.

The cheapest vinyl has a design pressed on a thin backing and is covered with a clear vinyl wear layer. Cushioned 'bouncy' type vinyls have a layer of foam between the vinyl and the backing making them comfortable to walk on. Some types can be loose-laid but should be stuck down in areas of heavy wear, and stuck or held with threshold strips in doorways. Patterns and colours are varied, from modern graphic designs to simulated wood and tiles.

Lino and vinyl are available in various widths up to 4m ($4\frac{1}{4}$yds) so choose the width to suit your room and try to cover a floor without a seam if possible. If one is inevitable, plan to have it in the least obvious place, even if that means two seams.

## Laying sheet material

As always with flooring, start with a clean, smooth, level, dry subfloor, and repair, line or otherwise correct as necessary. If a wooden floor has been previously treated with a stain, preservative or anti-woodworm fluid it should be left for several months to dry out.

Leave the vinyl or lino on its side in a warm room, loosely rolled with the top side facing outwards, for 48 hours to make it more supple.

The easiest way to cut the flooring is to make a template using brown paper or thick paper felt sold as cheap carpet underlay. If you have to join it, use masking tape. Lay the paper or felt on the floor of the room, mark the walls, door, and any recesses, and trace around objects

**LAYING SHEET LINO & VINYL**

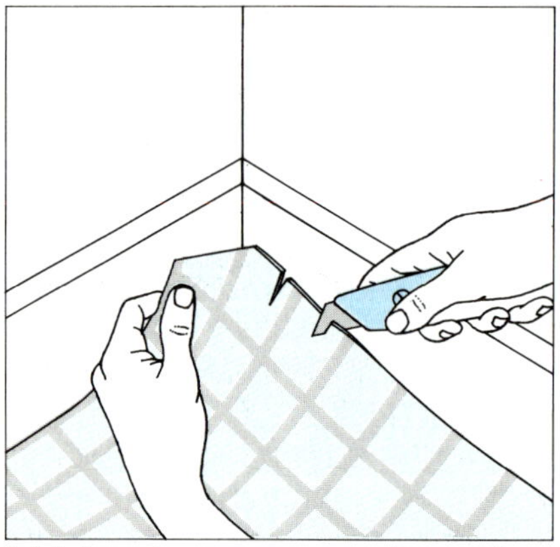

**1** Make release cuts at an internal corner to push the sheet against the skirting (baseboard).

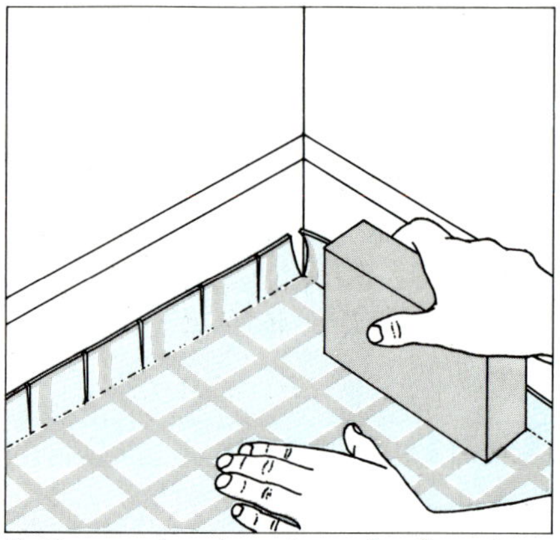

**2** Crease the sheet into the floor/wall angle with a block of wood and trim with a handyman's knife.

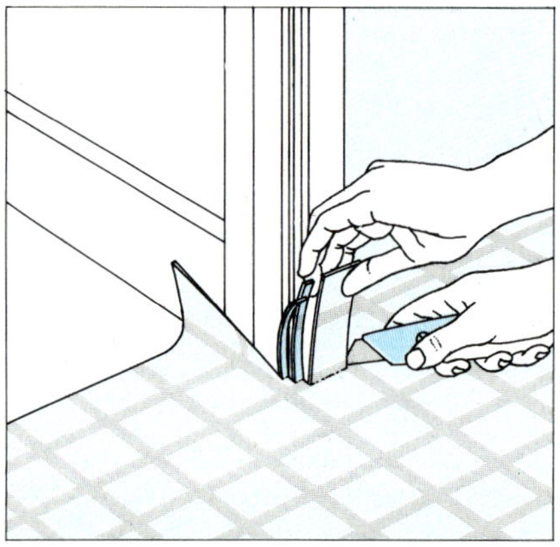

**3** At doorways, make a release cut for each angle of the frame and moulding and trim off the flaps.

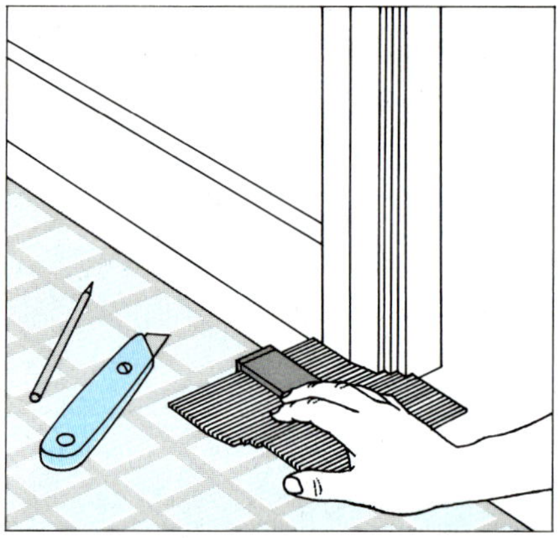

**4** Use a profile gauge by pushing the rods into complicated mouldings and using the shape as a template.

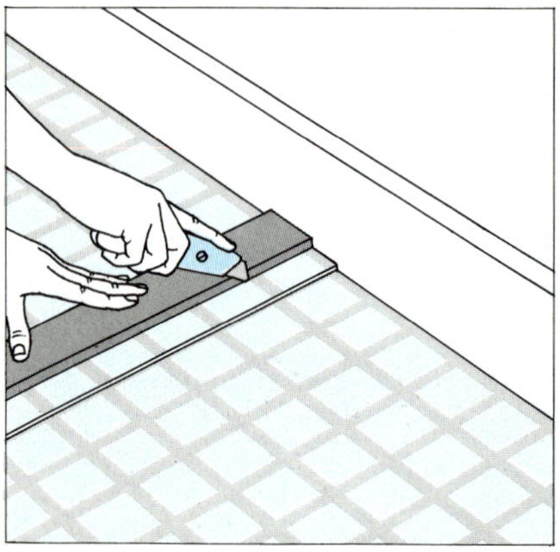

**5** Make joins between lengths by overlapping the sheets to match and cutting through both thicknesses.

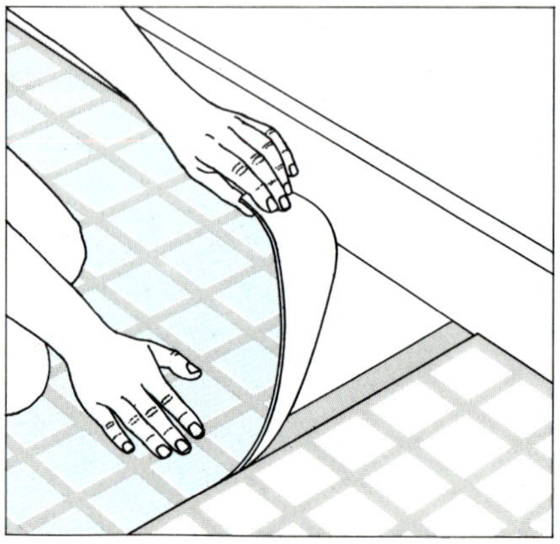

**6** Remove the surplus strips and stick the edges of the sheets to the floor with double-sided tape.

| | |
|---|---|
| PREPARING FLOORS | 84, 140 |
| SOFT FLOOR TILES | 140, 152 |


## INLAYING TILE PATTERNS

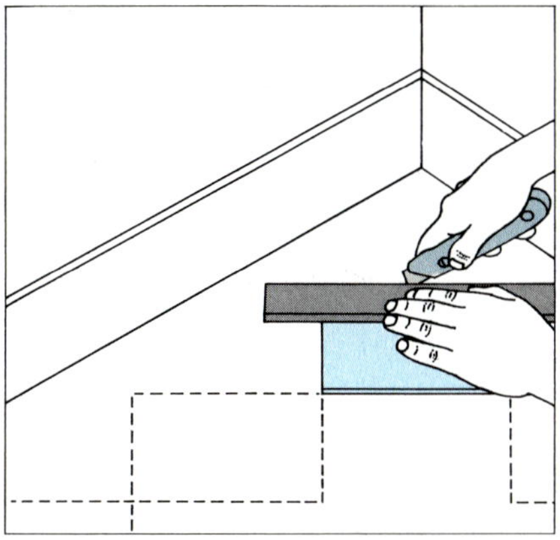

**1** Mark out the border pattern before overlaying each lino or vinyl tile and cutting round it.

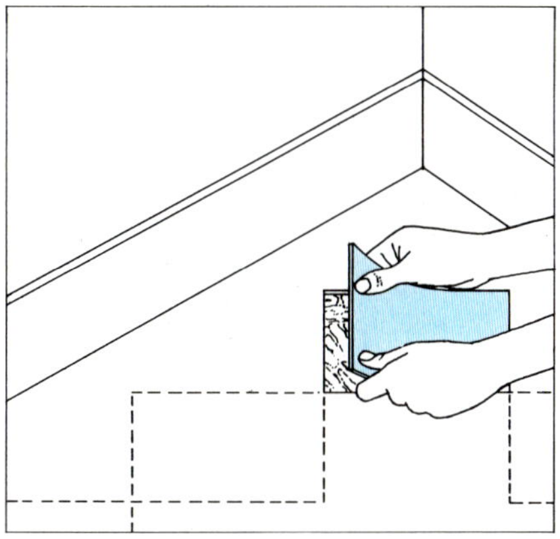

**2** Remove the pieces from the sheet and stick the tiles and surrounding sheet in place with adhesive.

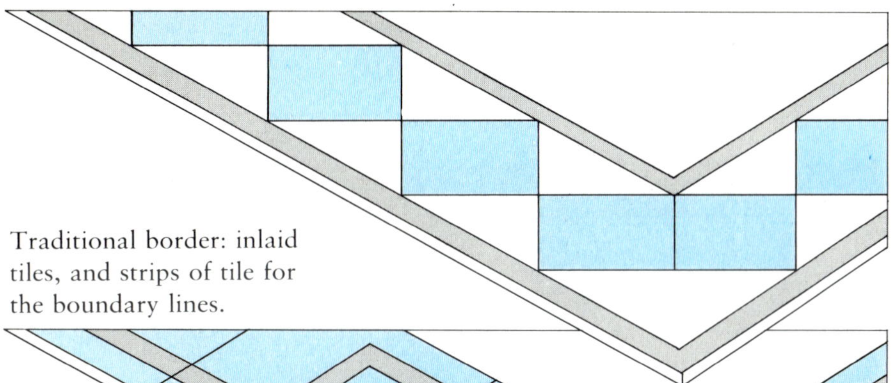

Traditional border: inlaid tiles, and strips of tile for the boundary lines.

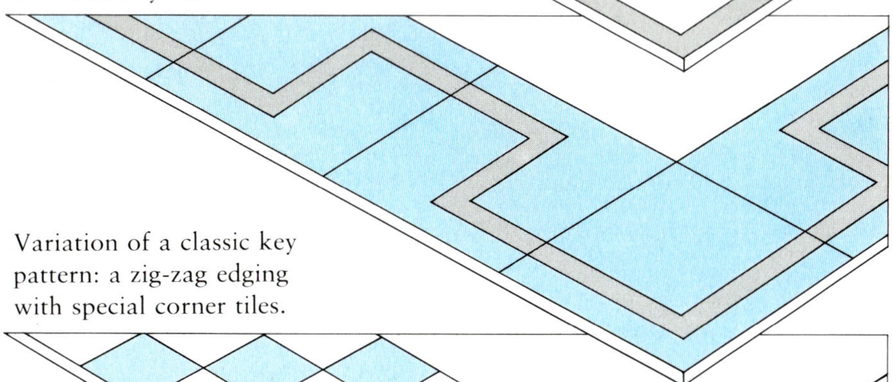

Variation of a classic key pattern: a zig-zag edging with special corner tiles.

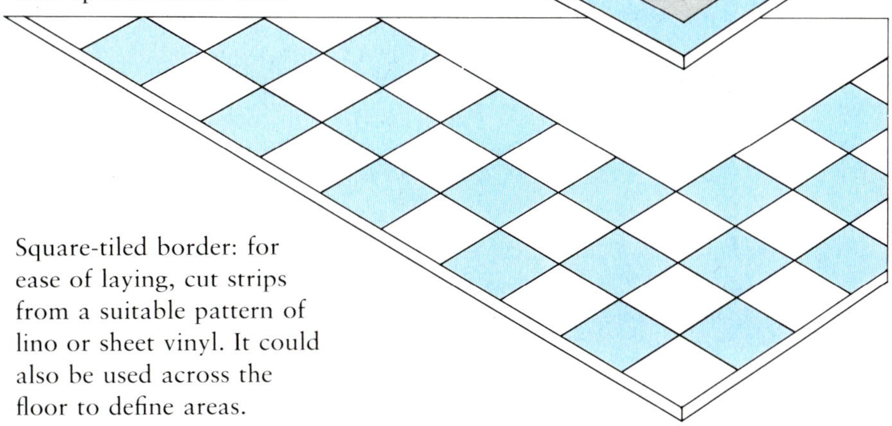

Square-tiled border: for ease of laying, cut strips from a suitable pattern of lino or sheet vinyl. It could also be used across the floor to define areas.

like pedestals and pipes. If the room was previously covered with sheet material or a carpet, this can be your pattern. If you can, take the flooring out of the room after it has been conditioned and lay it out flat on another larger floor or outside. Stick the template to the flooring with adhesive tape and cut the shape out of the flooring material. If you have to join sheets, overlap the edges by 25mm (1in) and adjust so that the pattern matches, then treat as one. As lino tends to stretch slightly in use, cut it exactly to size; vinyl tends to shrink so cut this 50mm (2in) larger all round.

Fit the cut sheet into the room, aligning the shape with the walls and smoothing from the centre outwards to remove any trapped air bubbles. Overlap two sheets by 25mm (1in) as before. Position the pre-cut holes round any obstacles, but leave the surplus.

Try to leave sheet material for a couple of weeks in position so that it stretches or shrinks.

Once settled, trim the overlapped sheets. Check finally that the pattern matches, then cut through the double thickness down the centre of the overlap, remove the offcuts and attach the edges with double-sided tape. Smooth the join with a seam roller. Next, adjust awkward shapes where necessary and trim the flooring to fit.

Pieces of lino or vinyl can be cut to shape on site in large areas. Overlap the widths and leave to settle before cutting, as before.

### Border patterns

The simplest way to liven up your sheet flooring is to inlay tiles of the same material to make borders or continuous patterns. Cut the tiles up to make more possibilities for yourself. Use the tile as a template for cutting, cut the hole, then stick.

# Glossary

## A

**Abrasive paper** Rough-surfaced material used to rub-down or smooth a surface prior to painting or staining. Known as glasspaper in UK and sandpaper in US.
**Adjacent colours** Colours found next to each other on a colour wheel.
**Advancing colours** Colours which appear to come towards you, making an area look smaller – 'hot' or 'warm' colours such as red, pink, orange, peach and yellow.
**Antiquing** A painted finish which gives a surface an old, well-worn appearance.
**Asbestos** Material made from fibres of calcium magnesium silicate, widely used for fireproofing and other building work until it was discovered to be a health hazard. Do not handle but call in expert help.
**Auger bit** Spiral-shaped tool for boring holes in wood.

## B

**Baluster** Pillar used to support the handrail of a staircase.
**Batten (US: Furring strip)** Narrow strip of softwood.
**Beam** Supporting structural member of a building, can be wood or metal. *See also* RSJ.
**Bevel** see CHAMFER
**Blistering** Bubbles which form on a painted or varnished surface, causing it to perish.
**Bonding** Joining of two surfaces, usually by adhesive.
**Bracket** Projecting support for a shelf; flat or angled metal plate for strengthening joints in wood.
**Bradawl** Sharp-pointed tool, like small screwdriver, for marking holes.
**Butt joint** Join of two edges such as wallcovering or sheet flooring, which touch but do not overlap.

## C

**Casement** A window which usually has a fixed pane, a side-hinged opening pane and a smaller top pane which also opens.
**Caulking** see MASTIC
**Cavity wall** Wall made from two layers with a gap between them.
**Chair rail** see DADO RAIL
**Chalk line** String coated with coloured chalk, stretched taut between two points, and 'snapped' to leave a chalk guideline.
**Chamfer (bevel)** Angled edge of board, metal, tile, etc.
**Chipboard (US: Particle board)** Building material made from wooden particles bonded together. Several different grades are available.
**Chuck** Device used to hold various drill bits in position in power and hand drills.
**Cold chisel** Wedge-shaped, hardened chisel used for cutting masonry and also metal.
**Colour matching** Putting colours together in sample form (sometimes on a colour board), and looking at them under accurate lighting conditions before deciding on a decorating scheme.
**Colour wheel** Method of showing the colours of the spectrum in sequence. Widely used in colour scheming.
**Colourwashing** Painting technique which involves applying a base colour and then adding several coats of a thinned wash or glaze on top.
**Combing** Painting technique where a wet surface glaze is 'teased' with a comb to reveal the base colour.
**Contact adhesive** Adhesive which is applied to both surfaces to ensure a strong, immediate bond.
**Corbel** Projection (usually decorative) from a wall, which supports a beam, cornice or moulding.
**Cornice (US: Crown moulding see also Pelmet)** Decorative horizontal band of plaster, wood or metal, placed at the junction of wall and ceiling or wall and roof.
**Countersink** To drill a cone-shaped hole in wood or metal, so that screws can be inserted leaving heads flush with, or just below the surface, and then filled.
**Coving** Similar to a cornice but much less decorative, and concave in shape.
**Cross lining** To line a wall or a ceiling horizontally with some lining paper, prior to painting or hanging a wallcovering.
**Crown moulding** see CORNICE

## D

**Dado rail (US: Chair rail)** Separates wall into two horizontally. The top half is then treated differently from the bottom half. Made from wood moulding, tiles or a wallpaper border.
**Damp proof** To treat a surface (floor, walls) to prevent water seeping through; provided by a damp-proof membrane (vapor barrier).
**Directional design** Pattern on wallcovering or fabric which creates a definite directional effect when joined on to the next width.
**Dragging** Painting technique for walls and woodwork, where an almost dry brush is dragged across a wet glaze to reveal the base colour.
**Drill bits** These fit into the chuck of an electric drill and are available, in different sizes, to drill masonry, wood and other materials.
**Drop (see also Pattern repeat)** Measurement taken from top to bottom of a wall to give the length of pattern on wallcovering or fabric required.
**Dry wall** see PLASTERBOARD and STUD PARTITION

## E

**Efflorescence** Powdery white substance which appears on the surface of brickwork and some newly plastered walls. Caused by the salts left after the moisture dries out.
**Eggshell** Finish on paint or stain which has a slight sheen.
**Emery cloth/paper** Abrasive material used to smooth metal.
**Emulsion (US: Latex)** A water-based paint used mainly for walls and ceilings.
**End grain** Wood grain exposed by cutting timber across the grain.

## F

**Feather edges** To abrade edges of chipped paintwork or to finish painting an edge with loose, diagonal strokes, so the join does not show when the next coat of paint is applied.
**Fidgeting** A process popular in marbling, when a brush is used to create zig-zag lines or branch effects.
**Flush** When adjacent surfaces are level and fit evenly; when grouting, a decorative fixing, or a trimming, is level with the main surface.
**Frame-fixing** A type of wallplug used when attaching wooden strips to a plastered wall. Instead of drilling through the wood *then* the wall, the hole can be drilled through both together.
**Frieze** A band, often horizontal, round a room. Can be positioned between cornice (crown moulding) or coving and picture rail, or above the dado (chair) rail. Made from plaster, paper and other material.
**Fungicide** Mould or fungus-destroying agent used in wallpaper paste for hanging vinyl and other wallcoverings. (fungicidal paste)
**Furring strip** see BATTEN

## G

**Glasspaper (US: sandpaper)** Abrasive paper in various grades, used to sand down woodwork, or painted or stained surfaces, between coats.
**Glaze** Application of a transparent, or semi-transparent, colour over a base colour to enrich and intensify. It is used in various painting techniques.
**Glazing** Process of fitting new glass into window and door frames.
**Gloss** Oil-based paint which dries with a high, reflective sheen. Used mainly for woodwork and metalwork. High-gloss and semi-gloss available.
**Grain** Direction of growth of timber. It shows on the cut surface as an attractive texture.
**Graining** Painted technique which imitates the natural effect of wood grain. It is often used to make poor quality wood look more expensive.
**Grout(-ing)** A filling worked into the joints between tiles after they are fixed, to seal them and create a continuous surface.
**Gypsum board** see PLASTERBOARD

## H

**Hardboard** Type of board made from compressed fibre, which is smooth on one side and has a cross-hatched rough texture on the other.
**Harmony** Blend of colours in a scheme which do not contrast strongly or clash.
**Hue** Pure colour as it appears on a colour wheel. It may be an original primary colour, or mixed with its neighbouring colour to create a secondary or tertiary colour.

## I

**Insulating board** A thick, compressed fibre board used to clad walls and ceilings to reduce noise and heat loss.
**Insulation** Thermal material used to reduce the rate of heat flow as in loft insulation. Also protective material used to cover wires and terminals, which is a poor conductor of electricity.

## J

**Jamb** Vertical sides of a door or window opening; the timber covering the sides.
**Joint** Connection between two or more pieces where they meet or overlap.
**Joist** Horizontal wood or metal beams used to support floors and ceilings.

## K

**Key** To roughen a surface to give a grip for succeeding coats of plaster, adhesive, paint or stain.
**Knot** Dark-coloured disc found in timber where a branch was formed.
**Knotting** Shellac primer applied to knots in timber to seal them.

## L

**Lacquer** Glossy finishing coat which is applied by brush; it dries as its solvent evaporates.
**Laminate** Tough surface material formed by pressing together layers of different substances. It is used to clad kitchen units, bathroom walls and cover countertops.
**Lap joint** Joint where two pieces of wood overlap forming a smooth single surface on one or both sides.
**Latex adhesive** Rubber which can be liquid or foam for backing flooring, or used for upholstery.
**Latex paint** see EMULSION
**Lath** Thin strip of wood.
**Lay(ing) off** Applying light finishing strokes to paint, stain or sealer to prevent runs and sags.
**Lintel** Supporting structural beam over a door or window.
**Live edge** Edge of paint which is still wet enough to be blended with adjoining new paint without the join showing.
**Load-bearing** Structural wall which supports a vertical load (usually the wall above). Before this type of wall is removed, the structure above it must be supported with a suitable structural member, such as a rolled steel joist (RSJ).
**Louvre** Horizontal slats made into doors, shutters and windows; also vertical slats made into window blinds.

## M

**Mantel (piece)** Shelf above a fireplace; part of a fireplace surround.
**Marbling** Painted technique used to give a surface the appearance of some real marble.
**Mask** To cover one area to protect it while decorating the adjacent surface.
**Masking tape** Low tack tape (does not adhere too firmly) used to mark off an adjoining surface when painting or stencilling to give a crisp edge.
**Masonry** Stone, brick, block or tile laid in mortar or concrete.
**Mastic (Caulking)** Sealing compound used to make waterproof joints round door and window frames; also used for glazing work.
**Matchless wallcovering** A textured or cleverly patterned wallcovering which does not need pattern matching across the widths.
**Matt finish** Non-glossy paint, varnish or other sealant.
**Microporous paint** A paint or stain, specially formulated to have a flexible surface. It allows the wood underneath to 'breathe', thereby controlling the moisture content.
**Mitre** To cut two pieces of wood, plastic, borders, beading, moulding, metal and other materials at matching angles where they meet at a corner.
**Mitre block** Special support and sawing guide into which wood and mouldings can be placed to make angled cutting easier.
**Monochromatic** Colour scheme based on different values of one colour.
**Mortar** Masonry bonding material made with sand and cement and water.
**Mortise (and tenon)** Rectangular or square recess cut in wood to receive a tenon, the other half of the joint.
**Moulding** Narrow piece of wood or other material used as a trim to provide a decorative surface. Also known as beading.
**Mural** Picture or pattern painted directly on a wall. There are various ways of 'cheating' including using photomurals and self-adhesive mural panels. Sometimes called wall patterns.

## N

**Nail punch** Tapered tool which is used to set nail heads below the wooden surface. Also called a nail set.
**Nails, cut** Flat, wedge-shaped nails used in flooring.
**Neutral** 'Colourless' colour. True neutrals are black, white and pure grey but beige, off-white and similar colours are also accepted as neutrals.
**Newel post** Post at top and bottom of a flight of stairs, supporting the handrail. It is the core of a winding or spiral staircase.
**Nosing** Rounded and projecting edge, usually of stair tread, but also used to describe a border of tiles at the top or edge of a tiled area.

## O

**Open plan** All-in-one living area without dividing wall.
**Out of plumb/true** Not a vertical surface.
**Overmantel** Decorative shelving, mirror (or combination of both) fixed on top of a mantelpiece which is on top of a fireplace.

## P

**Papier mâché** Moulded paper pulp which is easy to shape. It is used to make objects or to fill gaps such as between floorboards.
**Parquet** A type of wooden floor, usually laid in tile form.
**Particle board** see CHIPBOARD
**Pattern repeat** (see also DROP) The drop or distance interval at which pattern wallcovering repeats itself along the length.
**Pelmet (US: Cornice)** Decorative surround of wood, draped fabric or other material, placed at the top of a window to hide the curtain track or the fixing.
**Peninsular unit** Freestanding work unit which projects from a run of units.
**Picture rail** A narrow wooden rail fitted on walls in many old houses a short way down from the ceiling junction. It is shaped to allow pictures to be hung from it using some moulding hooks.
**Pigment** Colouring matter added to paint to give it the required colour.
**Pile** Surface texture of carpet or fabric which stands upright.
**Plane** Abrasive or cutting tool for levelling or smoothing wood.
**Plaster** Mixture of gypsum, putty lime or cement with sand. Water is added to produce a pasty mixture which is applied to walls and ceilings, and hardens to a smooth surface.
**Plasterboard (US: Gypsum board or Dry wall)** Standard size sheets of plaster, sandwiched between paper, used to surface walls, partitions and ceilings.
**Plate glass** High quality, very thick polished glass.
**Plumb-bob and line** Pointed weight on the end of a string line, suspended to determine a true vertical.
**Plywood** Thin wooded sheets glued together with the grain in alternate directions to form a strong and springy board.
**Pointing** Filling of joints with mortar, particularly of brickwork.
**Polyester** Synthetic resin used in alkyd paints and varnishes; synthetic fibre used in furnishing fabrics, usually blended with other fibres such as cotton.
**Polyethylene** Semi-transparent plastic sheet available in various weights.
**Polypropylene** Plastic material with good resistance to heat and solvents used in carpet manufacture.
**Polystyrene** Plastic compound used in its expanded form for insulation and decoration, for example ceiling tiles; used in its solid form for wall tiles.
**Polyurethane** Synthetic resin used in the manufacture of varnishes and paints, now synonymous with a clear type of wood varnish.
**Pounce** To apply colour to a stencil by dabbing on paint with a short-bristled brush.
**Primer** First coat of paint applied to a surface to seal and protect it and to prevent subsequent coats being absorbed.
**Putty** Special flexible mixture used to fix glass into frames. One type is used for wood, another for metal.
**PVA** Polyvinyl acetate, a chemical compound used in adhesives such as woodworking adhesive.
**PVC** Polyvinyl chloride, a plastic material which is found in many forms: electric cable sheathing; upholstery fabric; and in the manufacture of flooring and wallcoverings.

## Q

**Quadrant (US: Quarter round)** Beading with two flat sides at right angles and the third side curved.

## R

**Ragging** Painting technique where a texture is created on a wall by dipping rags in colour or glaze and then 'printing' them on the base surface.
**Random design** A design which does not have a specific repeat so it is matchless.
**Receding colours** Colours which appear to go away from you, making an area look larger, or more spacious ie. 'cold' or 'cool' colours, for example blues, greens, greys, lilacs.
**Relief decoration** Heavily textured wallcovering or plasterwork where part of the design stands out in relief from the backing.
**Repeat pattern** see PATTERN REPEAT
**Repointing** Process which involves replacing damaged mortar pointing in brickwork or similar.
**Reveal** Visible part of the side of a window or door opening not covered by the frame.
**Reverse hanging** Hanging alternate strips of wallcovering the opposite way up. This is only done if the texture or the paper finish requires this.
**Riser** Vertical part of a step on stairs supporting the front of the tread.
**Rose** Ceiling fitting to which a light fitting is connected, but can be a purely decorative relief decoration.
**RSJ** Rolled steel joist used to strengthen an opening in a load-bearing wall to take the weight of the walls above. See also LOAD-BEARING
**Rubbed colour** Coloured paint applied to a base coat with a rag and rubbed out thinly.

## S

**Sags (and runs)** Paint which has dripped and run down a surface leaving unsightly ridges. Cure by sanding and re-painting.
**Sand** To rub an area with glasspaper or abrasive sanding discs to smooth or strip back to the original surface. Sanding down plaster or woodwork is to rub down between coats to create a flat, smooth surface before putting up a new one.
**Sash** Window frame which slides up and down within the reveal.
**Score** To mark or incise along the cutting or breaking line.
**Screed** Thin layer of floor-levelling compound or cement (sometimes applied to plaster), laid prior to the top, finishing surface.
**Scribe** To mark the contours of a wall or floor, for example, on the edge of sheet material with a pointed tool or writing implement prior to cutting it to shape.
**Scrim** Thin material or gauze used for patching, or in some cases combined with plaster or filler for filling holes.
**Scumbling** Painted effect where a scumble glaze is applied over a surface colour and then textured or partly removed. This can be used to achieve a woodgrain effect.
**Sealing** Applying a seal or varnish to an area, particularly floors, to seal colour in or to protect the surface.
**Secret nailing** Nailing so that the heads go below the surface and are covered by an adjoining board or sheet. Used for attaching cladding. Also called blind nailing.
**Self-tapping screws (US: Countersunk screws)** Often used in dry wall construction.
**Shellac** A natural resin soluble in alcohol, widely used in spirit varnishes, knotting and French polish. It comes in white and orange polish and button polish form.
**Silk** Apart from the raw material used for furnishing fabrics and wallcoverings this term is applied to a slightly lustrous finish on paint, for example, vinyl silk.
**Sill** Horizontal piece at the base of window or door frames.
**Size** Gelatin-like substance which is used to seal a surface prior to decorating with wallcoverings.
**Skirting (US: Baseboard)** Border of wood, plaster or plastic which trims a wall where it meets the floor.

**Spectrum** Colours of the rainbow – pure hues of red, orange, yellow, green, blue, violet.
**Spirit level** A device which helps to give true horizontal and vertical measurements.
**Sponging** Decorative technique made by dabbing a top coat of paint or glaze over a base coat, using a sea sponge.
**Staple** Small metal pins which can be used to attach lightweight surfaces together or on to a backing, for example, fabric to battens. They are inserted from a staple gun.
**Stencilling** Way of patterning a surface with paint using a pattern with the motif cut out. Paint is dabbed or pounced through the hole.
**Stippling** Painted technique where the tips of the bristles of a stiff stippling or stencil brush are dipped into paint and dabbed on the surface, over a base coat.
**Straightedge** Levelling or marking board or rule, usually made of metal, with at least one true edge.
**Stud partition** Timber framework attached to floor, ceiling and sidewalls, and covered with a finishing material such as plasterboard to form a wall.
**Subfloor** The underfloor, to which a top surface is added. It can be boards, plywood, chipboard, hardboard or a cement or other solid floor.

## T

**Tamping** To agitate or push down freshly poured concrete or cement to exclude any air.
**Template** Shape cut from card, paper or other stiff lightweight material to follow the form of a particular item or area. It is used as a guide to cut a finished material – very similar to a paper pattern.
**Tenon (see also Mortise)** A tongue-like projection cut in wood to fit into a mortise.
**Thixotropic paint** Paint of jelly-like consistency, easy to apply as it does not drip or run. It should not be stirred.
**Tongued-and-grooved boards** Term applied to a type of wood cladding or floorboard which is easy to assemble – a tongue down one side of the board fits into the groove down the opposite edge of the adjacent board.
**Tread** The actual steps of a stepladder; horizontal part of the step on stairs.
***Trompe l'oeil*** Term meaning to 'deceive the eye' – a decorative illusion which makes something seem three-dimensional when it is, in fact, a flat surface. Can be a painted view or scene.

## U

**Undercoat** Coat of paint or stain which is applied to the surface between priming and the top, finishing, coat. It dries to a matt finish to provide a good key.
**Underlay** Resilient material laid under carpet to preserve it.
**Union** Type of strong, woven fabric used for covers and upholstery, usually with a printed design. Made from a blend of fibres such as linen and cotton, hence the name 'union'.
**Universal** Ceramic tile with chamfered edges, which are glazed on one, or two adjacent edges, so a wall may be tiled without using nosing tiles.

## V

**Valance** A frill of fabric used to cover a bed base, to trim the bottom of a chair cover or to top a curtain to conceal the track – a fabric PELMET.
**Veneer** Thin sheet of decorative material, usually wood, glued or pinned to low-grade timber or core-board to make it more attractive.

## W

**Wainscot(ing)** Interior wall surface, frequently of wood, usually to a height of about 1m (3ft 3in) from the floor. Creates contrast with the upper wall area.
**Warping** Distortion and twisting due to uneven shrinkage in wood.
**Welding** Method of joining metals by applying heat.
**Wet and dry paper** Abrasive paper which can be used with a lubricant (usually water) to rub down a surface prior to retreating.
**Whitewash** Wall finishing compound made from slaked lime and water.
**Wood graining** The process of applying a wood colour glaze to a base coat and using a graining comb and other tools to create the look of wood.

# Index

Page numbers in *italic* refer to illustrations and captions

# Acknowledgments

The publisher thanks the following photographers and organizations for their kind permission to reproduce the pictures in this book:

**6–7** Jean-Paul Bonhommet; **8** left Abitare/Christine Tiberghien; **8** right Jean-Paul Bonhommet; **9** left Conran Octopus/Simon Brown (architect Jerry Hewitt, Interior designer and soft furnishings Angela Hewitt-Woods); **9** right Elizabeth Whiting & Associates/Michael Dunne; **10** Jean-Paul Bonhommet; **10–11** Camera Press; **12** Susan Griggs Agency (designer John Stefanidis); **12–13** Jean-Paul Bonhommet; **13** Jean-Paul Bonhommet; **14–15** Deidi von Schaewen; **16** Syndication International/Homes and Gardens; **16–17** Elizabeth Whiting & Associates/Spike Powell; **17** Arcaid/Richard Bryant; **18** Elizabeth Whiting & Associates/Gary Chowanetz; **19** Jean-Paul Bonhommet; **20** left Elizabeth Whiting & Associates/Michael Crockett; **20** right Jean-Paul Bonhommet; **21** Jean-Paul Bonhommet; **22** Jean-Paul Bonhommet; **26** Elizabeth Whiting & Associates/Michael Nicholson; **28** Elizabeth Whiting & Associates/Neil Lorimer; **28–29** John Cullen Lighting; **30** Jean-Paul Bonhommet; **32** Jean-Paul Bonhommet; **33** Jean-Paul Bonhommet; **34** Annet Held; **34–35** Jean-Paul Bonhommet; **35** Fritz von der Schulenberg; **36** Arcaid/Lucinda Lambton; **38** Elizabeth Whiting & Associates/Rodney Hyett; **39** above Camera Press; **39** below left Pat Hunt; **39** below right architect Anthony Feldman (photographer Ken Tam); **41** Abitare/Ornella Sancassani; **46** Collier Campbell; **46–47** Jean-Paul Bonhommet; **48** Arcaid/Richard Bryant; **49** left Jean-Paul Bonhommet; **49** right Abitare/Christine Tiberghien; **51** above and below left Jean-Paul Bonhommet; **51** below right Arcaid; **55** above left Jean-Paul Bonhommet; **55** below left Camera Press; **55** right Abitare/Reiner Blunk; **56–57** Arcaid; **58** above Conran Octopus/Simon Brown; **58** below Annet Held; **59** Jean-Paul Bonhommet; **60** La Maison de Marie Claire/Pataut/Bayle; **61** left Antoine Rozès; **61** right Pat Hunt; **64** Conran Octopus/Simon Brown; **67** Jean-Paul Bonhommet; **68** Annet Held; **69** Jessica Strang; **70** Antoine Rozès; **71** Conran Octopus/Ken Kirkwood (architect Roger Mears, contractor CASP (D & P) Ltd); **72–73** Elizabeth Whiting & Associates/Rodney Hyett; **81** Susan Griggs Agency/Michael Boys; **83** Conran Octopus/Simon Brown (fashion designer Stephen King); **84** Pat Hunt; **86** Abitare/Gabriele Basilico; **87** Camera Press; **88** above Fritz von der Schulenberg; **88** below Susan Griggs Agency; **91** Elizabeth Whiting & Associates/Di Lewis; **93** Conran Octopus/Simon Brown; **94–95** Jean-Paul Bonhommet; **96** Vivian Boje; **96–97** Elizabeth Whiting & Associates/Michael Dunne; **97** above Vivian Boje; **97** below Conran Octopus/Simon Brown; **99** La Maison de Marie Claire/Korniloff/Olry; **102** Jean-Paul Bonhommet; **105** Abitare/Nini Mulas; **106** Lars Hallen; **108** Maison Française; **109** Michael Boys; **110** above Annie Morris; **110** below Conran Octopus/Simon Brown (François Gilles from I.P.L. Interiors – Paris – London); **111** Conran Octopus/Shona Wood (Laura Fortescue – colour washing by Penelope Beech); **113** Syndication International/Homes and Gardens; **114** The World of Interiors/T Leighton; **114–115** Dulux/ICI; **116** Elizabeth Whiting & Associates/Spike Powell; **119** left Lars Hallen; **119** right Jessica Strang; **120** Ianthe Ruthven; **121** right Ken Kirkwood; **121** left Jessica Strang; **122–123** Collier Campbell; **124** Elizabeth Whiting & Associates/Clive Helm; **128** Collier Campbell; **131** above Jean-Paul Bonhommet; **131** below Michael Boys; **133** Nairn Kingfisher Ltd; **134** Jean-Paul Bonhommet; **137** above Collier Campbell; **137** below Elizabeth Whiting & Associates/Clive Helm; **138–139** Jean-Paul Bonhommet; **139** above Elizabeth Whiting & Associates/Jerry Tubby; **139** below Abitare/Gabriele Basilico; **140** Jean-Paul Bonhommet; **141** Jean-Paul Bonhommet; **145** Michael Boys; **147** Jean-Paul Bonhommet; **148** Elizabeth Whiting & Associates/Tim Street-Porter; **149** Jean-Paul Bonhommet; **150** above Vivian Boje; **150** below Conran Octopus/Ken Kirkwood; **150–151** Jean-Paul Bonhommet; **153** above La Maison de Marie Claire/Eriaud/Comte; **153** below courtesy of Amtico; **154** Annet Held; **156** Annet Held; **157** above Camera Press; **157** below left Arcaid/Tim Soar; **157** below right La Maison de Marie Claire/Bouchet/Hourdin; **158** Pat Hunt; **158–159** Elizabeth Whiting & Associates/Richard Davies; **159** Abitare/Ornella Sancassani; **162** Annet Held; **163** Jean-Paul Bonhommet; **166** Conran Octopus/Simon Brown (Paul Hodgkinson, interior designers Simons Design Consultants); **168–169** Conran Octopus/Simon Brown (Paint effect by John Ebdon); **169** above Fritz von der Schulenberg; **169** below Jessica Strang (Oliver Morgan); **170** Arcaid; **171** left Pat Hunt; **171** right Abitare/Christine Tiberghien; **172** Conran Octopus/Simon Brown; **175** left Conran Octopus/Simon Brown (Ian Hutchinson architect); **175** right Jean-Paul Bonhommet; **176** Heuga; **178** Deidi von Schaewen; **179** Arcaid/Lucinda Lambton.

The publisher also thanks the following organizations for their kind help:

Laura Ashley, Braywick House, Braywick Road, Maidenhead, Berks, SL6 1DW (chart, page 125)
Colour Counsellors Limited, 187 New King's Road, London SW6 4SW
Comyn Ching, 19 Shelton Street, London WC2
Hodkin & Jones, 23 Rathbone Place, London W1P 1DB
ICI Paints, Wexham Road, Slough, Bucks, SL2 5DS
International Wool Secretariat, Wool House, Carlton Gardens, London SW1 (chart, page 173)
The Rawlplug Company, Rawlplug House, London Road, Kingston-Upon-Thames, Surrey, KT2 6NR
Wallpaper Paint Wallcovering Retailers' Association, PO Box 44, Walsall, West Midlands, WS3 1TD (symbols, page 125)